Global Movements

For Alain Touraine

Global Movements
Action and Culture

Kevin McDonald

Blackwell
Publishing

BLACKWELL PUBLISHING
350 Main Street, Malden, MA 02148–5020, USA
9600 Garsington Road, Oxford OX4 2DQ, UK
550 Swanston Street, Carlton, Victoria 3053, Australia

First published 2006 by Blackwell Publishing Ltd

1 2006

Library of Congress Cataloging-in-Publication Data

McDonald, Kevin.
    Global movements : action and culture / by Kevin McDonald.
       p.   cm.
    Includes bibliographical references and index.
    ISBN-13: 978-1-4051-1612-1 (hardback : alk. paper)
    ISBN-10: 1-4051-1612-9 (hardback : alk. paper)
    ISBN-13: 978-1-4051-1613-8 (pbk. : alk. paper)
    ISBN-10: 1-4051-1613-7 (pbk. : alk. paper)
    1. Social movements – Case studies.   2. Anti-globalization movement.
 3. Social movements – Islamic countries.   4. Falun Gong (Organization)
 5. Social movements – China.   I. Title.
 HM881.M33 2006
 303.48′4 – dc22

                                                        2005017742

A catalogue record for this title is available from the British Library.

Set in 10.5 on 12.5 pt Dante
by SNP Best-set Typesetter Ltd, Hong Kong
Printed and bound in the United Kingdom
by TJ International, Padstow, Cornwall

The publisher's policy is to use permanent paper from mills that operate a sustainable forestry
policy, and which has been manufactured from pulp processed using acid-free and elementary
chlorine-free practices. Furthermore, the publisher ensures that the text paper and cover board
used have met acceptable environmental accreditation standards.

For further information on
Blackwell Publishing, visit our website:
www.blackwellpublishing.com

Contents

Preface

This book is an attempt to understand shifts in the grammars of culture and action at work in movements. At its heart is the sense that contemporary movements confront us with a profound transformation, with a shift from the forms of organization and action characterizing the "social movements" of the last two centuries, to new grammars of experience. At stake are not only relationships between individual and collective, or a shift from hierarchies to networks, but ways of being in the world, of experiencing one's own and the other's embodied subjectivity. The attempt to understand these shifts pushes us to rethink not only what we understand by movement, but also what we understand as action as such. In the process, these movements open new ways of thinking about globalization, allowing us to move away from ideologies of the "borderless world" of simultaneity, and to begin to understand globalization in terms of multiple worlds, of embodied intersubjectivities, where civilizational ways-of-being interpenetrate in new ways.

In the early 1990s globalization was celebrated in terms of the expansion of the borderless economy, while later in the decade the theme of "resistance" became increasingly important. This understood globalization in terms of one center, while grammars of action were reduced to defending interests, traditions, or identities. This imposed a uniformity on movements and action, fundamentally regarding them as a defensive response, one to be understood in terms of the center they were resisting. Old intellectual frameworks were mobilized to think about them, some emphasizing opportunities and strategies, others identities and communities. In the process, emerging grammars of action, culture, and organization have tended to be ignored, in particular in the case of "non-western" movements that fail to correspond to models of "social movement" we are familiar with.

The decade that followed has seen the optimism of the 1990s replaced with new themes of violence, failed states, and the threat of terrorism, as the post-1945 order unravels. We are increasingly offered a choice between the borderless world or the "clash of civilizations."

Freeing ourselves from this choice is an intellectual, ethical, and above all practical, task, one this book hopes to make some small contribution to. It addresses people involved in creating, experiencing, and thinking about movements and who are living and trying to make sense of shifts in ways of acting, being, feeling, and organizing. It also addresses researchers, students, and teachers who are trying to think about movements in new ways. And it addresses people who are thinking about and feeling what globalization means, who wonder how to make real the possibilities it offers, of not living in one world, but of sharing many worlds.

This book has taken four years to research and write. It would not have been possible without the openness of many people to discuss and explore their action and experience, from people involved in Reclaim the Streets in Britain to antiglobalization convergences in the United States, to practitioners of qigong (a Chinese healing art) and Falun Gong, to people involved in forms of piety, or building puppets, or telling stories – a decision that in some contexts has exposed the person to potential risk. Nor would it have been possible without the opportunity to articulate and test ideas, to try to find ways to think about forms of action and experience that did not fit with older models of movement and globalization. Research Committee 47 of the International Sociological Association has played a key role in this, bringing together scholars from every continent in an ongoing attempt to understand movements and action in the contemporary world. The Centre d'Analyse et d'Intervention Sociologiques at the Ecole des Hautes Etudes en Sciences Sociales (EHESS) in Paris welcomed me for six months. There I was able to draw the manuscript together, and gain immensely from discussions and seminars with Michel Wieviorka, François Dubet, Yvon LeBot, and Nilufer Gole. The University of Melbourne offered a supportive intellectual environment, as well as financial support at critical stages for this research. At one point the university received a visit from a diplomat and political police from a country discussed in this book, who expressed concern about the directions of this research. The response of university leaders was to affirm the importance of social scientific work, and not waver in its support. This book has also benefited enormously from the support of people at Blackwell, its publishers. Phyllis Wentworth played a key role in helping reframe an initial proposal, while Ken Provencher has supported the writing, rethinking, and reworking with generosity and patience, combined with a demanding intellectual engagement. Readers gave generously of their time, responding to both the initial proposal and the draft manuscript, pushing me to think more clearly about what I was attempting to say. This experience underlines the critical role of publishers in the contemporary social sciences.

This book strives to understand the living, being, embodiment, and the senses at the heart of movements. These are also central to research and writing. In different ways traces of living with my three children, Gabriel, Lynne, and Sarah, are present in the chapters below. In a book that does not celebrate collective identity, but tries to understand ways that we become subjects through the experience of the other, there is an important presence of my partner Lorna Payne. This book would not be possible without the encounter I have had with Alain Touraine. He welcomed me as a doctoral student at the EHESS in the 1980s, and as a co-researcher in the period since. His commitment to understand the world in terms of struggles for freedom rather than systems of domination or strategies of interest shapes his intellectual and personal encounter with the other, from his role in the fight against the destruction of memory in South America, to the time and generosity he accords former students.

PART I

Movements and Globalization

CHAPTER 1

Globalization

I didn't cross the border, the border crossed me.
Los Tigres del Norte
Somos más Americanos

The beginnings of this twenty-first century have been dominated by contradictory and chaotic processes of globalization. But what is at stake seems extraordinarily difficult to grasp. Right across the planet there are signs of the changes at work, from the globalization of the economy or the rise of the Internet to the increasing importance of global fashion, architectural styles, consumption patterns, and celebrities. The rise of global media and extraordinary increases in travel and mobility have combined to produce new kinds of global events, from the Olympic Games, the World Cup, or the funeral of Princess Diana, to the September 11 destruction of the Twin Towers or the 1999 Seattle mobilization against the World Trade Organization (WTO). Our sense of living in a global world has been heightened by the increased awareness of the interconnectedness of new types of problems, from pollution, global warming, or failed states, to the increasing numbers of refugees and the emergence of global pandemics such as AIDS or the threat of terrorism. All these cut across borders, emerging from and constituting new types of networks and flows: of power, finance, information, people, experience, violence, emotion, and images. An older international context, where social life largely took place within the borders of nation-states, and where states were the main actors on the international stage, is increasingly giving way to a context involving new global actors, from NGOs, organized crime, or terror networks, and with it, to a whole series of debates attempting to interpret the nature of this emerging global world.

This book explores one of the most important dimensions of contemporary globalization: the emergence of new kinds of networks and flows of communication, action, and experience that I am calling global movements. Attempting to understand such movements is critical to the struggle to make sense of the possibilities and dangers reshaping our world. And while there is much we can learn from the frameworks social scientists have used to explore the social movements that emerged over the past century in western, industrial, national societies, attempting to make sense of emerging global movements demands of us new conceptual tools. We need to grapple with forms of sociality transforming the relationship between individual and collective; with grammars of movement that are better understood in terms of cultural pragmatics (Alexander 2004) and personal experience (Touraine 2002, 2005) than organization building and collective identity; with new forms of complexity and fluidity (Urry 2003); with civilizational grammars shaping ways-of-being and acting in the world (Eisenstadt 1999), interpenetrating in surprising ways (Bulliet 2004).

The forms of practice and communication we encounter in these movements are more embodied and sensual than deliberative and representational. They underline the urgent need to rethink our understandings of action in terms of touch, hearing, moving, feeling, tasting, memory, and breathing. They point to limits of the autonomous, secular subject and the models of intentional action that underpin major approaches to social movements. They confront us with forms of public experience that do not correspond to understandings of deliberative, rational, disembodied public spheres that have become increasingly influential over recent years (in the influential writings, for example, of Jürgen Habermas 1991, 1996). At the same time, the forms of action we encounter in these movements confront us with the limits of "identity" paradigms emphasizing communities, norms, and group cultures. Emerging global movements confront us with transformations in action and culture that demand a radical paradigm shift, pushing us beyond rehearsing largely familiar debates. In so doing, they confront us with the challenge of rethinking the way we understand globalization.

A Borderless World?

During the 1990s, dominant understandings of globalization were framed in economic terms. This reflected the importance of global corporations, the role of the finance industries, and the new forms of communication and information technologies integrating them. Influential management theorists (Ohmae 1990) championed the new "borderless world." Without any hesitation, this dominant view regarded the increasing integration of the world economy as leading to a convergence of societies. This formed the basis of what came to be known as the Washington Consensus, it shaped the policies of organizations such as the World Bank and the International Monetary Fund, and became the accepted wisdom in international think tanks such as the Swiss-based World Economic Forum. *New York Times* columnist Thomas Friedman was one of many journalists to popularize this argument, referring to globalization as a "golden straightjacket," where "once your country puts on the golden straightjacket, its political choices get reduced to Pepsi or Coke" (1999: 87). The political scientist Francis Fukuyama (1989, 1992) expressed the same argument in a more philosophical way when he argued that the collapse of the Berlin Wall in 1989 ushered in "the end of history," where countries would inevitably adopt a consumer culture and competitive political system as a result of their integration into the world economy. These arguments all implied that the emergence and triumph of globalization involved a universal, western, model of social and economic organization. Fukuyama was explicit, arguing that the end of history represented the "triumph of the west" (1989). Friedman's choice of beverages, Coke or Pepsi, conveyed a similar message.

Sociologists largely shared this same view. For the influential British sociologist Anthony Giddens (1990: 1), "modernity" is a type of society and culture produced by the west, while globalization involves its extension to the planet as a whole, continuing a process that has its origins in seventeenth-century Europe (1999). At the same time Giddens foreshadowed forms of defensive reaction to the "runaway world," in particular the emergence of fundamentalism, which he understands as "embattled tradition" (1999). Journalistic accounts offered a similar account, foreshadowing "backlashes" that would emerge in a desperate attempt to defend tradition against the relentless march of the global market (Friedman 1999). This view of a conquering globalization came to be widely embraced by radical intellectuals and populist leaders as well, from the theories of empire articulated by Toni Negri (Hardt and Negri 2000), the influential work of Noam Chomsky (2003) to French farmer José Bové's claim to defend local tradition and authenticity against invading homogenizing forces of the European Union and World Trade Organization.

Such celebrations and condemnations of globalization share a similar premise. As Robertson and Khondker argue (1998: 32), they perpetuate a view of the global as constituted by an active, dominant center, and defensive or subordinate reactions (groups or countries) forced to defend themselves against a process originating from outside. From this point of view, there is one source of globalization, "the west" or "capitalism." This understanding of globalization remains firmly within an older paradigm of modernization, understood as the universalization or diffusion of a dominant social model. Not only is there one source of globalization (the centers of global power), but also there is one process of globalization (the universalization of the model of these centers). Globalization travels in one direction, and to the extent it encounters obstacles, these are essentially defensive, subsumed within (and understandable in terms of) the generative process of globalization. As Karin Werner notes with regard to such analyses of fundamentalism, these construct an overall modernization project that is confronted with growing "fundamentalist holes," in the process setting up a framework where modernization is global, while universalizing fundamentalism "as a highly predictable form of antimodernity, which as such remains 'inside' the global modern orbit, whose references can only be reversed, not negotiated," an approach that "limits the cultural spectrum to either a modern or an antimodern option. Through this narrowness of focus it reduces the chance of recognizing hybridities, overlappings, and juxtapositions" (Werner 1998: 39–40).

Abstract Space, Homogenous Time

When Kenichi Ohmae celebrates the "borderless world," like Giddens, he understands globalization in terms of the expansion of borders, a process whereby more and more of the world comes to exist "within" the abstract space constituted by globalization. Writing at the end of the 1980s, Omae's metaphor for the globalizing world is a spatial one where a border expands, gradually encompassing countries and regions. This metaphor of an expanding border is particularly powerful because it frames globalization in terms we take for granted. It understands globalization as an extension of what Law and Urry (2004) call the "Euclidean world," where space is understood, and experienced, as empty and abstract, constituted by the borders that surround it. This understanding of space plays an important role in the political theory of Thomas Hobbes, who studied Euclid and mathematics while living in France, absorbing the principle that space should be understood as continuous and a continuum, uniform in all directions. Hobbes's Leviathan (1651) lay the basis for an understanding of the state where all subjects could be understood as functionally equivalent within a given abstract space. This idea would be influential in allowing the government of Charles II to conceive of taxation for the first time in terms of aggregates rather than individual cases (Poovey 1995: 29). This understanding of "abstract space," constituted by borders, would play a key role in allowing European states to construct nations, and would later be decisive in European colonization. Sunil Khilnani underlines the importance of such bordered, abstract space in the creation of "the idea of India":

> What made possible the self-invention of national community was the fact of
> alien conquest and colonial subjection. It was the British interest in determin-

ing geographical boundaries that by an Act of Parliament in 1899 converted "India" from the name of a cultural region into a precise pink territory . . . The arbitrary precisions of colonial techniques thus brought forth an historical novelty, a unified and bounded space called India. (2003: 155)

The new understanding of abstract space played a key role in the construction of what we now understand as "the social" (Poovey 1995). This was part of a wider transformation. Alain Desrosières explores the development of statistics and the "politics of large numbers," which made it possible to think in new abstract terms, allowing the integration of the different registers of reality into a single construction, with local singularities disappearing and becoming understood as parts of a greater whole, as manifestations of a general order (1998: 72). Law and Urry argue that it was this "Euclidean world" of abstract space that made possible the idea of functional equivalence, which led to an understanding of the world in terms of larger containers (states) within which there were other discreet entities standing in hierarchical or inclusive relationships – the behaviour of the smaller units had to be understood within the framework of the larger units within which they fitted. Here we see the origins of a new interest in categories and class, out of which would emerge the economic and social theory of Karl Marx. Pam Morris (2004: 3) sees this changed understanding of the world in the work of the British philosopher John Stuart Mill. In 1834 Mill describes Britain as a country made up of landlords, capitalists, and laborers, whose lives are so separated from each other that they experience themselves as different orders living in different worlds, in a world where such differences were experienced "as if they were one of God's ordinances not man's" (Mill 1834 320). Thirty years later, the philosopher observes a shift: "Formerly, different ranks, different neighborhoods, different trades and professions, lived in what might be called different worlds; at present, to a great degree in the same" (Works, 18: 274). This new understanding of inclusiveness did not, of course, deny difference and conflict – but this was understood as taking place within a new understanding of the social, corresponding to the nation, as one unified world. Today's celebrations of the borderless world extend this abstract space, seeing it at work every day in exchange rates, currency flows, and a host of economic data. The influential idea of "global society" is so credible, and almost self evident, because is yet another Euclidean container, "the largest yet imaginable" (Law and Urry 2004: 399).

The "global society" not only involves an extension of abstract space and functional equivalents to the planet as a whole; it also involves the extension of a particular experience of time. Benedict Anderson (1991) underlines the importance of newspapers in the formation of national societies, in particular their role in reporting daily events, arguing that they produced a powerful new sense of "imagined community." The philosopher Charles Taylor, drawing on Anderson, underlines just how much this modern understanding of society is grounded in a temporal experience. It is an experience of "one world," not only because of the abstract space that makes it up, but also because society is "a whole consisting of the simultaneous happening of all the myriad events that mark the lives of its members at that moment" (2004: 157). The culture of Anderson's "imagined community" is one of simultaneity, and there can be little doubt that this culture is a powerful process in the contemporary world. It drives global product launches, it is celebrated in simultaneous movie releases throughout the planet, it is at the center of pervasive cultural practices such as use of mobile phones or the Internet. Global culture is a culture of urgency (Laidi 2001), embedded in a background of the day-to-day, where television plays a role similar to the role Anderson attributes to newspapers. Microsoft's Bill Gates articulates this powerfully when he describes time itself as "friction," as a drag or impediment to the functioning of the network and the possibilities of instant access, information, and exchange that it brings (1996: 191).

Taylor underlines a critical dimension to this new time experience: its homogeneity. For society to consist of the simultaneous happening of a myriad of events, these events must constitute what he calls "homogenous time":

> this very clear, unambiguous concept of simultaneity belongs to an understanding of time as exclusively secular. As long as secular time is interwoven with various kinds of higher time, there is no guarantee that all events can be placed in unambiguous relations of simultaneity and succession . . . There is a close inner link among modern societies, their self-understandings, and modern synoptic modes of representation . . . Society as simultaneous happenings, social interchange as impersonal system, the social terrain as what is mapped, historical culture as what shows up in museums . . . (2004: 158)

This idea of the "borderless world" or "global society" combines the idea of expanding abstract space (bringing with it functional equivalence) with a new time-consciousness of simultaneity. In that sense, "global society" can be understood as expanding outwards from the center, in the way described by Giddens and Fukuyama. This idea of global society converged as well with the increasing importance of borderless networks structured in terms of simultaneous exchange (Castells 2000). But despite its power and its attraction to global elites, this account of "one world" and "global society" is less and less able to make sense of an increasingly complex world.

From Structure to Flow

Most nineteenth-century thinkers relied on metaphors of the machine or stable structures to think about social life. Karl Marx, for example, had a fondness for the image of the building, with its "base" and its "superstructure," while his conception of social change, as that of his contemporaries, was evolutionary or linear. Over recent years a paradigm shift has become increasingly evident in the social sciences, in the development of theoretical models attempting to make sense of new patterns of social life associated with networks and flows. One of the most important contributions has been made by the British sociologist John Urry (2000, 2003). He argues that the conceptual tools we use to make sense of "societies," as bounded areas of social life that correspond to the territories of nation-states, are less and less adequate to the task of making sense of emerging forms of social life and conflict that are increasingly global, and that increasingly take the form of flows. As opposed to the conceptual models that dominated the nineteenth century, evident in Marx's fascination with ideas of equilibrium or Freud's interest in energy and forces, Urry argues that contemporary forms of social life are complex and uncertain, and that the types of social systems that develop are unstable, and, drawing on the work of Prigogine and Stengers (1982), are better understood as in nonequilibrium, where small events can produce large and unpredictable effects, meaning that complex systems are increasingly subject to shockwaves (Mann 1993).

When we start to think about social life in terms of fluid and flows as Urry urges us, change is not linear, but shaped instead by "tipping points," where events occur that cannot be predicted, but that cause dramatic change and new patterns to emerge – such as, for example, the development of the mobile phone or the Internet. The patterns of change here are not expressions of an evolutionary logic that can be mapped out and projected out into the future, but take the form of complex systems reorganizing themselves in ways that cannot be predicted. Urry argues that increasingly complex social life is closer to a fluid moving across an uneven surface than to nineteenth-century metaphors of the machine. He draws on social studies of science (Mol and Law 1994) to suggest that social life can be analyzed in terms of *regions*, which take the form of spatial, bounded areas, such as cities or societies; *networks*, which stretch across regions, such as information systems for example; and *fluids*, which move through networks, but which can also spill over into others – for example, ideas that emerged in New Age networks have spilled over into management sciences (Thrift 1999).

The anthropologist Arjun Appadurai also points to the changing nature of contemporary experience. Rather than attach primary importance to the economic or the institutional, Appadurai (1996) argues that it is the cultural dimension that is most critical in shaping contemporary globalization, where increasingly it is the imagination that constitutes the field of social practices. Above all he underlines the importance of disjunctive experience, the sense that globalization consists of experiencing multiple places and multiple temporalities, dimensions that we will see as crucial to the "another globalization" movement that emerged over the 1990s. In an analysis that has important convergence with the work of John Urry, Appadurai proposes exploring contemporary globalization in terms of five "scapes," or global cultural flows: ethnoscapes, technoscapes, financescapes, mediascapes, and ideoscapes. The use of the term "scape" underlines the unevenness and unpredictability of flows and the importance of perspective, in much the same way as does the concept "landscape." Appadurai introduces these terms in the following way. *Ethnoscape* refers to the shifting terrains of people that constitute the world in which we live: tourists, immigrants, refugees, exiles, guest workers. *Technoscape* refers to the global systems and networks of technology, from the Internet to transport systems. *Financescapes* refers to the increasingly unpredictable flows of finance that rebound around the world. *Mediascapes* refers to the increasing importance of global media, from television, the Internet, magazines, to the flow of audio and video cassettes. *Ideoscapes* refers to the increasing importance of global flows of ideas and ideologies, concepts that are generated in one locality but then flow and take on extraordinary global significance (Appadurai 1996).

For Appadurai, what is critical to understanding the nature of contemporary globlazation is the increasing disjuncture between these different scapes, or between the flows of people, machinery, money, images, or ideas. In an integrated, hierarchical world, these flows all move together, as in Marx's model of ruling class and ruling culture, or in the theory of taste developed by Pierre Bourdieu, where the dominant class innovates and the rest of the population follows. In the contemporary world characterized by disjuncture, these movements diverge, collide as well as converge. Fashion, for example, is no longer generated by an elite and then descends the social hierarchy. While it flows along structures of social inequality, it is not determined nor produced by these – its grammar is experiential; it constitutes a structure of feeling.

Urry's analysis of networks and flow underlines two dimensions of particular importance. Rather than regarding technologies as an extraneous force breaking down communities (the traditional negative view that many sociologists have had with regard to technology), Urry argues instead that technologies increasingly are the media through which social relationships are constructed. The social, he argues, is increasingly characterized by forms of hybridity; it is no longer helpful to think of the social in terms of bounded geographic communicates, but it needs to be understood rather as forms of flow and mobility constituted through technologies, from the car to the Internet. Many social scientists still regard technologies as a factor breaking down the social world, from the radical analyses of the Frankfort school in interwar Germany to Robert Putnam's (2000) view that television is undermining "social capital" in the United States today. Urry, on the contrary, argues that it is increasingly through technologies that the social is itself constituted, and calls for the development of concepts able to develop analyses of the increasing hybridity of sociotechnological networks.

Network Society?

One of the most important attempts to make sense of what is at stake in the transformations at work in globalization is developed by the Spanish sociologist, Manuel Castells (1997, 2000). He argues that globalization represents a planetary shift to a network society, involving a shift from what he calls an "Industrial Paradigm" to an "Information Paradigm" (2000). Castells puts technological shifts at the center of this process; above all, the role of electronics-based information/communication technologies, while also suggesting an increasing role will be played by genetic technologies. These technologies bring with them new patterns of social organization that are informational, global, and networked. Networks, he argues, manifest technological and organizational superiority because of their capacity to deal with uncertainty and complexity, and because of this they inevitably triumph over other forms of organization such as hierarchy and bureaucracy. Networks dissolve centers and disorganize hierarchy, making the exercise of hierarchical power "increasingly impossible" (2000: 19). As a result, Castells argues, the nation-state increasingly finds itself bypassed and weakened by all sorts of emerging networks: of capital, trade, production, science, communication, human rights, and crime, to the point that the state can no longer remain a sovereign entity within a world increasingly organized in terms of networks. Other hierarchical structures find themselves similarly bypassed, whether schools, churches, or other forms of bureaucracy. The network/information logic is insatiable because of its superior efficiency – it absorbs or marginalizes all other competing forms of social organization.

Castells argues that in this emerging network society, the nature of power and conflict also changes. In this world, power is no longer vested in formal political institutions, but becomes decentralized (networks being decentered) and immaterial, taking the form of the flows and codes of networks. Networks possess a binary code of inclusion/exclusion: what is compatible with the network is integrated; what is not is either ignored or eliminated. While Castells argues that it is social struggles that assign goals to networks (reflected in their communication codes), once the network is programmed it imposes its logic on all its members. To challenge a network, actors have to challenge it from the outside. They may seek to counter it by building an alternative network based on alternative values, or develop a defensive, non-network structure or commune, one that "does not allow connections outside its own set of values" (2000: 16). Castells argues that social change occurs through each of these two mechanisms, both of which are external to dominant networks, and this has important implications for the way he conceptualizes contemporary movements and the way they challenge the forms of social domination and power associated with a global, network society. He sees a first type of challenge involving alternative networks, built around alternative projects, "which compete, from network to network, to build bridges to other networks in society, in opposition to the codes of the currently dominant networks" (2000: 22–3).

A second type of opposition involves a rejection of the network logic by affirming values that "cannot be processed in any network, only obeyed and followed." For Castells, the first form of challenge to emerging dominant networks is evident in alternative networks such as ecology, feminism, and human rights movements. He sees the second form of challenge, one that rejects the network logic, expressed by emerging forms of fundamentalism as well as other forms of "cultural communes" "centred around their self-contained meaning," such as "religious, national, territorial, and ethnic communes" (2000: 19, 22, 23). Both these new alternative networks and new defensive communes use new communications technologies such as the Internet. But it is not the technologies they use that make them networks; rather, the issue at stake is the extent to which they can communicate with different networks, beyond their self-definition.

For Castells this emerging networked world confronts us with a central dilemma:

> The fundamental dilemma in the network society is that political institutions are not the site of power any longer. The real power is the power of instrumental flows, and cultural codes, embedded in networks. Therefore, the assault to these immaterial power sites, from outside their logic, requires either the anchoring in eternal values, or the projection of alternative, communicative codes that expand through networking of alternative networks. That social change proceeds through one way or another will make the difference between fragmented communalism and new history making. (2000: 23)

Actors and Subjectivities

The social sciences, sociology in particular, played a key role in representing new forms of collectivity and aggregation, contributing to shaping the modern nation-state as a social world ordered in terms of clear boundaries, citizenship, and governance. Today there is a new uncertainty about fundamental categories to make sense of being and acting in the world (Wallerstein 1996). On the one hand, there are those who argue that the contemporary globalizing world is a "global society." This world without borders extends the logic of economic systems to the point where there is no actor, only behaviour, as individuals correspond to the systems of opportunity or incentive that they are part of. Or action becomes understood as "resistance" to this model. But this, as we have seen, places action "inside" the global orbit, and brings with it an understanding of the actor as engaged in purposive, instrumental action, where action is shaped by an understanding of interest and framed in terms of intention (Asad 2003: 73).

The core question that confronts us when thinking about globalization is whether we live in one world or in many worlds, whether we inhabit a "universe," or whether we are caught up in, and are helping to produce, what Law and Urry term a "pluriverse" (2004: 399). This means a shift away from paradigms of abstraction and generality, and means exploring globalization in terms of increasing pluralization and complexity. The themes of disjuncture and complexity imply a break with "one world," and to approach the world, as anthropologist Clifford Geertz argues (1998), in terms of particularization and singularities. This does not mean that a global world is made up of a myriad of incommensurable and mutually unintelligible experiences. But it does have implications for the way we attempt to understand general patterns that may be emerging in this context of complexity and pluralization. As Alberta Arthurs suggests, drawing on Geertz, "if the general is to be grasped at all . . . it must be grasped not directly, all at once, but via instances, differences, variations and particulars; in a piecemeal fashion, case by case. In a splintered world, we must address the splinters" (2003: 581). This does not mean we are faced with the choice of "one world" or a multitude of radically incommensurable worlds. Rather, contemporary globalization confronts us with the challenge of understanding new forms of partial connection, new experiences of border. This opens out as well the possibility of more complex ways of knowing, making possible a "fluid and decentred social science, with fluid and decentred modes for knowing the world allegorically, indirectly, perhaps pictorially, sensuously, poetically, a social science of partial connections" (Law and Urry 2004: 400). Rather than understand the world in terms of abstract space and homogenous time, this points to the importance of exploring what Talal Asad (2003) calls complex space and complex time.

A world understood in terms of complex space and complex time is not one where borders are made redundant, but rather one where borders traverse the subjectivity of persons who find themselves living in multiple worlds, as the Mexican-American band Los Tigres del Norte remind us. French sociologist Alain Touraine (2002) argues that in the emerging global world, it is the "individual's self-construction as an actor" that needs to be placed at the center of the struggle to understand the contemporary world. Over recent years the questions of what constitutes action have become increasingly central to social theory (Joas 1996; Asad 2003). Touraine argues that this lies at the heart of understanding the contemporary world, calling on the social sciences to radically shift focus, "from understanding society" (with a focus on systems, levels, and dynamics) to "discovering the subject," placing the struggle to become an actor at the center of the social sciences. This places the question of movements of action at the heart of the way we attempt to make sense of the contemporary world.

Global Movements

This book focuses on forms of action and culture that have emerged in different types of movement, each of which has globalized. The first of these became known as the "antiglobalization" movement at the time of the mobilization against the World Trade Organization that took place in Seattle, November 1999, but which now increasingly defines itself as a movement for "another globalization." Over the 1990s this movement became more and more evident through blockades and actions linked to the increasing importance of international summits and meetings of organizations such as the World Bank, the World Economic Forum, or the World Trade Organization, where these summits not only served as platforms for bankers and political leaders, but as key convergence points for emerging networks of groups and actors increasingly defining themselves in opposition to "neoliberal" globalization. These mobilizations accelerated after Seattle in 1999, reaching a peak in Genoa in July 2001, where some 200,000 people protested against what they saw as the agenda of the Group of 8 leaders of the world's most industrialized nations. For many analysts these massive mobilizations appeared to spring from nowhere, and many influential observers believed that they would disappear following the September 11 attacks in 2001 (*Wall Street Journal* 2001). Overall this has not been the case, with massive mobilizations taking place outside of the United States, such as in Barcelona in 2002 or Evian in France in 2003. But the very size of these mobilizations can be deceptive, overshadowing the crucial role of what Italian sociologist Alberto Melucci (1996a) refers to as "submerged networks" within such movements – in this case, new forms of media and Internet networks, the new humanitarian movement, and new forms of culture and direct action that emerged in ecological and urban action, and which are at the origins of the global networks that began to become more visible over the latter half of the 1990s. Once we begin to explore this process we encounter new grammars of action: a shift from older forms of solidarity to new grammars of fluidity (McDonald 2002).

The movement contesting neoliberal globalization involves significant dimensions and networks outside countries such as the United States, Europe, or similar societies. Below we explore one of the most important of these that played a key role in contributing to the emergence of a wider movement, namely the Zapatista movement that emerged in the Chiapas region of Mexico in January 1994, where a small group of indigenous insurgents, influenced by Latin American traditions of guerrilla strategy, took control of five towns. Many people in Mexico, including those sympathetic to the plight of the indigenous, were dismayed by these beginnings of armed conflict, coming at a time when a horrendously violent civil war in neighboring Guatemala was gradually drawing to a bloody close. Many external observers regarded this action as yet another ethnonationalist movement seeking to defend local, often archaic, traditions against their inevitable decline. In the period that followed, this indigenous movement showed an extraordinary capacity to transform itself into something new, with armed conflict effectively abandoned in favor of a new type of action. In particular cultural and communicative action able to link tradition and openness, which set in motion an extraordinary international dynamic that is still at work today. This is evident, for example, in the development of Indymedia, the Independent Media Center that began at the WTO mobilization in Seattle, but that had its origins in a call for independent global media that was made in the Mexican jungle. The originality of this movement has great implications for the way we think about contemporary globalization, movements, ethics, and democracy.

The second movement that this book explores emerged neither in the Americas nor in Europe, but in China. This is the movement of Falun Gong, a cultivation movement that has its origins in the wider qigong movement that emerged in China in the period following the Cultural Revolution. Falun Gong itself is based on a series of exercises developed in the early 1990s by a former public official, Li Hongzi. Over the following decade it was taken up as a form of practice by several million people in China, and received the support of influential sections of the power elite, before being declared an illegal cult and being subjected to very strong repression from April 1999 onwards. Amnesty International (2000) estimate that over five thousand practitioners were sent to labor camps in the two years following the ban. Despite the attempts to suppress Falun Gong in China, it has developed among the Chinese diaspora in East Asia and beyond, in particular through information technologies such as the Internet. It emerges in China through sporadic actions, such as the hacking into China's national television network in late 2003. Despite this repression, China specialists suggest that this movement represents the most significant challenge to the Chinese regime since the student movement of 1989 (Vermander 2001). What is distinctive about this movement is the extent to which it has taken shape around forms of embodied practice such as qigong exercises and meditation, and as such it is part of wider cultural and social transformations in China in the post-Maoist period. This movement is clearly not a "social movement" in the sense that sociologists have traditionally understood the term. But if it is one of the most significant movements to emerge in China over the past decade, we are confronted with the task of developing tools to explore its development and significance. In this case, the Falun Gong and the wider movement of qigong out of which it emerged confront us with critical questions about embodiment, memory, and subjectivity – questions posed within a different civilizational matrix to that from which sociology and western social science emerged. To explore its development, we need to "decenter" the western experience (Gole 2000).

Thirdly, this book turns to explore the development of new Islamic experiences emerging in the space between diaspora populations and Muslim majority countries. Analyses approaching the increasing significance of Islamic groups and networks do so in very different ways. The French political sociologist Gilles Kepel (2002), for example, argues we are seeing a shift in what he calls "re-Islamization" from above (an emphasis on politics and the state) to re-Islamization from below (an emphasis on piety and personal life). This suggests moving in two ways on the one path, opposing a dominant, western modernization. Other authors point beyond a reactive model, pointing to the emergence of new types of public space (Anderson 2003), the emergence of new types of "translocal" (Mandaville 2001) experiences and subjectivities, and the increasing importance of practices constructed in terms of autonomy, embodiment, and subjectivity (Mahmood 2004). These analyses point to something very different from the defensive ethnic or communitarian identities that understand Islamic movements as "holes" in the process of globalization.

One of the most important expressions of this globalized Islam is the development of what Olivier Roy has termed "neo-fundamentalism" (2004).

While Islam is part of a wider reconfiguration of religious traditions (Asad 1996), one where we encounter new subjectivities and public spaces, it is also associated with the emergence of new forms of antimovement (Wieviorka 2005a, 2005b). The "identity model" of social movements would suggest that these are defensive communities constructed against an invasive globalization (Castells 1997). But what is at stake appears very different, with contemporary forms of fundamentalism constructed *against* community cultures and histories (Meddeb 2002), while located in global flows of people and ideas. The chapters below explore the emergence of new forms of global Islamic experience, but at the same time focus in particular on forms of embodied subjectivity and practice at stake in globalizing piety movements that put into question understandings of action constructed in terms of disembodied grammars of representation.

Grammars of Culture and Action

The forms of action we explore in the chapters below cut across older understandings of agency and experience. The modern understanding regards action as shaped by intentionality or goals, understanding it in terms of movement to increased autonomy and freedom (Asad 2003: 71). Within this framework, the relationship to the body is an instrumental one where the actor experiences himself or herself as being "in" a body or being a self that "has" a body (Schoenfeldt 1999: 10). Movements, as we will see in the following chapter, have been understood within a recurring dichotomy, one understood either in *instrumental* terms (framed in terms of models of rational action) or in *expressive* terms (with an emphasis on identity, the symbolic or communities). Understandings of public space have emphasized the rational and the discursive, extrapolating an idealized model of the bourgeois public sphere understood as existing between state and society. The individual actor has been understood as secular, disembodied, and rational, and this paradigm as well was used to think about organization and the relationship between individual and collective experience. At the heart of this understanding we will encounter the category of representation.

In the movements we explore in this book we see a shift from older forms of organization to new experiences. We encounter in powerful form experiences of embodiment and embodied presence, and experiences best understood in terms of "embodied intersubjectivity" (Csordas 1993: 146) rather than models of representation. These underline the plurality of senses through which we experience the world, the other, and the self. But once we admit the possibility of acting sensually, we open the limits of intentional action, as sensory experience cannot be understood primarily in intentional terms. The senses pose a threat to intentional action, perhaps explaining why they have been effaced so thoroughly in the sociology of movements. Throughout this book we constantly encounter embodiment and the senses: dance, music, drumming, bicycle riding, experiences of vulnerability and physical confrontation, where the embodied actor and embodied intersubjectivity become critical to understand: from the embodiment of direct action in antiglobalization action to the embodied memory and embodied public experience in qigong movements or in practices of Islamic piety. These forms of action and culture allow us to break out of often repeated debates framed in terms of individual versus the community, opening out forms of individual autonomy that do not correspond to the rational, disembodied individual.

The movements we explore in this book are not identity movements, nor expressions of identity. The movements we explore are better approached in other ways, rather that in terms of "categories" and "aggregates," terms that as we saw, have their origins in particular time and place. Rather than strongly articulated senses of "us," we are more likely to encounter experiences of displacement, often accompanied by experiences of strangeness and what Margrit Shildrick (2002) explores as "encounters with the vulnerable self." Through engaging with these forms of action and culture, I attempt to understand more embodied grammars of subjectivity, intersubjectivity, and action. Rather than think of contemporary movements in terms of the paradigms of organization or community that were so influential over the twentieth century, I hope to open the way we think about movements to themes coming from studies of rhythm, music, and resonance. Paradoxically, while globalization brings with it the sense that we are living in different worlds, these movements suggest new ways of thinking about the worlds we share.

CHAPTER 2

Movements and Action

A paradigm is not only an instrument in the hands of the dominant; it is just as much the construction of defences, critiques, movements of liberation.

Alain Touraine, *Un nouveau paradigme*

Scale Shift and Political Process

In an important survey of approaches to social movements, Jeff Goodwin and James Jasper (1999) point to the importance of what is widely called "political process theory," which they suggest is currently "hegemonic" in English-language sociology. This view contends that "global movements" are essentially extensions of older forms of "social movement" that we are largely familiar with. From this perspective globalization involves new types of alliances between old types of actors, who remain located within the framework of nation-states and within grammars of action and culture that we are largely familiar with. And clearly this is a very important process, one of the driving forces of the extraordinary growth in the number of International Non-Governmental Organizations (INGOs) that has occurred over the past two decades. From this point of view, globalization is understood as a "scale shift" (Tarrow 2003), where national level patterns of action and organization extend out to new international contexts. Globalization is thus approached in terms of levels, while the task of social science becomes exploring and identifying the "mechanisms" that bring about shifts in these levels, variously conceived as "local," "national" and "international/transnational," or "micro," "meso" and "macro" (Tarrow 2003). Scale shift means that social movements not only focus on attempting to influence national political processes and organizations; they will increasingly move to focus on international organizations such as the World Bank, the International Monetary Fund, and so on, structures and organizations that constitute a new international "political opportunity structure." This essentially understands globalization in terms of a new level of institutions, which has several consequences. The emphasis on movements interacting with institutions leads to a focus on movements that most resemble those we are already familiar with at a national level, those most approximating the movements that have emerged in societies like the United States over the past decades. For many sociologists this is regarded as so self-evident that it scarcely rates discussion. This is because, for many sociologists, social movements are regarded as part of a wider process of modernization, understood as a process through which societies converge, become more like each other, and (although this is rarely articulated) become more like those societies that sociologists are most familiar with – those of Europe and North America.

The wider context can help us locate this "political process" approach. American sociologists and political scientists such as Charles Tilly, Sidney Tarrow, and Doug McAdam were attempting to break with earlier models that had dominated English-language studies of social movements, which to a significant extent had understood movements as expressions of social strain or dysfunction (Smelser 1962). Rather than see movements as expressions of social crisis, Tilly and others writing at this time conceptualized social movements as the rational action of excluded groups seeking to achieve political outcomes. Doug McAdam's analysis of the Civil Rights movement (1982) emphasized resource mobilization rather than relative deprivation, and these authors increasingly began to define social movements as instruments to mobilize and affect the political system, rather than expressions of social malaise. Tilly, as a social historian, argued that the development of modern political institutions serves as the key to understand these movements. For him, social movements become manifest through "deliberately formed, specialized, political associations" which emerge at the same time as the birth of modern electoral systems. As nation-states construct national political systems, their development leads to "the proliferation of created associations as vehicles for collective action" (Tilly 1984b: 304). For Tilly, the emergence of social movements parallels the historical emergence of political parties, these being two dimensions of the one process: "a social movement is essentially a political party with broad aspirations and a unifying belief system. A political party is a tamed, nationalized social movement" (1984b: 305). This analysis locates social movements firmly within political systems. For the influential German sociologists Rucht and Neidhardt, a social movement is "a mechanism for articulating and asserting certain collective interests . . . the functional equivalent . . . of political parties and interest groups" (2002: 20).

This political process analysis flows directly into analyses of globalization, where emerging international political institutions are understood as replicating developments that led to the constitution of national political systems.

French political scientist Florence Passy reworks Tilly's argument, affirming that just as modern social movements "emerged in the nineteenth century following a long period of construction of the national state," in the contemporary context "new power centres have been created at the supranational level." While emphasizing that such supranational power centers have not replaced the nation-state, for Passy the development of such "supranational structures offer social movements new political opportunities to address their claims" (Passy 2001: 13).

The Association, Public Space, and Representation

Tilly's account is more complex than the simple observation that new types of institutions create new "political opportunities." He attaches great importance to a new way of acting, and with this, to a new relationship between individual and collective experience. He sees both these at stake in the birth of *the association*. For Tilly the association involves "the *deliberate constitution* of new groups for the offensive pursuit of new rights and advantages" (1984b: 303–4; emphasis added). It is the deliberate constitution of these groups that Tilly regards as a decisive historical shift, pointing to the emergence of a new type of action and actor that he defines as the "social movement," and which he contrasts with earlier forms of action such as riots, and earlier actors such as communities. For Tilly what is so important about the association is that such groups are *"deliberately formed, specialist, manifestly political organizations as instruments of collective action"* (1982: 23). The idea of *deliberate* formation articulates an intentional understanding of agency; his emphasis on *specialization* captures the emerging division of labor that would be such a defining feature of the industrial society that was coming into birth at that time; the *manifestly political* identity captures the sense that these organizations were emerging in relation to the political system; while the idea of the association as instrument of "collective action" captures a cultural shift occurring at that time, one that allowed people not only to conceive of groups in new ways, but also to imagine acting together and creating *instruments* to achieve such action. This emphasis on associations came to define American approaches to social movements. So much so, that in the period following Tilly's work, American sociologists coined the expression Social Movement Organization (SMO) as a shorthand term to define what they considererd social movements. Over the 1970s William Gamson's (1975) contention that the key to a successful social movement lay in its capacity to build bureaucracy came to be regarded as self-evident. Successful movements build organizations and in the process they institutionalize. The Italian sociologist Alberto Melucci was particularly concerned about the implications of this approach (1996a). Reducing movements to their political dimensions has the effect of silencing their communicative content. Constructed in such a way, Melucci believed such analyses closed off the questions posed by movements. Instead, they become instruments to represent the interests of a group, where the study of movements becomes defined as identifying their "mechanisms" or "dynamics" (McAdam et al. 2001).

The political process model of movement is embedded in a wider understanding of action and culture. The dimensions Tilly continually emphasizes all refer to the emergence of a modern, western form of individual, one who is less defined by his or her community and more by his or her will and interests. The social movement, so understood, can be understood as an *act of representation*. Tilly insists that the groups making up a social movement must be "deliberately formed," as opposed to reflecting some community-based characteristic. One does not join an association on the basis of community characteristics, but as a member of a public sphere. The association that Tilly describes is one where those who participate do so on the basis of their *public*, as opposed to their *private*, selves. Hence the great importance that Tilly attaches to the role of the public meeting in the birth of the social movement. One of the key characteristics of the public meeting is precisely that it mobilizes "public" identities. We can see this in the way that decisions are taken – by a show of hands, not by a secret ballot. This understanding of public identities occurs equally in trade unions as well, that manifest a historical preference for voting through a show of hands, as opposed to secret ballot.

The public meeting has a particularly important role in the American political imagination, often associated with what is regarded as a pure form of democracy, the New England town meeting. Tilly's account of the public meeting resonates because it reconciles the modern individual with the community. As individuals free themselves from the constraints of tradition and community, they do not necessarily face anomie or disintegration, but the *reconstitution of a political community of free individuals* through association. Tilly's social movement echoes Alexis de Tocqueville's *Democracy in America*, with its emphasis on associations, hence the constant reference to the *deliberate* formation of the association, and the great pains Tilly takes to distinguish the association from other forms of collective that are expressions of preexisting communities. This also helps us understand the uneven resonance of the concept of "Social Movement Organization" – widely embraced in the United States, but much less so in countries shaped by other political traditions.[1]

While Tilly's followers at time seem to suggest that the creation of social movements is a simple product of the emergence of political institutions generating new types of participation, his own work on the association as a new type of vehicle for action and representation opens questions that go beyond the "political opportunities" created by new institutional arrangements. The association emerged over the 1800s as a wider grammar of action, well beyond a more narrowly conceived role as an instrument to take advantage of institutional arrangements. The historian Mary Ryan explores the United States in the same historical period, pointing to the importance of early associations of mutual support among workers, for example, to defray the costs of burial, which would lay the basis for the later development of trade unions. These associations emerged in the 1830s, declined with the depression of the 1840s, then blossomed in the 1850s, leading to the formation of the American Federation of Labor in 1886. Ryan points to the birth of American social movements in the areas of workers issues, women, and slavery, while emphasizing the same two dimensions that Tilly points to in Britain as the core of the "action repertoire" of these movements: the voluntary association and the public meeting. Tilly's theory of the birth of social movements is more than an account of the emergence of political institutions; it offers a more complex account of social and cultural transformations occurring during the 1800s.

The political process narrative locates social movements within a wider understanding of "western modernization" (Rucht and Neidhardt 2002), one that privileges organized relationships with political institutions and the forms of subjectivity, freedom, representation, and agency associated with this. With the advent of globalization, this is understood to be "scale shifting" from the national to the international level. In the process, the western experience of movement, or a particular understanding of this experience, claims paradigm status. This recurs in a series of very important ways: in how we think about the relationship between individual and collective experience; in what we understand by "the social"; in the ways we conceptualize action, where the model of freedom, autonomy, and agency that emerged within western culture is regarded as self-evidently universal.

New Social Movements?

There has been a countermodel to the dominant political process account, associated in particular with European sociologists such as Alain Touraine in France or Alberto Melucci in Italy. If American sociologists have largely focused on the relationship between social movements and the political system, this in part is explained by the United States' political system, which is open and characterized by relatively openly structured political parties, which tend to have weaker programs than their European counterparts (Buechler 2000). As a result the US system involves extensive networks of lobbyists and a whole culture emphasizing mobilizing to influence the political system, while the European model that developed over the twentieth century involved organizationally stronger parties tied to more clearly defined social groups or classes – evidenced by the importance of labor, social democratic, or communist parties over much of the twentieth century in Europe. So, while Americans naturally tended to conceive of social movements as mobilizing to influence the political system, European realities and intellectual traditions placed a much greater emphasis on social class and class structure when thinking about social movements. It is not surprising that Alain Touraine, one of the pioneers of European sociology of social movements, focused his first research on the labor movement (1955). For him, the key question to understanding movements was not the creation of associations, but labor mobilizations and forms of class-consciousness on the assembly line.

Touraine argues that it is critical to understand movements not simply as the products of social structure, but as actors sharing and contesting the types of creativity or "historicity" that constitute the core resource in different types of societies. For Touraine preindustrial societies are organized around access to and control of land. With the shift to industrial society, Touraine saw the core resource shifting to the control and organization of labor, and so conflicts at the center of industrial societies would take place in workplaces. For Touraine, labor in industrial society is not only a resource; it is a form of creativity and a grammar of ethics. Hence Touraine's paradigmatic model of social movement was the labor movement (1996).

Over the late 1960s student and worker conflicts swept across Europe and the United States. For many observers this represented more than a simple event within the political cycle, but pointed instead to more profound social change (Crouch and Pizzorno 1978). Serge Mallet (1975) writing in France argued that the rise of the student movement and its alliance with new categories of workers pointed to a broader shift due to the increasing importance of intellectual work, and Mallet adopted an older language of class to argue that new professional groups represented a "new working class," their emergence ushering in new types of conflicts around control and creativity at work, framed in a language of autonomy and creativity. André Gorz believed that emerging conflicts and changing patterns of the organization of production meant it was time to say "farewell to the working class" (1982). Touraine also believed that the conflicts emerging in the late 1960s pointed to a shift away from the forms of organization and consciousness that had characterized the action of the labor movement in industrial society. He argued that the student movement of the late 1960s and the women's movement which emerged from it pointed to a profound shift in societal type, from industrial to postindustrial society (1971, 1974), a view that was being developed at the same time in the United States by Daniel Bell (1973). On this basis, Touraine argued that the forms of action emerging in the late 1960s and over the 1970s involved what he termed "new social movements."

For Touraine, the question of "identity" was central to these new movements. By this he meant that the decisive conflicts generating "historicity" were no longer located in the workplace, but were taking place at the level of culture and its models of creativity and knowledge, the core resource in postindustrial society (1981). Hence Touraine attached particular importance to student and ecology movements, which he saw as potentially contesting the way new forms of technocratic power were attempting to shape and control models of social creativity. In a type of society increasingly organized around communication codes, identity for Touraine was above all a field of conflict, where processes of social creativity were at stake. Of critical importance to emerging movements was their ability to manage the tension between identity's "two faces"; namely its defensive and the creative dimensions (1988). This tension had proved central in Touraine's analysis of the labor movement. On the one hand his earlier research had encountered a "proletarian" identity, shaped above all by the experience of deskilled work, where work is experienced as domination, where the worker is stripped of creativity by systems such as the assembly line. In this context worker action typically ranges from withdrawal to sabotage, all characterized by the theme of rupture, of trying to be free from a meaningless and often destructive experience. But at the same time Touraine's research had pointed to an identity associated with skilled workers for whom work is an experience of creativity, and who develop forms of action that can easily become absorbed into forms of "market unionism." For Touraine these two sides of identity, an experience of the creativity of work and a new form of social suffering brought about through loss of creativity, are both brought into being by industrial society's culture and social organization. Neither of these dimensions alone can create a workers' movement. Touraine argued that a social movement of workers comes into being when these two dimensions of creativity encounter and transform each other in the context of social conflicts. This synthesis is not the culture of a community, but the product of a social struggle, one that is able to affirm the creativity and ethic of work while at the same time naming the form of domination at stake in systems of work organization that sought to strip workers of their creativity. Touraine's research underlines just how this synthesis is fragile, is constantly being remade, and can only be achieved through social relationships. Just as Hoggart (1957), Touraine argues that community culture is often opposed to social movements and conflicts. Movements, he insists, do not defend collective identity; they contest social relationships. The new social movements, he believed, foreshadowed a new central conflict that would parallel the central conflict between industrialists and labor movements in industrial society.

From Organization to Identity

By the mid-1980s the distinction between "European" and "American" approaches (Klandermans 1986) to social movements increasingly became understood as an opposition between an "identity" paradigm and a "strategy" paradigm (Cohen 1985). The political process approach was increasingly criticized, in particular from within, as failing to accord sufficient importance to questions of identity, above all in the context of American "identity politics." Taylor and Whittier's analysis of lesbian feminist communities (1992, 1995) played a key role in terms of integrating the theme of identity into the political process approach. Identity increasingly became understood as a resource that could be mobilized (Tilly 1993–4), or a factor that reduced the costs of mobilization (Tarrow 1994), it was the way movements "transform their members into political actors" (Taylor and Whittier 1992: 104). In the process, identity increasingly became defined as the characteristic of a community, *"the shared definition of a group* that derives from its members' common interests, experiences and solidarity" (Taylor and Whittier 1992: 105; emphasis added), becoming the functional equivalent of ideology (Taylor and Whittier 1992: 104; Taylor 2000). As political process theory became "hegemonic" among English-language approaches to social movements, identity increasingly became defined as "collective identity," establishing itself as a new orthodoxy within the study of social movements, the process whereby "social actors recognize themselves – and are recognized by others – as part of broader groupings. *On the basis of such allegiances*, they give meaning to their own experiences" (Della Porta and Diani 1999: 85; emphasis added).

The embrace of "identity" by American sociologists reflected changes occurring within the American political system, where in a context of increasing cultural pluralism political mobilizations increasingly aimed at creating the status of a minority (Berbrier 2002), effectively using "identity" as a "political resource," where often successful entry into the political system required constituting a "community," such as the "deaf community" or the "gay community" (Berbrier 2002). Joshua Gamson, examining American political culture, makes a similar point when he argues that the "political opportunity structure" requires "clear categories of collective identity . . . for successful resistance strategies" (Gamson 1995: 391). This intellectual shift is summed up by McAdam, Tarrow, and Tilly when they argue "actors take action in the name of identities" (McAdam et al. 2001: 137).

Over the 1990s the *Social Movement Organization* transformed into the *Social Movement Community*, held together by identity rather than organizational structure. But there is a large continuity between this understanding of community and earlier models based on organization. Snow and McAdam, key proponents of the political process model, develop an account of identity when they argue that for a movement to be successful there must be "correspondence" between the "I" and the "we," where *"before individuals become serviceable movement agents* . . . it is necessary that personal identities dovetail with a movement's collective identity" (2000: 52; emphasis added).

It is difficult, if not impossible, to imagine applying this model of "identity" correspondence and community, a product of American political culture, to emerging global movements. For that reason, important figures within the political process tradition argue that there can be no "global movements," only "domestic organizations who choose to move into transnational activism" (Tarrow 2002) in order to strengthen their position within the national political system. But as the language of movements is one of community, successful transnational strategies will involve "mechanisms" of identification and attribution of similarity:

> as institutions from the World Bank to the IMF to the WTO to the G8 adopt the provisions of global neo-liberalism, contenders around the world with little else in common can begin to attribute similarity to themselves and others who have in common with them only an antagonistic relationship to one of more of these institutions. In this sense, international institutions not only provide an opportunity structure for contention but provide unifying themes and identities for those who oppose them. (Tarrow 2002: 32–33)

This essentially instrumental understanding grounds attempts to frame identity within a "social mechanisms" model that increasingly looks to cost-benefit models of microeconomic rational choice (Tarrow 2002).

The models of social movement introduced in this chapter carry a very important legacy of the time and place of their construction. Touraine's attempt to develop a theory of new social movements was developed in the context of the decline of trade unionism and the social conflicts that emerged in France in 1968 and its aftermath, where he suggested at first that the new movements would be a new "class actor." In the United States understandings of social movements were influenced by the critique of "organization man" and new types of identity movements, community and minority, emerging from the 1970s onwards. These traditions are evident in ways of conceptualizing movements: French political culture remains deeply ambivalent about ideas of community and minority, paralleling American culture's antipathy to the question of class.

Civic and Industrial Grammars of Action

To think creatively and usefully about the idea of "social movement" we need to go beyond these more obvious oppositions, and be alert to the ways our understanding of "social movement" is located within a wider trajectory of western cultures and societies. We have seen that the category of the "social" emerged in Europe over the nineteenth century, linked to a new awareness of "generality," of shared condition and experience, linked, as we have seen, to a new understanding of large numbers. This made possible the new ways of conceptualizing risk and of pooling resources to deal with this, the basis of new types of association to share the costs firstly of funerals, later, of injury. As political philosopher Pierre Rosanvallon argues (2002), this new understanding of risk and the possibility of insuring against it led to the formation of the welfare state at the end of the century (Rosanvallon 2000).

This awareness of generality was also present in cultural shifts that framed the way newly emerging social groups understood their relationship between each other. The American historian James Sewell explores the emergence of working-class culture and action in France, and argues that a critical dimension of this process was a new moral grammar produced in the context of new social relationships. He argues that this is particularly evident in the way the meanings of the word "exploit" changed from 1760 to 1860. In the early part of this century, the term "exploit" had a morally neutral meaning, referring to the way a farmer would make use of his fields as a resource. As the industrial order emerged, the term was used to describe the way emerging industrialists made use of their workforce as a resource. At first this was used in the same way as the farmer exploits the land, but with developing labor organizations and action the term took on a new, modern meaning, where "exploit" came to describe a form of action denying the dignity and worth of those workers who were exploited. A shift had occurred, the understanding of "the social" in terms of a new awareness of generality and categories framing a new moral language constructed in the context of new social relationships.

Poovey, Morris, and Rosanvallon all argue that a new understanding of collectivity and inclusion was a critical factor in the emergence of the modern category of "the social." This was central to the new understanding of class as category that developed in the early nineteenth century, one that was taken up by Marx who argued that class could be understood as a totality, as an actor, or what would later be called by twentieth-century political ideologies a "class subject" (Negri 1991). The cultural changes at work in the first half of the nineteenth century did more than recognize generality as a category – they made possible thinking about "generality" as an actor. This concept still plays itself out today in the ways we think about movements, in particular through what Boltanski and Thévenot (1991) call the civic and industrial grammars of action that framed a new way of thinking about the relationship between collective and personal experience. And here they underline the key role of the political philosopher Jean Jacques Rousseau, and the way he changed how collectivity was thought of.

For Rousseau, civic peace depends on the authority of a sovereign who stands above the selfish and particularistic lusts of individuals, and who is thus able to secure the common good. Rousseau's political philosophy can be understood as part of a wider process of secularization taking place in Europe over the eighteenth century (Eisenstadt 1999). He was close to Jansenism, a French religious movement with parallels to Calvinism's understanding of predestination of the elect, or the "community of saints." As Riley argues (1986), before Rousseau, divine will was made manifest through the body of the king, who as sovereign stood above the lusts and disorders of particularities. Through developing the concept of the "general will," Rousseau disembodies this concept of sovereignty, and transfers it from the king to the citizens, whom he understood as a collectivity, as the convergence of the human wills of citizens who *give up their particularities* and devote themselves to the common good. For Rousseau, the quality of the good citizen is not achieved through talent, fame, or rank, but instead through the qualities of virtue and sacrifice, which in turn assure the "mutuality" of social practices (Boltanski and Thévenot 1991). For Rousseau, such civic action frees the individual from the dependencies of hierarchical relationships or personal obligation, and allows them to become detached from one another and thus become able to achieve the status of citizens. Good citizens are able to disassociate themselves from personal interests, and place themselves in the position previously occupied by the sovereign, acting uniquely in terms of the general will. Rousseau lived from 1712 to 1788, but his work captures processes that extend into the nineteenth century and beyond, in the ways, for example, that the universal French state set about abolishing particularities of custom, region, and language, and turning "peasants into Frenchmen" (Weber 1976).

It was during the nineteenth century that the previous moral primacy claimed by the sovereign came to be claimed by new expressions of the collective, the most obvious example being the state. But this principle of the moral primacy of the collective over the individual would also be at the center of a wider "civic world" of action and organization, one that played a crucial role in emerging trade unionism. Boltanski and Thevenot write:

> The peculiarity of the civic world is to lay stress on beings who are not individual beings but collective ones. Individual human beings can be seen as relevant and worthy only as they belong to a group or as they are representatives of a collective person. In this world, important persons are, therefore, federations, public communities, representatives or delegates. Their qualities are to be official or statutory. The relevant objects are either immaterial, for example, rules, codes, procedures, or material, as union premises or ballot boxes. Praiseworthy relationships are those which involve or mobilize people for a collective action. (1999: 372)

As Pierre Rosanvallon argues (2000), the modern capitalism that emerged over the nineteenth century equally drew on this principle of generality and equivalence, envisaging new ways of organizing labor, where one worker could be substituted for another. The response of labor movements across very different cultures and political traditions was to construct defensive collectivities, forms of action and organization that embraced the emerging civic grammar, where actions are of worth not when they are undertaken in the name of an individual, but when they are taken in the name of the collective. Within this grammar of action, singularities and particularities threaten division. Solidarity is achieved through renouncing particularities – overcoming particularity makes solidarity and acting collectively possible (Boltanski and Thévenot 1991: 237). This ethical model has a direct impact on the way the group structures itself and acts. If the moral principle upon which action is based is the collective or what is held in common, then "relationships between people are of merit when they set in place arrangements that de-singularize them" (1991: 143). From this perspective, interpersonal relationships are subject to suspicion, as are forms of private communication taking place between individuals: "every person-to-person relationship that is not mediated through the relationship to the totality of the political body serves as an obstacle to the general will, degrades it, or pulls it in the direction of the particular and thus constitutes a plot that must be denounced" (Boltanski and Thévenot 1991: 144). This leads to forms of organization that emphasize vertical relationships of delegation, mandate, and representation, while horizontal relationships threaten the unity of the movement. The member relates to "the totality," or to actions, symbols, or structures manifesting the totality – declarations, resolutions, conferences. Person-to-person relationships and private indentities are excluded. This form of movement seeks to constitute itself as a totality, as a "collective subject."

The moral imperatives of the civic grammar profoundly shaped the birth of trade unions (Sewell 1980), and remain important today, evident above all in the relationship between individual and collective. It is the civic moral imperative that is at the basis of the importance within trade union culture attached to treasurers, branches, secretaries, members, statutes, resolutions, and meeting procedures. All these are strategies that desingularize participation. At the same time trade unions embraced key features of the emerging industrial grammar, which places value on efficiency and the division of labor as a way to achieve goals. Embracing the industrial ethic of organization allowed the labor movement to develop a form of structure where power resided in the collectivity, structured in a logic of representation and delegation, where each level of the organization elects the level above it, while decisions proceed downwards, where those at the summit are able to view and act upon the interests of the collectivity as a whole. In an industrial organization one acts in terms of executing a function (Hage and Powers 1992) as opposed to acting on the basis of personal loyalties, relationships, or characteristics. This form of organization succeeds in combining the principle of equivalence (all members can be interchanges) with the fact that some positions, such as president, will exercise greater power than others: while possessing unequal power as a result of the role occupied each member is in principle equal. Power inequality resides in the positions, not the persons, reflecting the imperative of efficiency. The importance attached to the collective underlines the significance of programs, policies, and resolutions of conferences – instances through which the collective manifests itself. Within the civic grammar, when people act, they do so in their official capacity as secretary, president, and so on. Hence the importance of references to conferences and resolutions – people act to execute a function; they act through putting into practice decisions made by the collective.

The moral imperative of solidarity means that once the collective has taken a decision, all will execute it. It is impossible, from the perspective of the civic grammar, for this to be otherwise. Failure to act out a decision made by the collective constitutes a moral fault: it attacks the very core of the civic grammar. In that sense, *the collective acts through the individuals who make it up*. Renouncing particularities means that involvement is based upon what is held in common; hence the importance attached to voting by public show of hands, as opposed to secret ballot. Formal meetings, minutes, and practices such as addressing the chair (who incarnates the collective) are all ways of ensuring that relationships between members are mediated through their relationship to the totality. The culture of this civic, industrial form of action is faceless; it seeks to build a form of strategy that celebrates the collective, while being suspicious of the personal, the singular, and the private.

This civic grammar continues to exercise a significant impact in the way recent theories of social movement conceptualize the relationship between individual and collective. We see this, for example, when Snow and McAdam affirm that social movements require a "collective identity" described in terms of "correspondence" between the "I" and the "we," and when they affirm that "before individuals become serviceable movement agents . . . it is necessary that personal identities dovetail with a movement's collective identity (2000: 52). For such theories of social movement, the collective involves overcoming singularity.

From Generality to Subjectivity and Experience

Many areas of contemporary social life suggest that we are no longer in a logic of generality and equivalence. Castells' work underlines just how much emerging network logics engage with personal experience rather than categories and groups. The industrial paradigm sought to exclude individuality from the workplace, whether through the standardized responses of the bureaucrat or the utopia of the assembly line, which Henry Ford hoped would completely remove personal creativity from the workplace, making all workers interchangeable (Ford 1929). Contemporary work patterns point to their increasing individualization, from the increasing flexibility of personal work histories, the importance of self-employment and short-term contracts, and the increasing individualization of rewards through individual contracts. Ulrich Beck (2000) in Germany and Boltanski and Chiapello (1999) in France explore these same processes. Boltanski and Chiapello underline in particular the shift from long-term career to short-term project, and the increasing integration of personal capacities into the work task, where increasingly work involves people's capacity to embrace change, their ability to communicate, their sense of humor, their mobility. Work processes typical of what they call "network capitalism," they argue, break down older distinctions between public and private; work is less and less about interchangeable persons exercising a function, but about subjects increasingly responsible for their "self-production": responsible for their body, their image, their success, and their destiny. Industrial capitalism was characterized by a strong separation of private life and working life, family and work, personal opinions and work ability. This separation is increasingly blurring, not only in terms of the way time is organized, but also in terms of the changing nature of work itself, which increasingly demands commitment, creativity, and that one invest *oneself*. Ideas such as "competency" blur personal qualities and work capacities, while increasingly work mobilizes personal capacities such as openness, sense of humor, the ability to relate to the other, making demands on workers that are very different from the strong separation of public and private at the basis of the bureaucratic workplace. This underlines the importance the relationship that individuals construct *with their selfhood* as increasingly decisive for their ability to successfully navigate the contemporary social world.

These transformations impact upon the very nature of subjectivity in the network society. Industrial work systems seek to expel private dimensions from the workplace, with a view to making each worker interchangeable. Such work processes produce *generality*, a powerful sense of sameness that was a critical dimension to the solidarity and class-consciousness that formed the labor movement. Today's emerging network paradigm no longer produces *generality*, but rather *individuality*, a process captured by Alberto Melucci when he argues that "individuals are becoming the core of what once would have been called the 'social structure'" (Melucci 2000: 45): a transformation that has decisive implications for contemporary forms of conflict and movement. In a similar way, Alain Touraine, while pointing to a globalized economy and technologies, emphasizes the increasing importance of intimacy, sexuality, embodied experience – all dimensions of an experience of privatization and of the weakening of the role of institutions in social life. Global flows, Touraine argues, are accompanied by an equally important search for personal experience (2000: 28). Indeed, Touraine argues that the processes involved in globalization threaten the subjective unity of the person, a process he describes as "desubjectivation" (Khosrokhavar and Touraine 2000). The growing importance of personal life in a globalized world is not necessarily defensive cocooning, but may also represent the basis of recomposition of social action: "in a world of permanent and uncontrolled change, there is no other basis of support (for action) than the individual's effort to transform lived experiences into the construction of a self as an actor." For Touraine, subjectivity increasingly constitutes the core of contemporary social conflicts. Such conflicts, he argues, are less concerned with defending *collective identities*, the pattern of social movements in industrial society, and increasingly take the form of a struggle for *coherence of selfhood*: "in a society of rationalization, we appeal to the dignity of work. In today's world, we live an opposition between the world of finance and consumption, and the aspiration to make of our own existence a meaningful whole" (2000: 145).

Action As Sign: the Paradigm of Representation

Charles Tilly argues that what we now understand as social movements emerged with the creation of the association in the first half of the 1800s. Touraine underlines the emergence of new forms of labor conflicts and organization. While exploring different social terrains, and constructed within different political cultures, both these accounts point to new forms of social representation as crucial to what we now recognize as movements – both these forms of practice underline the importance of public voting, whether in the public meeting or the trade union assembly. Both the trade union and the public association involve a new form of representation as action.

French sociologist Pierre Bourdieu (1985) helps us understand what is at work here in his exploration of the "genesis of groups." He places representation and the symbolic at the center of his analysis, arguing that actors construct the social world by means of the "work of representation." He takes as an example the "working class." While new work processes and conditions meant workers were subject to a new work regime in factories, a working class was brought into being by the action of groups and individuals claiming to represent it. The claim of emerging trade union leaders to speak on behalf of and through this *to represent* the working class, Bourdieu argues, is the form of social practice that actually constitutes the social category. The "capacity to make entities exist" (1985: 729) involves making public what had previously existed at an individual or isolated level. This "work of categorization" is at the center of the struggles through which "agents clash over the meaning of the social world and their position in it." It is through this action of making public, Bourdieu argues, that groups are brought into social existence. For Bourdieu, social power works through this power to name. But equally importantly, from this point of view, it is *through the action of representation that groups are made a social reality*. And here Bourdieu (2004: 37) draws on the work of Thomas Hobbes, the thinker of abstract space:

> A multitude of men are made one person when they are by one man, or one person, represented; so that it be done with the consent of every one of that multitude in particular. For it is the unity of the representer, not the unity of the represented, that maketh the person one. And it is the representer that beareth the person, and but one person: and *unity cannot otherwise be understood* in multitude. (*Leviathan*, Chapter 16; emphasis added)

Bourdieu suggests that the origins of this understanding are to be found in the emergence of modern law and what he calls the "mystery of ministry"

(2004) or "the mystery of the process of transubstantiation whereby the spokesperson becomes the group that he or she expresses." The minister, whether a minister of religion or of state, "functions as a sign in the place of the whole," "an entirely real substitute for an entirely symbolic being" (1985: 740).

> By the minister's mere visible presence, he or she constitutes the pure serial diversity of the separate individuals (*collection personarium plurium*) into an "artificial person" [*une personne morale*], a *corporatio*, a constituted body, and through the effect of mobilization and demonstration, may even make it appear as a social agent . . . the spokesperson, in speaking of a group, on behalf of a group, surreptitiously posits the existence of the group in question, institutes the group, through the magical operation that is inherent in any act of naming. (Bourdieu 1985: 741)

The existence of groups and classes is not, Bourdieu insists, the simple effect of social structures. Groups are brought into being through slogans and mobilizations, where the leader of the political party, the trade union or the social class "personifying a fictitious person, a social fiction, raises those whom he represents from the state of separate individuals, enabling them to speak and act, through him, as one man. In exchange, he receives the right . . . to speak and act as if he were the group made man" (Bourdieu 1985: 740). This lies at the heart of this conception of action, only possible through representation. In this account, action occurs through the constitution of groups. At one level Bourdieu is arguing that social groups exist through leaders and spokespersons representing them, and will cease to exist as groups once they cease to be represented. But at a deeper level, Bourdieu proposes a conception of political action defined in terms of the symbolic: "Politics is the site par excellence of symbolic efficacy, the *action that is performed through signs capable of producing social things, and in particular, groups*" (1985: 741; emphasis added). Such political efficacy involves a form of dispossession: "Individuals cannot constitute themselves (or be constituted) as a group, that is, a force capable of making itself heard, of speaking and being heard, unless they dispossess themselves in favor of a spokesperson" (1991: 204). This form of action, Bourdieu argues, is ultimately to be understood in terms of the categories of *will* and *representation* (Wacquant 2004).

Thus understood, action is *performed through signs*, and is performative; that is, it brings about a new state of affairs. The trade union creates the class through representing it; the association creates the social movement through representing it. In the process, as Hobbes argues, the multitude becomes one person. This understanding of action as fundamentally symbolic is crucial to theories of social movement: the mob or the riot is not understandable within a grammar of representation; the deliberately formed association is. Very different theoretical approaches are located in this understanding of the centrality of the symbolic and the act of representation as performative. While first articulated by Hobbes, and theorized by Bourdieu, it recurs in the work of gender theorists such as Judith Butler (1997), for whom gender is a performative sign, producing what it claims to represent. Political theorist Nancy Fraser is concerned about the authoritarian and communitarian directions being taken by contemporary "identity politics" in the United States, but at the same time understands action as "the power to represent" (2000: 112). Political process theories of social movements, while emphasizing its instrumental dimensions, equally underline this understanding of action as the construction of the category: McAdam et al. ask "Why, for example, do participants in social movements spend so much of their energy in public affirmations of shared identities: marching together, displaying shared symbols, acting out solidarity?" Their response: "a successful claim of collective worthiness, unity, numbers and commitment brings recognition as a credible political player with the capacity to make a difference in the next political struggle" (2001: 147, 148).

Shifting Paradigms

Despite internal tensions and debates it is possible to point to a dominant paradigm of "social movement" constructed in terms of transformations in western society and culture. On the one hand, there is a central priority to the formation of groups, which may take the form of association, organization, or, more recently, community. We can locate this process within a wider emergence of western modernity, in the understandings of abstract, bordered space made up of functionally equivalent members, and within a new, modern understanding of representation out of which emerges a modern understanding of symbolic action that recurs in decisive ways in approaches to social movements. Implicit in this is the idea of the movement as a form of totality (whether organization or community), that claims a form of sovereignty that previously had been understood in religious terms, and located in the body of the sovereign. The paradigmatic example of this grammar of action is the trade union, with its emphasis of delegation, representation, the functional equivalence of members, the importance of relating to the totality, and the distrust of horizontal, person-to-person relationships, where one acts as a delegate or as a representative, not as a person. We see this same grammar at work in models of identity that understand the member as a "serviceable agent of the group." These are very powerful grammars of action that not only penetrate organizations but intellectual traditions. Action as the symbolic, through the ideas of representation, identity, delegation, and solidarity that flow from it, shapes an intellectual universe.

The forms of action that we encounter in this book all involve a break from this paradigm where groups are constituted through the act of representation. Rather than "the power to represent," we encounter other grammars of action: healing, touching, hearing, feeling, seeing, moving. We encounter grammars of embodiment, as experience, as mode of presence and engagement in the world (Csordas 1993: 135). Exploring these forms of action means breaking with the Cartesian separation of body and subject, placing the senses and body within action. This, as we will see, puts into question the autonomous subject defined by their will. This also opens out the question of other forms of structure, where the subjects do not relate to the totality as in the civic model, and dispossess themselves in the way described by Bourdieu. Many authors are attempting to bring about a shift in the way we think about movements, underlining the importance of network. While networks are clearly important, this book points to placing the embodied subject at the center of action, and once we do this, current concepts of "network" appear disembodied, and too located in a culture of simultaneity – typically researchers attempt to "map" networks in a way that disembodies them and locates them in a one-dimensional time (see Diani 1995; Diani and McAdam 2002). Other types of structure may allow us to think of action in terms of bodies and time, and in the concluding discussion I explore metaphors of music and rhythm rather than looking to networks to replace an older conception of structure of representation.

Global Modernities

Increasingly comparative studies underline the problems of thinking about globalization as the diffusion of western forms of individuality and "civil society." The Israeli sociologist S. N. Eisenstadt draws on the work of Karl Japsers to use the concept of "civilization." Jaspers distinguished between what he calls "axial" and "non-axial" civilizations. The term "Axial-Age" refers to the civilizations that crystallized during the period of 500 BCE to the emergence of Islam. The civilizations that emerged in this period manifest a new awareness of the distance separating the day-to-day or mundane world and the transcendental or divine order. Compared with the transcendental, the mundane world was incomplete, inferior, polluted or in need of reconstruction. Principal examples of these civilizations being ancient Israel, second-commonwealth Judaism, and the Christianity that emerged from it, ancient Greece, Zoroastrianism in early Iran, early imperial China, Hinduism and the Buddhism that emerged from it, and Islam (Eisenstadt 1999). Rather than being a simple reflection of the social order (as nineteenth-century secularists from Karl Marx to the French sociologist Emile Durkheim believed), Eisenstadt insists that the distinguishing feature of these civilizations was the tension between the transcendental and the mundane. This critical vision of the social world, this call to conversion or change made in the name of higher principles, was associated with the emergence of different elites or social groups, such as religious officials, clerics, or intellectuals who claimed access to the transcendental and who used this in some way or other to criticize day-to-day social organization (Eisenstadt 1999: ch 1).

This meant that the social order was no longer seen as manifesting or reflecting eternal or transcendental principles, but was seen to be in need of some kind of change or conversion or completion so that it could correspond to the possibility opened out through the transcendental order. This tension between transcendental and mundane had important dimensions for conceptions of power. Where such civilizations developed, the God-king disappeared, and while the king or ruler may have retained important sacral dimensions, the ruler was in principle accountable to some higher order. As a result, in these civilizations as Eisenstadt argues, the possibility of calling a ruler to judgment appeared (1999: 6) – examples being the prophets in ancient Israel or the Chinese concept of the mandate of heaven. But these civilizational dynamics took on very different forms, developing very different conceptions of accountability and radically different conceptions of what it meant to reconstruct the world. In "other-worldly" civilizations, principally Hinduism and the Buddhism that emerged from within it, this took the form of renouncing the world and reconstructing the inner experience of the believer. In these civilizations, the critique of the mundane world would rarely focus directly on the political system, and where movements that emerged out of these cultural models addressed the political, this rarely took the form of attempting to reconstruct the political, but rather took the form of calling upon rulers to adhere to the moral principles upon which existing regimes were based (Eisenstadt 1999: 15). Confucianism, which Eisenstadt proposes exploring as a "this worldly civilization" and became institutionalized with the development of scholars and literateri, did not aim at reconstructing the political domain, but emphasized instead the importance of individual responsibility and moral cultivation – themes, that as we shall see, are central to the forms of movement that emerged in China in the period following the Cultural Revolution, and which have since globalized. For

Eisenstadt the major monotheistic civilizations – Judaism, Christianity and Islam – all combine important dimensions of both this- and other-worldly paradigms. Each possesses a powerful orientation toward reconstructing the mundane world, and each attaches a significant importance to the political domain as the means to achieve this.

This civilizational analysis has important implications for the way we think about emerging global movements. Firstly, it underlines the limits of analyses that are constructed in terms of "universalization." An awareness of the extent to which social patterns are constituted through civilizational grammars alerts us to the extent to which many claims to "universal" status in fact are the product of specific experiences and historical trajectories. European modernity is one form of increasingly multiple forms of modernization. The strong link between nation-state and collective identity, which played such an important role in many European countries, was not evident, for example, in countries such as India that did not develop a nation-state. Other cultural matrixes develop a radically different conception of action, as is evident in the understanding of cultivation. Not all matrices look to reconstruct the mundane world through privileging the political, nor do all develop the same type of civil society that emerged in Europe. Nor do all develop the particular relationship between individual and collective experience that emerged with the modern association, to which Tilly rightly attaches such importance in the case of the European social movements.

The way we understand the concept of action itself is deeply embedded in civilizational matrixes. Tilly, as we have seen, understands action in terms of *intentionality* – a recurring theme in his emphasis on deliberation, while Bourdieu emphasizes representation and action as symbolic. An awareness of civilizational grammars opens us out to different ways of being selves and experiencing the world, to different ways of experiencing embodiment and relationship to the other, to different grammars of social critique. All these suggest that movements may not necessarily follow the trajectories that we are familiar with in western modernity. If we define the "social movement" as the "functional equivalent" of political parties and interest groups, we have defined core conceptions of action, communication, and relationship to the other in the terms that emerged in western societies. This mutilates our regard, filtering out all the experiences and movements that do not correspond to the grammars of action and culture that emerged in the context of Euro-American modernization, or regards them as defensive expressions of an inability to cope with modernization and its demands. This imposes a mode of sameness that is increasingly experienced as a form of violence, as a refusal of recognition. This is not simply an intellectual question; it is also an ethical one.

NOTE

1   While central to the American political imagination, contemporary research suggests that actual cases of the New England public meeting were far fewer than
their role in the American imagination would suggest (see François and Neveu
1999).

PART II

From Antiglobalization to Grammars of Experience

CHAPTER 3

Direct Action: from Community to Experience

The origins of direct action predate the large mobilizations of the late 1990s. It first emerges in the American antinuclear movement of the early 1970s and played a key role in the Clamshell Alliance action against nuclear power in Seabrook, New Hampshire. From there it generalized across the United States through a series of occupations of sites scheduled for nuclear reactor construction, most notably at the Diablo site in California (see Jasper 1997), in a process illustrating the model of fluidity proposed by Urry (2002). In the United States it played an important role in the emergence of Earth First!, which over a decade played a key role in developing new forms of action. While in the United States Earth First! became increasingly closed and inward looking, resulting in its effective collapse, out of its culture and action emerged the Ruckus Society, which would later converge with traditions of cultural action exemplified by the Californian-based network, Art and Revolution, from which would emerge the Direct Action Network, which played such a critical role in the success of the Seattle action against the World Trade Organization.

The direct action that emerged in the United States spilled over into Britain in the early 1990s, when British university students embraced Earth First! and its model of action. But in Britain this became radically transformed through the encounter with youth culture and antiroads action. So, while in the United States Earth First! effectively collapsed, in Britain it mutated into Reclaim The Streets, which would later play a key role in the emergence of the People's Global Action network. In continental Europe, direct action follows a different path again, because of the absence of significant antinuclear movements. In France, for example, direct action emerges out of the "new humanitarianism" that developed in that country over the late 1980s and early 1990s, linked to the "no-borders" culture of networks such as Médecins Sans Frontières, or the appeal to direct action against hunger and homelessness, networks leading to the development of forms of association such as the Association for a Tobin Tax for the Aid of Citizens (ATTAC), which can be seen as a new form of action framed within an older form of organization. In Italy the Centri Sociali (social centers) play a key role, acting as convergence points for alternative youth cultures. In northern Europe alternative youth cultures also play a key role, where the relationship to violence occupies an important place in forms of direct action – as in sabotage and actions developed by Animal Liberation (Peterson 2001).

These forms of action and movement are shaped by national contexts and traditions. They are not examples of a new global cosmopolitan culture. The new humanitarianism that emerged in France in the 1980s has no parallel in the United States; the antinuclear movement that was so important in Britain and the United States has not been significant in France. Direct action's development is an example of Therborn's (2003) "tangled" paths or Urry's "partial contacts." While Earth First! effectively collapsed in the United States, the model of action it developed became transformed in the context of British antiroads struggles, giving rise to Reclaim The Streets, which in turn in the late 1990s returned to the United States, as well as in countries such as Italy or Australia. The affinity groups and spokescouncils that were first developed in the context of the Clamshell Alliance in Seabrook in 1975 played a key role in Seattle 1999, emerging also as a key form of organization in the Evian action against the G8 in July 2003. The "roadshow" developed by Earth First!, involving traveling between cities to develop networks and organize action, is a precursor of the important place of "caravans" in antiglobalization action, and underlines the importance of a grammar of experience associated with displacement and the voyage. Forms of action flow from one network to another, in a process amplified by the Internet and communications networks such as Indymedia in the United States or the Tactical Media Crew in Italy. In this chapter we begin to open out these experience flows, where music plays a more important role than meeting procedure, where instead of associations we encounter tangled networks of voyage and intensity.

The Clamshell Alliance: Affinity Groups and Exemplary Community

The origins of "direct action" are to be found in the American antinuclear movement and the strategy it developed over the 1970s of occupying sites scheduled for reactor construction. One of the most important of these was the Clamshell Alliance that took place in Seabrook (New Hampshire) from 1975 to 1977, inspired by site occupations that had taken place in France and Germany. Those involved in this action had a history of involvement in the student antiwar movement, and the occupation at Seabrook was strongly influenced by traditions of nonviolent civil disobedience developed by the American Friends Service Committee (Quakers) that had played an important role in both peace and civil rights movements of the decade earlier.

A key form of structure of this action was the affinity group. These had been emersed in civil rights action in particular, and were small groups made up of people who pledged to support each other during confrontations with police and others who might be hostile. Often they were formed through a process of "trainings." They had played a key role in responding nonviolently to police violence during the civil rights period, and were taken up in particular by the Quakers, who organized trainings for activists at Seabrook. Rather than loyalty to an abstract organization, or an experience where the activist was alone among thousands of unknown faces, through the affinity group each activist constructed strong bonds of support with a small number of people, and during the action, which was potentially shaped by violent confrontation, their loyalty would be directed toward this small group.

In the antinuclear action beginning at Seabrook, during the occupation of a site, affinity groups would cluster in particular areas, with each "village" of affinity groups sending a representative to participate in a "spokescouncil" that would deal with issues arising, and be responsible for negotiating with police. This points to a shift in their role. Rather than simply a way of organizing action – nonviolent resistance to arrest – these groups were becoming principles of organization. At Seabrook this extended further, because, following arrests, activists demanded to stay as part of their affinity groups while they were in detention (Epstein 1991: 68). In the process the affinity group, a technique of action designed to allow people to successfully and nonviolently resist arrest, became a principle around which a community was to be organized. In defending the affinity group, the actors were defending their community – themes that prefigure the identity politics that would emerge in the United States.

The Seabrook occupation was soon emulated across the country, playing a key role in the birth of the American antinuclear movement by combining site occupation and exemplary community. At Seabrook three powerful American traditions converged: religious-based moral protest; the counterculture and communal living movement that was critical of American culture, while involved in exemplary and at times utopian action; and the defense of local traditions and local democracy, with a great importance attached to town meetings and local referendums (Epstein 1991). The action did more than oppose the construction of a nuclear plant. It promised community. This became increasingly important in what became a "subculture" of direct action, "defined by egalitarian, pacifist, and ecological values, and by internal procedures centred on consensus decision making and efforts to create community" (Jasper 1997: 189). Researchers who have explored this movement argue that as it developed it become increasingly closed in on itself, remaining largely embedded in a cohort from the movements of the 1960s, this closure epitomized by the constant references to forms of utopian community constituted through the experience of jail (Joppke 1993: 84).

Despite this, the theme of direct action, affinity groups, and "spokescouncils" emerged powerfully in the antiglobalization action of the late 1990s. To understand this, we need to explore the development and transformation of direct action in environmental action. And here the key reference point is Earth First!

Nature's Warriors – Earth First!

Earth First! was created during a camping trip undertaken by five young men to the Pincarte Desert in 1981. The aim was to break with talk and discussion, and act. Earth First!'s first significant action took place on the morning of the spring equinox of 1982, where a 109 yard black plastic wedge, tapering from 12 to 2 feet in width, was rolled down the face of the Glen Canyon Dam in Colorado. In the context of controversy about the dam and the destruction of wilderness that the damming of rivers involved, this action received national publicity because of the power of the image of what appeared to be a huge crack running down the face of the dam, evoking the power of the river breaking free of its man-made imprisonment (see http://www.hcn.org/allimages/1995/mar20/graphics/950320.001.gif).

This was the first of a series of actions, all aimed at protecting or freeing dammed rivers or threatened forests. These early actions were followed in June of that year by a "Road Show," a three-month tour to spread the message and involve new people. Earth First!'s action followed a very different evolution from the American antinuclear movement. The reference to town meetings was absent; instead themes of tribal society (at least as imagined by the activists) were dominant, as were themes of music and poetry. Music played (and still plays today) a key role in Earth First! in the United States, together with Road Shows and an annual "tribal gathering," the "Round River Rendezvous" (based on a legend of a river flowing into itself, use of the term "Rendezvous" to describe traditional American Indigenous meetings). These rendezvous were associated with powerful experiences of breaking free of social norms, in the early years associated with significant alcohol consumption.

The young men who created Earth First! were clearly influenced by Edward Abbey's 1976 novel *Monkey Wrench Gang*, which describes the heroic adventures of a group of nomadic environmental defenders who blow up bridges to defend wilderness. In 1985, David Foreman, who had been at the center of Earth First!, published *Ecodefence: A Field Guide to Monkeywrenching*, with an introduction by Abbey. In it he sets out his vision of direct action, implying support for spiking trees, sabotaging forest logging operations, and blowing up dams. For Foreman and Earth First!, action was decisive: "Action is the key. Action is more important than philosophical hairsplitting or endless refining of dogma . . . Let our actions set the finer points of our dogma" (quoted in Lee 1995: 57). Earth First! rejected industrial society and organization, and insisted that it was a movement rather than an organization. It combined a strong control over key orientations with a culture that emphasized local autonomy and action.

Foreman increasingly came to regard human beings per se as the cause of the ecological destruction of the planet. Over the 1980s the apocalyptic dimension of Forman's writings in the *Earth First!* journal increased, advocating compulsory sterilization of people in the United States following the birth of a first child. Over the period 1987–90 this, combined with increasing pressure being applied by the FBI, provoked increasing tension within Earth First! One group around Foreman became increasingly apocalyptic, believing that industrial civilization was about to collapse, and that out of this collapse would emerge a new type of human experience, embedded within the natural world rather than dominating it. Another group defined itself as "social," looking to link with workers' organizations and regarding environmental destruction as more a product of capitalist pursuit of profit rather than a consequences of the human species as such. The biocentric orientation increasingly began to interpret events in terms of a coming, inevitable, and desirable destruction of human civilization, one that would lay the basis for a freed Earth. It was from this perspective that Daniel Connor, a close ally of Foreman, asked in an article in 1987 whether AIDS was "the answer to an environmentalist's prayer," interpreting the development of AIDS as "Gaia's response" to overpopulation, pollution, and species distinction. The December 1987 issue of *Earth First!* carries an article written by Foreman affirming that "the AIDS epidemic, rather than being a scourge, is a welcome development in the inevitable reduction of human population" (quoted in Lee 1995: 110). In June of that same year, ACT-Up was formed after a Gay Pride march in New York. That radical environmentalists were discussing the benefits of AIDS from the point of view of the planet underlines the extraordinary distance that lay between these two currents of direct action. Over 1990 Earth First! underwent a series of fractures and schisms, ultimately splitting apart as the social ecology group triumphed over the deep ecology group.

Martha Lee (1995) argues that Earth First! is best understood as a millenarian movement. That is, Earth First! came to view industrial society's technological development and destruction of wilderness as leading toward imminent ecological collapse, which would bring with it the end of industrial society. The collapse of EarthFirst! became inevitable once the biocentric current welcomed AIDS as Gaia's action to rid herself of the human pest. This millenarian current within Earth First! increasingly embraced a form of survivalism, with a recourse to language of the saved and damned, pure and impure. This opposition also became increasing evident in the later writings of the movement's intellectual source, Ed Abbey, who in the 1980s called for the closure of the border between Mexico and the United States, describing immigrants as polluting the country. Nature's warriors were increasingly being drawn into the spiral of a sect, the saved in a world of the damned. But what is critical to recognize about Earth First! is its appeal to a kind of individual experience, one that is wild (hence the importance of alcohol) and free of the inhibitions of social norms. The emphasis on action, as opposed to debate, strongly contrasts with the extraordinary importance given to articulating and discussion at the center of American exemplary communities. Earth First! pioneered a powerful grammar of action from its first act against a dam domesticating a wild river. The movement drew on Dionysian themes, where to be free is to be wild; hence the importance of freeing nature and the extraordinary importance of wilderness to these young people. The experience of *being in wilderness* was critical to the birth and development of Earth First!, where people can come alive. But while Earth First! destroyed itself in the United States, it underwent a radically different path in the United Kingdom, where the contest with industrial culture converged with youth culture, creating a new form of action constituting public culture – the British antiroads movement.

Antiroads

While Earth First! in the United States was becoming more and more trapped in the opposition between the saved and the damned, its leaflets and magazines were circulating internationally. Drawing on existing networks in the British peace movement (Welsh 2001) and on its tradition of occupying sites that had been developed in particular at Greenham Common (see Roseneil 1995), in late 1991 a newly formed British Earth First! attempted to set up a blockade at the Dungeness nuclear power plant. The aim was to build a link between peace and environmental concerns by arguing that the nuclear plant would endanger the site's fragile ecological balance (in a way reminiscent of the Clamshell Alliance in 1975). As Wall (1999) notes, as one of the most remote regions of England, the location was among the closest sites to

"wilderness" in Britain. This action failed. Despite their efforts, the organizers could muster only a small group of some 60 people, and it became clear
that the attempt to defend wilderness the way this had been done in the
United States was not going to build momentum. Action then moved to
blocking Malaysian timber imports (Wall 1999). That year also saw the first
action against the G7 emerging out of the environmental movement: a pole
was climbed, a banner unfurled in an action involving some 20 people. But
in 1997, the next time the G7 would gather in Britain, it would be met by
some 60,000 protestors. Following the summit there were a series of actions
against rainforest timber importation and processing, generally taking the
form of occupying timber yards (Wall 1999).

The critical event was to shift to action opposing the car. In the late 1980s
the British government foreshadowed a massive increase in the extent and
importance of motorways in the country, with road transport at the center
of state strategies for economic modernization, in much the same way as in
1972 when Richard Nixon unveiled an ambitious program of nuclear power
construction. This was more than an economic strategy. It involved an image
of Britain, densely traversed by a network of motorways, bringing with it
economic opportunity and an integrated country. Cars and motorways were
at the center of a modernizing imagination, in much the same way that
nuclear power took on such a symbolic importance in the American or
French modernization of the 1970s. In Britain, this modernizing imagination
involved a destruction of the past, foreshadowing the destruction of some
800 scheduled ancient monuments (SAM) by 2025.

Earth First!'s first action against the car took the form of occupying a
bridge in the resort town of Brighton at Christmas 1991. This first action
focused on the role of the car as a polluter, as a source of toxic chemicals.
But quickly the themes involved changed. Four months later, in April 1992,
Earth First! initiated a "Reclaim The Streets" campaign, the aim being "to do
imaginative and nonviolent direct actions, and to reclaim the streets of
London from cars and traffic and give them back to the people" (Earth First!
flyer, in Wall 1999: 63). In August of 1992, a car was destroyed in London's
Hyde Park, the action involving readings from Heathcote Williams's *Auto-
geddon*, emphasizing the social as well as environmental destruction caused
by reliance upon the car.

The idea of direct action and compelling experiences that had been at the
center of Earth First! in the United States had a powerful resonance among
young activists in Britain. But the American conception of wilderness had no
parallel in Britain. This is because "wilderness" is not simply a category of
landscape, but a cultural model: it is the other to the civilized; it is raw power
and danger opposed to domesticity; it is freedom against routine. Earth
First!'s initial action in Britain, one that sought to link peace and environ-

mental movements through defending wilderness against nuclear power, failed not simply because of the lack of "wilderness" in Britain. The meanings of landscape in Britain are radically different to the wilderness we encounter in the United States. This would emerge powerfully in the antiroads campaign.

Twyford Down

The early period of Earth First!'s opposition to the car was constructed in two quite different ways. The first is evident in early themes developed in 1992 when Earth First! members joined with local associations in Twyford Down to stop a proposed freeway extension. The newly formed group issued leaflets condemning the car as the "linchpin of capital accumulation," describing the car as the key industry in "the Fordist mode of production" (South Downs Earth First!). This more or less traditional form of Marxism emphasized a traditional class analysis, one where the car was the technological infrastructure to the capitalist order. This would be transformed through the action at Twyford Down.

Twyford Down, in the chalk hills of the South Down area of England, is located near the medieval city of Winchester in Hampshire. The M3 motorway (linking Southampton to London) was scheduled to be extended through the area, one of high architectural, archeological, and wildlife value. While Twyford Down's chalk cliffs were subject to environmental protection, this had been administratively suspended to allow construction of the motorway. Traditional lobbying and representations to Members of Parliament had failed to stop the planned extension. Two "new travelers" had come upon the site while traveling, and had decided to pitch camp and get to know that area better. While local conservationists had been trying to prevent the motorway through lobbying and representation, the "new travellers" had other links and networks, deciding to camp there and look to involve others in defending the site. Following a small demonstration, some one hundred people succeeded in opening a water lock at the construction site, flooding construction equipment. This action attracted media attention, underlining the power of direct action as opposed to lobbying and letter writing. Following this success, those present at the site determined to establish a protest camp.

The camp had become an important protest repertoire in Britain, in particular since the long-running camp undertaken by women at Greenham to oppose the introduction of cruise missiles into the country (Roseneil 1995). Women who had played a key role at Greenham were part of the early action at Tywford, and played a key role in the decision to establish a camp. The strategy also drew on forest occupations that had been developed by the Australian rainforest movement (Wall 1999: 67). The camp would last some two years, at its peak involving several thousand people. People would come and visit the site, stay a few days or weeks, and in the process contacts and networks gradually widened, setting in motion a process where from 1992 to 2000 some 70 antiroads occupations occurred in Britain.

Through the mobility of people coming and going, as well as through media coverage, these camps connected with other forms of cultural change occurring in Britain. One in particular involved the growing networks of "New Age travellers" (Herrington 2000), the other being the festival culture that had emerged around historical sites such as Stonehenge. Over the 1990s traveler culture widened to become a cultural laboratory centered on developing new nomadic lifestyles, an eclectic culture including urban radicals, the rave and drug scene, dance culture, sound systems, festivals, spirituality, squats and vegetarianism, environmentalism, as well as mystical feminism (for a participant's account, see Dearling 1998). At the same time, important sections of the traveler culture are made up of people who have been excluded or damaged by urban culture, the homeless and deinstitutionalized who do not find a place in the postindustrial city (Martin 2002). The increasing numbers of travelers converged with the growth of cultural and music festivals centered on sites regarded as charged with mystical forms of power and significance: Stonhenge, Rollright Stones, Avebury, Cissbury and Chanctonbury Rings, the Malvern Hills. There had been a recent history of conflict around access to such sites, with violent clashes at Stonehenge in 1985 leading to an "exclusion zone" that lasted over 10 years. During this period, a network of largely anticommercial music festivals had continued to develop, linked with cultural experiments around healing, food, and natural religions, many of these festivals linked to celebrations of natural cycles such as the solstice.

Over the 1980s, the British environmental movement essentially took the form of a "conservation" movement. It was largely integrated into the system of interest groups, meeting regularly with policy makers (Rootes 1995) and undergoing the changes that Gamson (1975) regarded as critical to successful social movements, bureaucratization and professionalization. Organizations such as Greenpeace and Friends of the Earth embraced business practices from mail-order management of members (Jordan and Maloney 1997) to integrating legal advice in campaign strategies. Sociologists who attempted to make sense of why the environmental movement had not significantly developed in Britain over the decade of the 1980s suggested that this was because the powerful political institutionalization of the Labour and Conservative parties meant that social life and political culture in the country remained dominated by the opposition between business and labor, with newer themes such as ecology remaining marginal in a political culture dominated by a commitment to economic growth (Eyerman and Jamison 1991). To the extent that the British environmental movement existed, it appeared to be following the trajectory mapped out by political process theorists, "maturing" from a social protest movement to an interest group within the political system.

The action at Twyford Down would radically transform this process. Over the two-year period that the Twyford Down site was occupied, we encounter the development of forms of action that would also emerge in other antiroads actions, constructed in terms of embodiment and imagination. Forms of embodied action were most obvious in the efforts undertaken by protesters to put their bodies at risk in order to block the destruction of sites, from "locking on" to machinery (to prevent this being used) or to trees, or through building and occupying tunnels that would have to be cleared before destruction and construction could begin, or constructing tripods or treehouses that had to be accessed and dismantled before construction can take place.

As Doherty (1999) underlines, such forms of action involve manufactured vulnerability that confront authorities with weeks to remove activists from sites, and produce dramatic television stories that potentially run for weeks or even months, as opposed to the several hours required to clear more traditional forms of blockade or protest. The relatively small number of people involved illustrates Melucci's (1996a) argument that in an information society, the power of an action does not come from the physical mass and presence of the number of people mobilized, but through their ability to "challenge codes" or to "change how experiences are named and perceived" (Doherty 1999: 290).

Embodiment, Memory, and Myth

The British historian Simon Schama (1995) underlines the importance of landscape to memory and myth, from the Californian tall trees symbolizing American freedom and liberty, German forests as a symbol of collective strength, French forests as a symbol of state order and planning, or Polish forests as a symbol of national identity capable of enduring invasion. Arguably the extraordinary resonance of Earth First!'s action in defending individual tall trees in California, by putting nails in them to stop chain saws, was not only due to the controversy caused through the risk caused to loggers cutting them down, but also to the place of these trees in the American imagination, when compared, for example, to the defense of clams in New Hampshire.

Alain Touraine argues that in industrial society, the workplace is the critical location where we see key social movements and conflicts develop, because it is there that the "historicity" of industrial society is produced, and it is there the core actors of industrial society, the labor movement and industrialists, encounter each other. Is there any parallel between his argument and the forms of action that have emerged in forests and other landscapes over the past two decades? Macnaghten and Urry's (2000) research underlines the extraordinary resonance of practices associated with woods and forests in England, and the ways in which different social groups engage with and perform with their bodies in them. Being in the forest increases the intensity of the experience of embodiment, of being vital, active, corporeal, and mobile. In particular, they argue, the experience of *being* in woods is one that is sensual, it is one where people use all their senses directly (sight, hearing, touch, and smell), offering the possibilities of unmediated relationships: with the other, as, for example, when two companions go for a walk through a forest, where they can share the experience and each other's company without the need for language. They argue being in a forest, a wood, or a "natural environment" is a time when one can experience one's own body, one's self, without the need for this to pass through interaction with others – through experiences of solitude such as walking alone, for example, that are not readily available in the city, or where the immediacy and intimacy of the smell of trees or earth, or the sounds of geese or water flowing, take the person back to private memories of childhood.

Practices such as walking or being in the forest involve access to forms of embodied memory. The smell of earth; the feel of moisture in the air through the skin; the sound of wind in leaves; sensing the time-presence of trees; the silence that can be experienced only in a forest, one that is full rather than empty; the rhythmic bodily activity of walking, where body awareness is radically different from that experienced in the city; all these open out grammars of embodied experience, and with these, the possibility of experiences of memory that are not accessible through cognition. As with music, the memory that we experience through the forest is embodied – we remember something that was forgotten, and in the process we experience ourselves in a different way. Also as with the experience of music, there is something elusive about the experience of the forest – we can feel that something remains beyond: there is something about being in the forest that is hidden (Garner 2004). Hence the importance of the forest, as Macnaghten and Urry (2000) emphasise, for myth and story: from Hansel and Gretal to Tarzan or English children's novels (for a more psychoanalytic exploration of the meaning of forests and their place in myth, see Bettleheim 1976).

Macnaghten and Urry underline the increasing importance of *embodied experience*: from wild food to camping, to the interest in extreme sports, a dimension that they analyze in terms of a yearning that takes different forms, but one that is closely constructed in terms of woodland experience. "Many people," they write "appear to be articulating . . . a desire for deeper, more continuously engaged connections with the life and continuities of woodlands in their areas," forms of experience in almost all cases constructed in terms of forms of embodied, "unmediated experiences" of nature, less constructed in terms of humans saving nature (conservationism) than in a language of "nature saving us" (2000: 180).

These themes emerge at the center of the occupations developed in the antiroads action. The embodiment of the actor in this action goes beyond manufactured vulnerability as an instrumental media strategy, to the point where bodies and embodiment occupy the center of activist experience. The accounts of people involved in the camps continually focus on embodied experience: keeping warm, keeping dry, cooking, cleaning, problems of waste and excrement, physical exhaustion. The body keeps recurring, to the point where it threatens to take control of experience.

If the first attempts to articulate what was at stake in the action at Twyford Down were constructed in terms of a somewhat archaic Marxist technological determinism, myth and memory soon emerge as central in participants' accounts of these occupations. One participant describes the site in precisely those terms:

> It was just such a beautiful place, but quite small really, no impressive 500-year old forests or anything like that; just the hard cleanness of chalk and flint, a place where the Down met the sky, the sense of space, and where the footprints of past generations who'd lived in the landscape were literally visible – the barrows [large hills believed to be built on ancient graves], the field systems, and dewponds, and the worn-deep iron-age trackways locally known as "dongas." (Plows 2002)

At the peak of the occupation of the site some 2,000 people were involved in preventing earth-moving machinery gaining access to the area that was to be cut. But the core of the group consisted of a group of between 30 to 50 people who came to call themselves the "dongas tribe," naming themselves after a term used by local people to describe the pathways that crisscrossed the fields. Interestingly, the term "donga" was introduced to the area in the 1970s by a South African school teacher, who was reminded of tracks in his native South Africa that were called "dongas." Alex offers a sense of the kinds of meaning and culture produced through this action:

Underpinning the political direct actions of the Dongas was an ethical frame-work, an explicit spirituality – or to be precise, a political paganism. The Dongas explicitly articulated a sense of connection to nature; nature was seen as sacred. Crucially, the Dongas saw themselves and all life as part of this web: nature was not some "other." These concepts (most people were familiar with Lovelock's "Gaia" theories) were linked to ideas about significant landscapes and earth energies. The Down and the nearby hillfort St Catherines' Hill were "powerpoints," markers for currents of earth energy or leylines. The Dongas were not alone on this; the founder of Winchester College, also a Mason, was also a keen sacred geometrist, and to this day, Winchester College schoolboys hold a service on the Hill on Summer Solstice morning. The Dongas felt that these beliefs would have been shared by the Bronze and Iron Age people who had lived on the Down. Identifying with sacred landscape thus meant identi-fying with these earlier "tribes." They felt such a connection to the place and its history that they produced stories, poems, songs and myths about wheels come full circle, new tribes, old ways. Conscious parallels were also made with the beliefs and political, land rights struggles of indigenous tribes worldwide. Magic reality, myth-weaving and sympathetic magic melded into direct action. Believing themselves protected by the land they physically defended with their bodies, they symbolized this protection and called it into being with the use of significant images and objects. Music, especially drumming, and invoking protection through chants and songs, often preceded action, and went on during it. (Plows, 2005: 204)

There are similarities between the rituals described here and those per-formed a generation earlier in the United States; for example when Starhawk, now a well-known American practitioner of ecopaganism, led demonstrators in a celebration of the Sun during the 1979 occupation of the Diablo Canyon site in California (see Jasper 1997). We encounter the plurality of belief systems characteristic of global culture and the New Age: the Goddess, European legends of the dragon, Masonry's solar rituals, North American indigenous herbal magics. But this is more than an eclectic ecopagan cultural movement that could easily become reduced either to a consumer trend or a simple countercultural discourse.

The power of this experience confronts us with the question of magic and myth and the emergence in action of what we can call, drawing on Bell (2003) "mythscapes." The action developed by the occupiers of the site allows a kind of connection with a past that would otherwise be lost, and is about to be destroyed through the physical destruction of the site:

The Dongas felt that these beliefs would have been shared by the Bronze and Iron Age people who had lived on the Down. Identifying with sacred landscape thus meant identifying with these earlier "tribes." Everyday nature, the facts of life, growth and change, were at the heart of what was seen as magical. Similarly, the Dongas observed and celebrated natural cycles such as full moon and Winter Solstice with fire, music, drumming, circle-dancing, and often the ingesting of "magic mushrooms"; an indigenous hallucinogenic mushroom which, whilst "recreational," also enabled shamanic connection to the earth/universe, increasing the sense of sacredness. On such nights (and on many others), protection "spells" for the Down were made up on the spot during drumming and chanting sessions like performance poems, very differently from formalized ritual . . . they were symbolic ways of reestablishing connections to nature, and, as importantly, to history. (Plows, the Dongas tribe)

The embodied experience of being opens up a form of imagination that is at the center of the action. The magic conjures the presence of people and tribes. Rhythm and drumming are central to this action.

We Dance Fire

In 1995, one of the largest green spaces in the Scottish city of Glasgow was occupied to prevent its destruction for a freeway. Geographer Paul Routledge was a participant, and captures this experience in his personal journal:

Glasgow. It's a cold, grey Saturday in February, 1995. South of the River Clyde, an ecological encampment stands amid the woodlands and parklands of Pollok estate, Glasgow's largest green space. From the roadside hangs a huge red banner proclaiming "Pollok Free State" and, amid the tall beech trees, stand carved totems of eagles, ravens and owls, and a confusion of tents, benders (do-it-yourself shelters) and tree houses. Pollok Free State represents a material and symbolic site of resistance to the proposed M77 motorway extension that is planned to run through the western wing of Pollok estate. Here, several hundred people have assembled to await the arrival of four cars being driven from several parts of England by environmental activists. Warming themselves around the flames, folk present a confusion of colour and style. A group of musicians strike up some impromptu celtic folk music. An air of expectancy hangs amid the woodsmoke and the winter wind. The four cars that are arriving at the Free State are to be buried, engine down, in the M77 road bed alongside the five that have already been buried. Once buried, the cars will be set alight, burned as totems of resistance and on their charred skeletons anti-motorway slogans painted.

Amid the sounds of car horns, whistles and cheers from the assembled crowd, the cars arrive. The cars line up beside a tree which flies the Lion Rampant. As the crowd proceeds to march towards the burial site, a band strikes up a cacophony of bagpipes, horns, drums, whistles and shouts. We march up to the road bed and, one by one, the cars are manoeuvred into the tombs that have been dug for them. Engine down and with earth and stones packed around them, the cars are buried vertically in the road bed. A resident of the Free State swings a sledge hammer and dispenses with the windscreen. Another cheer rises from the crowd. We are a rhythmic crowd, moving to the visceral beat of the drums. We revel in the burial of the car, encoded as it is with our resistance to the environmental consequences of excessive car use and to the construction of the M77 motorway. Once the cars are buried, petrol is poured over them and they are set alight. Voices of celebration fill the air, accented with Glaswegian, London English, Australian, Swedish, American. People dance in the firelight, their shadows casting arabesques of celebration upon the road: we dance fire, we become fire, our movements are those of flames. (Routledge 1997)

We encounter each of the senses in this account: cold is felt, woodsmoke is smelt, voices shout, cries are heard, colors are seen. The action is modulated to the rhythm of drums; the metaphor is a dance, not a march. What is striking is the way the body and the senses are at the core of this action. The action and presence of others, the location and one's own self are all experienced through the body. The senses and an experience of embodiment are amplified in the way described by Urry and Mcnaughton. The action is held together by the rhythm of the drum and the dance of fire, not the organization and its delegates. After they are burnt, the cars are left standing as evocative monuments. The action leaves a physical presence that is part of the landcape and the myth it contains. Later another five are added, creating a circle of nine cars that come to form the center of the occupation, ancient stones evoked through the term "Carhenge."

The grammar of this action is not one of "claims about the group." The car in the ground does not represent a group, it evokes memory, feeling, hope, imagination. If we want to begin to make sense of what is happening here we need to break with the identity paradigm. With good reason, Routledge looks to the work of Italian sociologist Alberto Melucci. For Melucci, social movements are less and less intelligible in terms of claims made on the basis of identities; instead he argues movements are better understood as communicative actions that disrupt and contest the dominant codes that shape human experience – movements are not fundamentally about making claims, but are increasingly temporary, and their action is a message that society has to interpret (Melucci 1996a). He points to three key dimensions of such action. The first he calls "prophecy," where movements carry a message that what is possible is already real in the experience of those proclaiming the message. The second he refers to as "paradox," where the authority of dominant codes is made manifest through their exaggeration. The third he calls "representation," by which he means "a symbolic reproduction which separates the codes from the contents which habitually mask them." From this point of view, "collective action is a 'form' which by its very existence, the way it structures itself, delivers its message" (Melucci 1989: 76–77). This is a very different form of action from the group being created through the action of representation, in the model of symbolic action proposed by Bourdieu.

Routledge suggests, following Benford and Hunt (1995), that this action is a form of "dramaturgy" – "the staging and performing of political action to gain public attention." This terms clearly does capture the type of action successfully pursued by groups such as Greenpeace, which combine direct market principles with modern television values. But it is less sure that the Pollok action is a case of "staging." Routledge's own account goes beyond a model of tactical use of the media. He notes himself the importance of intensity, referring to an early occupation leaflet that refers to activists being "alive to the aliveness of life." Another emphasizes, "we are living it, rather than just talking about it." Intensity combines with immediacy. The camp experience involves some sort of time compression. As Routledge notes, the events as experienced at the camp are "immediate: experienced in the present without mediation" (1997: 371). "We dance fire, we become fire, our movements are those of the flames." What does this mean?

Ritual?

Rather than focus on an instrumental concept of "staging," Bronislaw Szerszynski argues that the best way to make sense of what is happening in these forms of action is in terms of *ritual*. An example he cites is the protestor sitting atop a tripod to block construction equipment – here the aim is not simply to block access to a bulldozer, but to dramatize the danger that the protester is encountering, his or her own vulnerability. He underlines as well the importance of what he calls "connotative meanings." One particularly evocative example that he cites is the case of two semi-naked protestors blowing rams' horns in a ritual of lament beside the fresh scar of the roadworks that cut across Twyford Down after the camp had finally been cleared. Szerszynski underlines the visuality of such communication, its ability to express and evoke experiences of desolation, grief, and powerlessness at the destruction of the Down – a powerful form of communication that can be mediated by television in particular. Drawing on religious rituals, Szerszynski argues that ritual involves four dimensions: firstly, it is repeated or rule-bound behaviour, referring to some kind of ongoing tradition that transcends the individuals directly involved; secondly, it is "performed" behaviour, "executed with a heightened sense of being for display"; thirdly, that it is partly or wholly noninstrumental or symbolic; and fourthly, that it communicates through "condensing symbols" rather than through elaborate speech, through connotation rather than denotation (2002: 54).

Through ritual as a form of action, Szersynski argues, actors can achieve five things in particular. They can construct a relationship between what is and what could be, closing the gap between the way the world is and the way it should be, between the indicative and the subjunctive. Szerszynski quotes Clifford Geertz: "in a ritual, the world as lived and the world as imagined, fused under the agency of a single set of symbolic forms, turns out to be the same world" (2002: 56). Through ritual, the possible world becomes part of the real world.

Secondly, argues Szersynski, through ritual, actors can generalize beyond particular actions to link with universal or cosmic meanings. Striking workers in a small factory might begin to sing "The International," for example, the song written by Eugene Pottier following the fall of the Paris Commune of 1871, referring to the International Working Man's Association (1864–76). Through singing this song, these workers not only affirm that they want to be part of a wider historic struggle of workers; they for a short time become part of this struggle. At Carhenge the burnt-out cars are placed in a circle to remake the circle of the ancient stones. The ancient past and its magic is no longer lost, it is pulled into the present, made real again, placed at the physical center of the camp.

Thirdly, Syerszynski argues that rituals allow certain things to be achieved that can only be done through symbol, above all allowing forms of communication that are *connotative* rather than *denotative*. Denotative communication strives for clarity, and, to avoid ambiguity, it aims at being clear and transparent, involving a message to be agreed or disagreed with. At the core of this kind of communication is argument, the paradigmatic example being rational, discursive discussion or discourse. Conative communication on the other hand is evocative, involving metaphor. Syerszynski writes:

> protest action seen as connotative rather than denotative would thus be viewed not as simply bearing a message to be agreed or disagreed with, but as engaging the viewing subject through complex processes of connotation and metaphor in which the meaning of the action, like that of a work of art, cannot be detached from the action itself. (2002: 59)

In conative communication, information is not simply transmitted; instead meaning is constructed, the receiver of the message has to *experience* the message, or, as Szerszynski argues, receivers of a message have to call forth personal memories and associations in order to produce new meanings for themselves. In that sense, movements as Melucci argues, are a message, but a message that is closer to a work of art than to an academic argument. To explore the implications, as Alexander and Jacobs (1998) argue, we need to move from a cognitivist framework to a cultural one.

This use of ritual is an important attempt to make sense of what is happening in these forms of action. It alerts us to the central place of communication. Yet it largely remains within the paradigm we began to explore above, where action is understood to "represent." But at the same time, Szerszynski's own account points beyond this emphasis on "representation," noting, as does Melucci, that the work of art does not "represent"; rather it is a form of communicative experience that calls on the viewer to produce new meaning. The understanding of ritual as "symbolic behaviour" does not seem to capture the importance of embodiment and the senses of grief and desolation that are felt more than being represented.

Cultural Networks, Experience Flows

Rather than look for the social group that a movement represents (the identity paradigm), we need instead to look at the communication flows through which a movement emerges and transforms. In the case of Britain, cultural festivals played a key role. By the late 1990s there were several hundred such festivals each year in Britain, involving literature, music, dance, traditional folk cultures, ecological farming and agriculture, art (over 400 festivals are listed each year at www.festivaleye.com). These meant that the music, recovery of historic traditions, and forms of experience of the natural world at the center of the cultural processes involved in the Twyford occupation and others like it could connect to wider networks in and beyond Britain. One participant describes his encounter with the Dongas at a Rainbow festival in Ireland:

> Music is everywhere. Dance workshops. Rebirthing. Healing. Spiritual teachings. Everyone is smiling and open faced. You can be crazy and nobody minds, like Everton, the black Londoner who since the age of 6 had just wanted to walk around holding a stick meditating on it – so that's what he was doing here; or the American gent who wants to go about with no trousers on. There is constant drumming – really good. I am seized on by a clown who's drawn to my drum and find myself sitting down with this group playing the most amazing music. I look up at their flag and find they're the Dongas Tribe. The Rainbow Festival is billed as a gathering of the tribes of Europe, and I'm mind-blown by Dongas because they're the amazing people who've been protesting the motorway rape of Twyford Down in England. I feel I've come home. (McIntosh 1994)

Emerging out of an older English tradition of fayres (McKay 2000), these festivals served as a critical link to broader youth culture, a bridge to other cultural flows.

The City

Grammars of experience that had been emerging in antiroads action moved from English rural areas to suburban London with the action against the extension of the M11 freeway. A campaign against the extension of the freeway, which would involve the destruction of houses and parkland, began in September 1993. A year-long campaign developed, focusing on occupying houses in Claremont Road, the principal street scheduled for destruction. Nets and tripods were introduced, ropes and aerial cross-paths linked different houses, just as in forest occupations areal paths allow people to live and move about in trees. As in the rural actions, occupation served as a focus for visitors and networks, producing a powerful effect. One visitor, Charles, describes the experience:

> Claremont at that time was so funny. Not outrageous or loud or ghastly, but just fun and enormously happy. A big friendly commune of welcome and greeting. Just like London used to be, but maybe with its eccentric and creative overtones. Sofas and chairs in the street, a no-car zone apart from the street's very own green "Rust in Peace" car, full of art and flowers. A cafe, an office, and a thriving little community, all asking me for "Any spare change." Busking in the sunshine, dogs yapping, the breeze in the trees, and artistic happenings aplenty. It was a very dynamic and yet meditative atmosphere. I may not be a tattooed punk, but I loved it there. (available at http://www.geocities.com/londondestruction/index.html,)

The eviction of Claremont Road involved 700 police, 400 security guards and 200 bailifs, who required four days to remove 500 protestors from the site. As Doherty (1999) notes, the occupiers achieved major national news coverage over these four days, as well as significant tactical successes, such as maintaining power supply through a secret tunnel that went under police lines. One participant describes the streetscape:

> The street was painted and filled with psychedelic sculptures, barricades, above them the nets, tree houses, aerial walkways and towers went up; inside the houses, bunkers, lock-ons and tunnels were hidden in tons of rubble. (quoted in *Roadblock* 1995: 25)

It was in the middle of this period that the Criminal Justice and Public Order Act made unauthorized repetitive music (i.e., rave music) in public places illegal. In the final days of confrontation between protestors and police, a sound system was set up, playing the repetitive beats of Prodigy. The claim to the street was being made not only through the physical occupation of the site (the scaffold tower and lock-ons), but also through creating a sensorial space through music. We can get a sense of the power of this experience through the diary of "Aurora," who became involved in the occupation toward the end. She gives us access above all to a sense of the strange power of the experience, one where music is part of constituting a world she had never experienced before:

On my 30th birthday, in 1994, I made my first ever visit to a protest site. Claremont road E1. Site of the then proposed M11 extension. I guess I'd been watching the campaign on TV and I think it was a kind of a mixture of birthday panic combined with sustained curiosity that brought me there, and I found myself literally stepping into another world.

The terraced street of squatted houses was closed to traffic, barricaded at each end. The only cars remaining had been speared with scaffolding poles or filled with earth and sprouted with flowers, the trees were decorated and had tree houses, the houses painted, the place was alive with art and vision. Out of one houses sprouted a huge tower and within this structure, was a sound system.

And it was while I was taking all this in that I heard the Prodigy for the very first time. It blasted out of the tower . . . "what we're dealing with here is a total lack of respect of the law . . ." It was the very first techno I'd ever heard. My mind really was glowing. This music was the perfect accompaniment to the anarchic, utopian, visionary world that had intoxicated me. The lyrics expressed rejection of authority and the prevailing order, and yet had answers. They had the poison and the remedy . . . In "Break & Enter" a woman sings, "give the planet love" accompanied by the sound of smashing glass. This was direct action in musical form. Nothing has ever moved me so much since, and thus started a long love affair with both the anti-road movement and techno.

To this day when I get up to go on an action, or come home from a political event, I will open all the windows in my council flat and blast it out top volume as a kind of battle cry, a message to everyone of the possibilities . . . "Fuck 'em and their laws." (Green 2002)

The accounts of these two visitors go beyond the idea of embodiment as a "tactic." They underline instead the sensual and experiential nature of both the action and of response to it. The street is turned into a work of art, one that is experienced and felt, not simply a message to be agreed or disagreed with. People find themselves pulled into the experience. Not only is this not primarily cognitive (a message to be agreed with or not), but this opening of the senses and embodiment involves a form of action that is nonintentional.

A number of people who had been involved in the Claremont Road occupation met together in the weeks immediately after the final expulsion in February 1995, and determined to carry on the action through reforming Reclaim The Streets. And this time music would be central.

Cars Can't Dance

On May 14 1995 an old car enters one of the busiest intersections in London, a five-way intersection at Camden, only to collide with another car in a similar condition. The two drivers get out and start arguing, while traffic banks up around them. Then, to general astonishment, each reaches into their car, brings out hammers, and begins destroying the other's car. Other people begin streaming into the intersection from the subway. A party begins, lasting five hours, with participants taking it in turns to participate in smashing the cars. A solar powered sound system provides music. A second "crash in" follows on 23 July at the Angle intersection in Islington. Press estimates suggest that some 2,000 people were involved in the party that followed, this time with a much more powerful sound system, where banners were put up, stalls were established, and sand was poured onto the road to turn it into a children's playground.

These first two actions set off an extraordinary development. Over the next year similar actions were repeated across British cities, culminating in an occupation of the M41 freeway in the summer of 1996, which press estimates suggest involved some 7,000 people (*Guardian*, July 16, 1996).

Not only did the occupation center on dancing, but sections of the road were dug up and trees were planted. The aim was not simply to occupy the site, but to create an extraordinary experience, something of which is captured in press reports:

> There are transvestites snogging in the fast lane, stilt-walkers partying in the slow lane, and parents encouraging their children to play in the overtaking lane. By a sound system on the hard shoulder, a 24-foot high pantomime dame sways to music, skirts billowing yards of pink fluffiness. Welcome to a typical street. Not. (Griffiths 1996)

The action against the extension of freeways could have taken the form of the opposing rural community to the impersonal city, or traditional life against the imperatives of the market. But the grammar of action we encounter here is different in two important ways: the street party replaces the march or the demonstration, while the action opposes embodied inter-subjectivity (Csordas 1993) such as dance or hearing together to functional imperatives:

> The road is mechanical, linear movement epitomized by the car. The street, at best, is a living place of human movement and social intercourse, of freedom and spontaneity. The car system steals the street from under us and sells it back for the price of petrol. It privileges time over space, corrupting and reducing both to an obsession with speed or, in economic lingo, "turnover." It doesn't matter who "drives" this system for its movements are already pre-determined. (http://rts.gn.apc.org/prop02.htm)

This is an ethic of the present. It is committed to living differently now, as opposed to programmatic or linear attempts to shape the future. This experience of turning an abstracted functional space into a space of embodied communication would become immensely powerful, globalizing along networks of information and emotion. In Europe it traveled rave and music cultures: August 1997 saw a two-day blockade of the A33 autoroute in Germany, building on an earlier "antiroad rave." A first Reclaim The Streets took place in Finland in May 1997, a second in August. The years 1996 and 1997 saw a significant extension of road blockades across Europe and the use of the Internet for "action updates," which were forums where activists could call for support, post pictures, and tell their stories. Some 44 street parties were held between the first urban occupation of Camden High Street on May 15, 1995, and the first "Global Street Party" of May 16, 1998, where simultaneous street parties were held in 24 cities across four continents.

A participant at a blockade of the World Economic Forum (WEF) in Melbourne, Australia, in September 2000 (which brought together some 10,000 people over three days) recounts his experience of reclaiming the streets:

> it's just like the city belongs to the community. It's like saying, "You might have the power, but when we get together, especially with the numbers we had down there, the world is ours." It's a way of being able to prove that on the ground we do have power and there is that [pause] perceptions are kind of cracked [pause] just to think that you can occupy that kind of space and you can just change the way the whole world operates and all of a sudden what was a street becomes a dance floor. There is the power to be in that space in terms of having culture and community and all kinds of other things. (Pip, videoactivst)

This action does not necessarily require large mobilizations. Bear, a forest activist with a long history of tree-sits, was a DJ in one of the spaces occupied at the WEF blockade in Melbourne. For him, turning the street into a dance floor aims at changing the codes that govern the urban:

> The urban environment is so locked in that there is no space for people to just erupt into a party. It's like, we had a house in High Street, and our little fun thing was to have a whole group of people over and we would have a drink and dinner and stuff, and it would just erupt into a party and so we would just open the front doors to the house and move the furniture onto the footpath. Leave enough room for everyone to get by, pull out the drums and have a party on our sidewalk in front of our house. People would be driving past and go "yeah" and it's just the ability to be able to go out on the street and express yourself because it is essentially our street. Responsibly too – just bring the city back to the people rather than the people being stuffed into the city.

These were the networks that decided to hold a "global street party" to correspond with the Birmingham G8 in 1998.

Back to the United States: Critical Mass

The Global Street Party timed to coincide with the Birmingham G8 is the clearest sign of the emergence of a global movement embedded in cultural flows. It was this that led to the first Reclaim The Streets action in the United States. While in Britain RTS had emerged out of Earth First!, in the United States the remnants of Earth First! had increasingly come to define itself against the city and urban culture, and had nothing to do with the development of RTS in that country. Instead, RTS emerged from a new kind of urban movement, Critical Mass.

Critical Mass began in San Francisco in September 1992. It was originally an idea of a single cyclist, who discussed the idea with other people involved in an already existing network of bicycle messengers. The aim right from the beginning was not to create a group, but to create an event – a monthly bicycle ride through the city, in order to claim space on the roads for bicycle riders. The initial name of the event, "Commuter Clot," communicated the idea that the riders would aim at slowing down the flow of urban traffic. Flyers were photocopied and distributed in workplaces, suggesting that people "ride home from work together." The original ride gathered together between 40 and 50 people, who rode together to slow the traffic and demonstrate that bike riders existed. From this first ride idea of a regular, once-a-month ride emerged. This then began to spread, first to other cities, then internationally, with 10 years later critical-mass rides taking place in every continent. The term "critical mass" was adopted after several participants saw a documentary on bicycles and bicycle culture by American film maker Tedd Bliss, *Return of the Scorcher* (1992), who used the term "critical mass" to describe the way bicycle riders in Beijing bunch up into a large group, and then proceed to cross busy intersections, the size and the density of the group allowing them to cross the traffic.

The people involved in Critical Mass describe it as an "unorganized coincidence," and strongly reject any suggestion that it is an organization. And they are right. It is precisely because it is not an organization that Critical Mass has developed into a form of global action. The Internet plays a key role in events, information and experiences being shared, through what is described as "a worldwide critical mass hub" (http://criticalmassrides.info/index.html). The hub give details of monthly rides and most of these rides have discussion pages where participants discuss issues.

But while Critical Mass is an example of action spread via the Internet, it predates it. In 1992, the people involved in Critical Mass described it as a "Xerocracy," as we see from a leaflet produced by people involved in San Francisco in 1994:

> Organizational politics, with its official leaders, demands, etc., has been eschewed in favor of a more decentralized system. There is no one in charge. Ideas are spread, routes shared, and consensus sought through the ubiquitous copy machines on every job or at copy shops in every neighborhood – a "Xerocracy," in which anyone is free to make copies of their ideas and pass them around. Leaflets, flyers, stickers and 'zines all circulate madly both before, during, and after the ride, rendering leaders unnecessary by ensuring that strategies and tactics are understood by as many people as possible.
>
> Xerocracy promotes freedom and undercuts hierarchy because the mission is not set by a few in charge, but rather is broadly defined by its participants. The ride is not narrowly seen as an attempt to lobby for more bike lanes (although that goal exists) or to protest this or that aspect of the social order (although such sentiments are often expressed). Rather, each person is free to invent his or her own reasons for participating and is also free to share those ideas with others.' (http://www.scorcher.org/cmhistory/howto.html)

In this case, primacy is attached to the horizontal, to the *encounter with the other person*, not to the encounter with symbols or instances of a collectivity constituted through the act of representation. We encounter action experienced as embodied flow, as we see in the account of an action in San Francisco:

The cop was standing in front of me as I turned around.

"Excuse me," he said with professional reserve, "are you one of the organizers here?" I had been passing out flyers of the route to the 500 or so bicyclists gathered for the monthly Critical Mass. I was also handing out my zine.

"I don't think there are organizers," I said hesitantly.

"Because last time you guys kept riding through intersections even after the light turned red and you caused gridlock. Is that one of the organizers over there?" The motorcycle cop pointed to another person handing out flyers. A Channel 7 reporter was trying to interview her.

"Not that I know of. Why does something like this need an organizer? It's pretty unorganized."

"OK sir, well we're not going to let that happen again because the mayor heard about it and he's very upset. When the light turns red we're going to clear the intersection by force if necessary."

I mumbled something non-confrontational and slunk away, unsure what this ride was going to be like, hoping against hope that the police would not instigate anything. The other rides had been so calm. I didn't want to get arrested.

About half an hour later the bike ride poured into the street. Police were escorting us on motorcycles on both sides, same as before. Even though we as a mass with our corkers could block traffic with no problem on our own, they thought we needed their "escort" for protection, or maybe they were just trying to make us think we needed them.

Riding towards the middle of the slow moving mass, I noticed the light at our first intersection turning red just as I was getting there. I cringed. Eight motorcycle cops pulled into the crowd with menacing faces. I looked around to see what everyone else was going to do. Everyone looked very calm about the whole thing, which relaxed me. I saw one, then two bicycles slip between the motorcycles. Then I was weaving my way through. The blockade was leaking like a sieve. The cop on my right tried to back his motorbike into my way. But his bike was too heavy and he was too slow. I was through! (http://danenet.wicip.org/bcp/cm.html)

Critical mass is not an organization – it is an event. The metaphor "critical mass" captures the idea of "tipping point" as opposed to linear, cumulative process. It is an event that, when it occurs, changes reality, including itself.

The paradigm is one of flow and liquidity. The riders "pour" through gaps in police lines, the blockade set up to contain riders "leaks like a sieve"; the flow of the riders is opposed to the heaviness of the police; the technique the riders have developed for controlling the flow of cars around them is described as "corking," drawing on the image of retaining fluid in a bottle.

Since beginning in 1992, Critical Mass has become a global event. On the last Friday of every month, rides take place in over 300 cities.

Collisions and Convergences

The RTS proposal of a Global street party in 1998 generated thousands of emails, while RTS London set up a web site where people could find links to other groups setting up parties in other countries. Reports of the day were posted (http://rts.gn.apc.org/global3.htm), giving a sense of the globalization of the movement, where people recounted their stories. In Valencia, Spain, for example, those involved report that they had heard of the initiative only three weeks before, as a result of a friend from London visiting who was also involved in RTS. While there was no RTS in their city, there were networks of people attracted to the opposition they saw at the center of the action:

> the street is a space that belongs to people, but has been stolen by the car; the street is lifeless and depressing, it must be transformed into a space of creativity and freedom, through a party! (http://rts.gn.apc.org/g-valenc.htm)

In Darwin, Australia, there was an attempt to set up the day, initiated as well as a result of a visitor from London who had been involved in RTS. In this case there were no local networks to sustain the event, and despite distributing some 2,000 leaflets, only the three people who tried to set up the event ended up at the meeting point. They decided to go to the beach after no one came. In Prague, capital of the Czech republic, several thousand people took control of the street, several were arrested, cars and a McDonald's store were trashed. But where did the concern with the General Agreement on Tariffs and Trade (GATT) and its successor, the World Trade Organization (WTO), come from? The WTO is a long way from defending the chalk hills at Twyford Down or Claremont Road in London.

Over this period, new flows and intersection points between networks begin to be visible. The Zapatista struggle in Chiapas, Mexico, had set up a first international Encuentro or encounter in 1996, followed by a second Encuentro in Spain in 1997. This emerged out of a year-long process of consultation and discussion, where the Internet had begun to play a critical role, converging with more traditional nongovernmental organizations (NGOs). In 1997 several European youth NGO's had organized the "Hunger Gathering," a countersummit to the Food and Agriculture Organization (FAO) food security summit that was being held in Rome at the same time. The Hunger

Gathering focused on the impact of biotechnologies in agriculture in countries such as India, underlining the impacts in terms of reduced biodiversity, the increasing vulnerability of peasant farmers, and the role of Transnational Corporations and the WTO. The WTO had been increasingly targeted by development NGOs since the "50 years is enough" campaign aimed at the World Bank, which had converged with ecology groups also who opposed the Bank's policies regarding dams and large-scale industrialized agriculture.

These networks were widening and interpenetrating, new experiential grammars emerging. From social base our focus has shifted to cultural flows, and from movement reflecting identity we have begun to explore movement as experience. Thus far we have focused on the emergence and transformation of direct action in the environmental movement, which has moved from the Untied States to Britain, and from a rural to an urban context. But we need to understand wider shifts in grammars of direct action. These become more evident in two critical processes: the emergence of new humanitarianism, and the development of new types of action above all evident in the Zapatista movement that emerged on the other side of the planet, in the remote border areas of Mexico.

CHAPTER 4

The New Humanitarianism

Without television, contemporary humanitarianism would not exist.

Bernard Kouchner, founder of Médecins Sans Frontières

In May 1991, some 20 people protested against the London meeting of the G7, principally focusing on the importation of Malaysian rainforest timber. Yet when the G8 (with the inclusion of Russia) would return to Britain, in Birmingham in 1998, it would be met by a gathering of some 60,000 people, including a "human chain" of some 7,000 people calling for the abolition of Third World debt, as well as an RTS street party involving several thousand people. While the vast majority of those participating were British, European-wide networks had been mobilized, following the successful mobilization against the G8 two years earlier in the French city of Lyon. In France, different networks had converged in the Lyon mobilization, from new worker "coordinations" such as Solidaires Unitaires Démocratiques (SUD), new types of campaign networks against poverty such as Droits Devant!! (DD!!), and forms of humanitarian organization such as Médecins Sans Frontières.

Once again the diversity of such groups would appear to support the thesis that these are nation-based groups that principally have in common the fact that they have, for different reasons, opted to include an international dimension to their strategy. Once we start to look, however, certain themes begin to reoccur: the shift from hierarchy to network; the personalization of commitment; the move from long term to short term; the shift from organization to project; the critical importance of the media, above all television, for the mediatization of action; the shift from the organization to event. The shift from 20 people protesting the G7 in 1991 to 60,000 in 1998 is not primarily a shift in scale: it points to a shift in paradigm.

Beyond Counterexperts

The origins of the G8 lie in the crisis of the post-1945 system of economic and political regulation, a crisis that became increasingly evident during the early 1970s with the collapse of the Bretton Woods system of fixed exchange rates and in the oil crisis following the Arab–Israeli war of 1973. Finance ministers of the United States, France, Great Britain, and Germany met in April 1973 at the White House library, followed by a first meeting of the heads of government, which was held in France in 1975, where Italy joined the group as well, the discussion focusing on inflation. A dynamic of annual economic summits was established. For almost the entire first decade of its operation, these summits were ignored by NGOs, social movements, and others, while the summits ignored them as well (Hajnal 2001).

The first signs of a shift occurred at the London Summit of 1984, when the G7 was identified by British NGOs as a target for lobbying and opposition. The 1983 summit had given an important place to the issue of international debt, structural adjustment, and the role of the IMF, in a context where food riots and structural adjustment programs were leading to increasing contestation of IMF policies. The Economic Summit had reaffirmed its support for such policies, and by the mid-1980s it was emerging as an instance of global governance. The increasing public role of the Economic Summit, and the emerging opposition to IMF structural adjustment policies that it was championing, set the context in 1984 for the inauguration of The Other Economic Summit (TOES), a gathering of development NGOs and radical academic economists largely based in Britain. A second TOES was held in 1987, and over the next decade the TOES network organized an annual countersummit, largely drawing on international networks of radical academic economists, while involving international development NGOs as well. In something of a paradox, the counternetwork referred to itself as a counter economic summit at precisely the time when the agenda of the Economic Summit was widening beyond the economy, to include questions of terrorism, international politics, and pollution, following Chernobyl in 1986.

A significant shift occurred in relation to the G7 and its opponents in 1989, the year the Summit was held in France. It was the bicentenary of the French Revolution, and the French government under President Mitterrand mediatized the event, holding it during the peak of the Revolution's commemoration on July 14. Action against the Summit also mediatized, with a concert and a countersummit bringing together people from the seven poorest countries on earth. But this was largely framed within debates about the heritage of the French Revolution. A mass concert was held at the Bastille, modeled on the 1986 Live Aid concert, where in the words of the organizers, "the rev-

olutionaries of 1989 could celebrate those of 1789." The aim was to symbolically frame opposition to the Economic Summit in terms of the heritage
and categories of the traditional French left. But despite the success of the
concert, the action had almost no lasting impact. But next time the Summit
came to France, in 1996, it would be met by a new type of actor: the new
humanitarians. This chapter explores key instances of this form of action and
culture that played an important role in the 1996 action against the G7: Restos
du Coeur (Restaurants of the heart) and Médecins Sans Frontières (Doctors
without Borders).

The New Humanitarianism – the Restos du Coeur

The Restos du Coeur were founded in France in 1986 by a comedian and
entertainer, Michel Colucci, more frequently known by his stage name,
Coluche. Coluche had shocked the French political establishment when he
stood in the presidential election of 1981, presenting himself as a candidate
for those who believed that politicians were no longer serving the people.
Four years later, in September 1985, Coluche was lending his support to the
French campaign against hunger in Ethiopia, the same international campaign that had led to the Live Aid performance in Britain earlier that year.
While participating in a radio show raising funds for the Ethiopia relief
appeal, Coluche was challenged by a caller to not only respond to hunger in
Africa, but also to respond to what the caller insisted was the increasing
hunger and poverty in France itself. This period in France was marked by an
increasing sense of the breakdown of the postwar period of prosperity, and
extensive public debates about poverty and new forms of "social exclusion"
understood in terms of the weakening of social connection (for an overview,
see Paugam 2000).

The day after this event, Coluche went to visit Abbé Pierre, a long-time
figure in the French charitable tradition within the Catholic Church, who had
been responsible for providing free meals to the poor in France since the
1950s. Following this meeting, Coluche went on national radio, and together
with Abbé Pierre launched a national appeal to bring about an end to hunger
in France. The show was inundated with calls, not only from individuals offering food, but also from major food retailers, who pledged to provide food for
the new food distribution centers that Coluche was calling for. Over the next
few days other celebrities associated themselves with the action, critical intellectuals signed up as well. A network of food distribution centers was to be
formed, to be known as the Restos du Coeur, the aim being to mobilize 5,000
volunteers over the coming winter and distribute some 8.5 million meals to

the hungry. The three French national television stations joined the mobilization, all supporting the new restaurants that were springing up across the country.

In March 1986, several months after this extraordinary mobilization, Coluche was killed in a motorcycle accident. His death served to accelerate the movement he had started, such that in the 1986 winter that followed, some 10,000 volunteers took part in the Restos du Coeur, while the number of meals distributed over the winter tripled to reach 27 million. A decade later, in 1996, the Restos were distributing 60 million meals to over half a million people, involving some 30,000 volunteers. By 2003 the association consisted of some 40,000 volunteers, had over 2,000 restaurants and meal distribution points across France, and distributed some 60 million meals, most during winter. The Restos du Coeur points to a form of action characterizing the "new humanitarianism" that would play a critical role in the development of mobilizations around globalization, three dimensions in particular.

The first of these involves the relationship with the political process and the state. As a candidate in the 1981 French Presidential elections, Coluche was a symbol of the disillusion with politics and the political process – he was an outsider, standing for election against the political establishment of both Left and Right (such figures have become increasingly frequent across western political systems in the period since). One of his first actions on taking up the challenge of responding to poverty in France was to seek out the imprimatur of Abbé Pierre, a Capuchin monk who had been involved in food distribution to the poor for more than three decades, and who was generally regarded as politically conservative. Coluche was in many ways associated with the generation of May 1968, a generation whose vocabulary and concepts were fundamentally political. Abbé Pierre was a symbol of an older form of charity, of the importance of direct response to those in need rather than programs of political change. In affirming the urgency of direct distribution of food to those in need, Coluche was affirming that this was a more human and more ethical response than involvement in a political system regarded as unauthentic. In the French case this is particularly significant, the Restos du Coeur involving a break with what was known as the "republican model." Rather than seek the mediation of the state, reflecting a civic morality where the state assures the welfare of the citizen, the culture of this action focused on establishing a direct relationship with the other, and with it the affirmation of a *value of authenticity through the directness of this relationship* (Salmon 1998: 23). It emphasizes a direct relationship with the other, one not mediated by the action of the state.

The second significant dimension of the Restos du Coeur, as noted by David Salmon, is the extent to which this movement is a "media association."

The development of the Restos du Coeur did not involve the formation of an association, followed by media interest. Rather, the association emerged first of all *in the media*, its early development depending crucially on "media personalities" or celebrities. Not only were celebrities critical for the early development of the movement; it is possible to argue that the culture of Restos du Coeur was critically shaped by the culture of the media, in particular by that of television. Critical dimensions of this movement emphasize urgency and immediacy, dimensions central to the communication codes of contemporary television.

The third dimension of this movement that would prove increasingly significant lies in a series of characteristics associated with the "personalization" of commitment. Several important dimensions become evident in research undertaken with people involved in the Restos. Firstly, the culture is neither one of "pity" nor "devotion" to the figure of an imaginary "poor person." Poverty is seen as pervading French society, to that point that volunteers in the Restos underline that what is happening to people who are poor could also just as easily happen to them as well. But at the same time there is no attempt to construct a "collective identity," one that takes the form of "us" in classical models of social movement. Rather the culture of the Restos is one where people involved do not seek community, but rather a recognition of a shared experience. The culture of the Restos is one where those involved communicate with each other on a first-name basis, using the familiar form of address *tu* rather than the formal *vous*. This form of address in France is more common among younger people rather than older people, but this is not the profile of the Restos – which in fact have a significant proportion of retired people involved as volunteers. Rather Ravel and Ravon's (1997) ethnographic study of the Restos points to the extent to which *only* first names are used, with membership lists and rosters consisting of first names and telephone numbers. At meetings and planning sessions, whether one is involved as a volunteer or a service-user is not spelled out (and in fact one can be both), and the culture of not using family names is part of a culture where there is in fact an avoidance of markers such as profession, family name, status, and so on. The preference for first names and the use of *tu* do not point to a youth culture of informality, but to a culture that is personalized, one that *avoids a collective identity based on references to socially shared identities* (volunteers avoid seeking out information about such things as family status, family name, locality, or employment status).

Médecins sans Frontières

Important dimensions of the culture and action present in the Restos du Coeur are also evident in the organization that arguably serves as a paradigm case of the "new humanitarianism," Médecins sans Frontières. Médecins sans Frontières was formed in 1971 by a group of medical doctors led by Dr Bernard Kouchner, following a period working with the International Red Cross in Biafra. The context for the birth of MSF was the changing nature of conflicts and the increasing limitations this imposed on the action of the International Committee of the Red Cross. Until the early 1960s, the ICRC had essentially limited its role to monitoring the application of the Geneva Convention in relation to civilians and prisoners, and in fact did not send medical teams to conflict zones. The ICRC's role in conflict zones had developed in a context where organized and disciplined armies fought against each other, one where medical services were provided by the military combatants. But in 1960s Africa, during the period of decolonization and civil wars, it was clear that the nature of armed conflict was in a process of transformation, involving guerrilla conflicts, food shortages, and a blurring of the distinction between armed forces and noncombatants. This is evident in changing patterns of casualties of war over the twentieth century. In the First World War, only 5 percent of those killed were civilians. In the Second World War, this had increased to 50 percent of those killed. In the wars of the 1990s, in the order of 90 percent of those killed were civilians (Tilly 2002). Wars are increasingly conducted in cities, not in remote locations, and blur distinctions between regular and irregular forces. In the Biafran war, even the most basic medical supplies and trained staff were absent. The older model of medical assistance to be effected through armies could not respond to this emerging situation. At the same time, the ICRC policy did not permit emergency staff it sent to work in crisis zones to make critical public comment on the actions of member states, as its continued presence depended upon the good will of those states.

Kouchner had been a member of a French Red Cross team sent to Biafra that consisted of some 50 doctors. On returning to France he was part of a group of "Biafran veterans" who organized a "Committee against the Biafran genocide," and believing that similar situations were likely to continue to develop in Africa, the group established the Group d'Intervention Médicale et Chirurgical d'Urgence (Emergency Medical and Surgical Intervention Group), the aim being to develop a capacity to intervene in similar emergencies. In 1971 this group joined with a doctor who had similar experiences in Bangladesh, creating Médecins Sans Frontières. Looking back on the period of formation of MSF, Rony Brauman, who became President of MSF in the mid-1970s, underlines the importance of the increasing ease of access to international travel as well as that of the media. What Brauman is talking about is what the geographer David Harvey (1990) refers to as "space compression" – the world becoming smaller as a result of travel technologies. But above all Brauman underlines the critical impact of television in the devel-

opment of MSF: "the instantaneous visibility of disasters and conflicts on television made it less and less acceptable either to do nothing or to offer only
a confused effort at emergency assistance" (Brauman 1993). Kouchner
himself goes further, arguing that without the media, and above all television, the humanitarian action that developed over the 1980s simply could not
have occurred (1991: 112). These key actors in the development of MSF
underline the critical role of television as a form of mediation, one described
by Michael Ignatieff in the following terms:

> Whether it wishes or not, television has become the principal mediation
> between the suffering of strangers and the consciences of those in the world's
> few remaining zones of safety. . . . It has become not merely the means
> through which we see each other, but the means by which we shoulder each
> other's fate. (1998: 13)

It is clear that television played a key role in the emergence of new forms
of humanitarian action, first of all in France, and later other countries. Media
theorists like Thomas Keenan (2002) are critical of this development, arguing
that this humanitarianism has replaced political solutions to conflicts, where
food and blankets replace durable political solutions. Others such as Luc
Boltanski (1999) argue that the response to distant suffering is more complex,
while insisting that television increasingly shapes both the contemporary
public sphere and forms of action that develop within it. The Restos du Coeur
and Médecins Sans Frontières both owe their origins to charismatic figures,
and both began as "media associations." Despite the impact that MSF had in
French, and later international media, over most of its first decade there was
a large gap between its media profile and its actual capacity for action: over
the period of 1971 to 1978, MSF on average sent out only a few dozen doctors
each year (Brauman 1993). Right from the beginning, however, the teams it
sent also included a press officer, whose role was to compete for media presence, dramatizing the situation and the role of MSF doctors (there is an
obvious parallel between MSF and Greenpeace). This strategy has received
extensive critique, with MSF accused of "commodifying tragedy," with MSF
accused of being increasingly integrated into a media-driven system, playing
out a model of hero (the MSF doctor) and victim (see Leyton 1998).

Both MSF and the Restos emerge out of a culture of urgency. The ethic
of action to which both appeal is framed in terms of the imperative of acting
now. In the case of the Restos, the appeal to act is not addressed to the long-
term needs (employment, salaries, changing the relationship between work
and income), but to the immediate needs of the coming winter. In the case
of MSF, the appeal to action focuses on the current emergency, as opposed
to the long term. Bernard Kouchner's emphasis on emergency and immedi-

ate response can also be seen as related to changes in French medicine over the 1960s, the period when Kouchner trained, and during which emergency medicine emerged as a separate medical specialization. The first association established by Kouchner was conceived in terms of an international medical emergency, and his preference for emergency medicine shaped his period as French Minister for Health.

The importance of emergency also points to a less evident dimension: the search for risk and the relationship with violence. French political scientist Johanna Siméant (2001) explores the personal trajectories of key people involved in the formation of MSF. A surprising number of the older group involved in its formation had either been involved in the French Resistance during the Nazi occupation, had been former marines, or, in the case of younger members such as Kouchner or Brauman, had played a role in maintaining order for political organizations during the events of May 1968 or earlier. Kouchner's grand parents were killed in a concentration camp, and he became politically active through antifascist action. One his first involvements was being member of a group physically defending the apartment of Simone de Beauvoir against a possible Organisation Armée Secrète attack in the late 1950s (the Secret Armed Organization, an armed group that opposed France's decolonization of Algeria, was responsible for several hundred deaths, as well as an attempted assassination of France's President General de Gaulle in 1962). In 1961 Kouchner, together with Régis Debray, volunteered at the Cuban embassy to join an international brigade to defend the island nation against the United States. Kouchner did not finally join the brigade, but in 1964 traveled to Cuba as part of a delegation of French Youth (Siméant 2001). During the traumatic events of May 1968 Kouchner moved between different groups, distributing leaflets at factory gates, and was involved in the Union of Communist Students while also maintaining involvement in the medical milieu (Siméant 2001). The book he co-authored, *Savage France*, which celebrated the struggle of May 1968, paints a picture of a looming confrontation between the forces of contestation and the forces of order, where Kouchner declares "each Frenchman is individually a rebel" (Kouchner and Burnier 1970: 9).

Kouchner's celebration of *Savage France* manifests the "virile culture" that Siméant argues would later play a critical role in the emergence of MSF. This is evident in an ethic of adventure, in a love of fast cars (more often borrowed than owned), in a detached relationship to money, and in an intolerance of timidity, bourgeois manners, and hypocrisy. While a continent away in terms of political tradition and culture there are evident similarities between Kouchner's culture of virility and that of Dave Foreman, the founder of Earth First!, who equally emphasized urgency and action rather than the long term and talk. Kouchner would later contrast the experience of emergency work in Biafra with the humdrum life of work and metro in Paris, writing, "despite our ironies and our doubts, we had created an aristocracy of risk. Once again, the male hormone . . ." (1991: 324).

MSF, as DeChaine (2002) argues, has played a key role in the construction of a global imaginary, envisioning a world "without borders." Central here is the idea of "humanitarian space," an understanding of space where we encounter the other as a person, not as a citizen of a given country – MSF's action seeks to deterritorialize and humanitarianize space (DeChaine 2002), where the recognition of the humanity of the other also sets in place the conditions that allow MSF to act – in an image of a globalized, borderless world modelled on the image MSF has of itself.

Action Networks

Themes that had played a key role in the emergence of "media associations" such as the Restos du Coeur and MSF are equally evident in other action networks that took shape in France over the 1990s, which would play a key role in the emerging theme of antiglobalization later in the decade. In France, rather than be associated with defense of rural sites, direct action emerged around housing struggles, in particular through Droit Au Logement (DAL) and new types of mobilization of undocumented immigrants or *sans-papiers*, as well as worker co-ordinations, one of the most important being SUD, emerging first among workers in high-technology sectors of the economy, one that maintained a strong work-based identity.

For some authors, these networks represent little more than the return of a generation of the extreme left that had been hibernating during the 1970s (Poulet 1999). And it is clear that a number of the new coordinations that emerged over the early 1990s were animated by members of extreme-left political organizations, with members of older political organizations prominent, such as Christophe Augiton, who is a member of the Political Bureau of the Ligue Communiste Revolutionaire, a Trotskyist political group founded by Alain Krivine (who still remains its leader) in 1968. Aguiton is a founder of SUD-PTT (Solidaires, Unitaires et Démocratiques – Post, Telegraphs, Telephones), as well as AC! (Agir Contre le chomage – act against unemployment). AC! played a prominent role in the development of the Marches against Unemployment, while Augiton is a co-founder and spokesperson for ATTAC, the Association for a Tobin Tax for the Aid of Citizens, one of the principal organizations playing a key role in the development of the antiglobalization movement in France

These movements allowed themes that had developed in humanitarian action to enter a wider field of debate. The type of action they undertook was direct action, and highly "mediatized," the aim being to produce communicative events (such as occupations) or symbols (such as dragons, clowns) rather than build organizations. Boltanski and Chiapello (1999: 434) argue that these forms of action in many ways parallel the shift to a network capitalism. The grammar of action that they employ underlines the theme of *presence* rather than *distance*, *short-term* and immediate rather than *long-term* action; a focus on *events* rather than *programs*. The form of organization is one of networks built up around events, the mode of action is open to heterogenity and plurality rather than an emphasis on sameness. There is no need to construct a "collective identity" across the action. Christophe Aguiton insists on this plurality within action networks, calling for "a form of organization symbolic of this situation: the network, where one works together with others, while maintaining one's own identity" (Aguiton and Bensaïd 1997).

There is a strong sense that the actors involved are aware of a paradigm shift at work, away from an older model of building an organization, to a new pattern of networks, one where the temporal experience is focused on the present rather than the future. Aguiton writes:

> Today we are in the middle of a profound rupture. We are in a culture of networks . . . It is the defence of values, more than a model of society, that makes up the ideology that underlies the mobilizations. When parties, trade unions or associations were holding up a project of social transformation – whether revolution, self-management or common program – what counted was reinforcing one's own group, widening the scope of influence of one's party or trade union. Today what is at stake is defending values, the structure takes second place, instead different forces come together, *"all together for the battle of the instant."* (Aguiton 1996; emphasis added)

These new networks were at the origin of the "social summit" that corresponded with the G7 meeting held in Lyon in 1996.

Antipoverty

On Saturday, May 16, 1998, some 10,000 people formed a 6 mile human chain around Birmingham city center during the G8 Summit of the leaders of industrialized nations (see http://www.indymedia.org.uk/images/2004/06/293206.jpg). The human chain, part of a wider action involving some 50,000 people, paralyzed much of the downtown area. The action was organized by a coalition of largely Christian aid and development groups that made up the "Jubilee 2000 Coalition," the principal demand of the coalition being the annulling of Third World debt. This coalition had been formed in 1996 in an attempt to broaden an earlier coalition of British development NGOs, the Debt Crisis Network, which had been campaigning on the issue of debt in Africa, and that in 1996 had organized a series of visits of African leaders to Britain to speak on issues of debt, a visit that received high level support from British church leaders. The formation of Jubilee 2000 aimed at broadening the base of the coalition beyond development organizations. The coalition of organizations had adopted the name "jubilee" in reference to the Christian biblical injunction to free slaves and release people from debt in a "jubilee" every 50 years. Those participating in the human chain were calling on the G8 to ensure that debt was annulled by the year 2000.

The action aimed at symbolizing the importance of "breaking the chain" of debt. A constant theme in the campaign was the reference to debt slavery, with campaign leaders likening their action to the British campaign for the abolition of slavery during the nineteenth century. We encounter the human-itarian imagination: the link between people directly, not relying on the medi-ation of governments or states. This action also alerts us to the ways that global action mobilizes national traditions. In the British case, action on debt was focused on Africa, with constant references to the "chains of debt," "the slavery of debt," and the struggle to abolish debt, emphasizing historical par-allels with the struggle to abolish slavery. Over the period leading up to the Birmingham Summit activists increasingly refer to themselves as "New Abo-litionists." The core theme is one of compassion for the suffering caused through debt, the basis of a new form of slavery.

It is significant that this form of mobilization did not extend to the United States, despite the efforts of the campaign organizers. The obvious reason is the much lower awareness of Africa in the United States (where there is a far higher awareness of South America). But more impor-tantly is the absence of the kind of "abolitionist" identity that this British movement was attempting to mobilize. The failure of this campaign to develop in the United States alerts us to the different understandings of suffering within different cultures. In the United States, as Hannah Arendt (1973) observes, the opposition of the Founding Fathers to slavery was constructed uniquely in terms of the theme of liberty. Arendt notes that we do not find any concern expressed by the American founders that slavery may also be associated with a powerful form of suffering (see also Boltanski 1999). This means not only the identity that the activists were constructing (the new abolitionists) was a specific British one, constructed through a rela-tionship with Africa, but also that the type of compassion that the campaign was seeking to build would resonate more in some cultures and less in others.

Celebrities and Media

In the year that followed, the Jubilee campaign broadened out to involve celebrities such as Bono, Muhammad Ali, and film star Ewan McGregor. Ali toured Britain in February 1999, laying a wreath at a refugee center in Brixton to those who have died as a result of debt-induced poverty. This event received significant coverage in the British media. Significantly, press reports on the day focus on the tears of those involved: "He came over smiling and I was crying with joy" (one participant quoted in the *Sun*, February 18, 1999), while one of the organizers of Ali's two-day visit to London described the experience in the following terms: "I've never known two days quite like it. Ali is just awesome. Like Princess Diana, he has the ability to inspire and unite. He brings people together, a true world citizen" (*Mirror*, February 18, 1999).

The reference to Princess Diana and the wider role of celebrities in the Jubilee campaign is important to understand. The sociology of the media has made great developments since early representations of the media as a system of manipulation, increasingly exploring the response we make to television images, in this case, images of often brutal suffering. Many analysts link the increasing incidence of images of suffering to the emergence of contemporary humanitarianism. Alain Touraine (2000) suggests that as the global world becomes more and more complex and less intelligible, increasingly celebrities play the role of mediator, serving as a link between us as observers and "nameless humanity." In a particularly dark analysis, Gilles Lipovetsky argues that the sentimentality and moralizing associated with media treatments of suffering, where the action of eliciting a response is associated with almost narcissistic gratification, means that while we become sensitized to forms of suffering presented in an increasingly televisual format, we become desensitized to those forms of suffering that are not mediated and turned into entertainment. For Alain Touraine, the increasing mediatization of suffering accelerates the decomposition of social life, rendering actual social relationships less and less visible:

> Television has gained such a central place in contemporary life because it directly relates the most private dimensions of life with the most global of realities, the emotion when confronted with suffering or the joy of being a human with most advanced military and scientific technologies. Such a direct relationship eliminates the mediations between the individual and humanity, and runs the risk, through decontextualizing messages, of actually contributing to the process of desocialization. The emotion that we all experience when confronted with images of war, sport or humanitarian action does not become transformed into motivations and taking positions. (Touraine 2000: 18)

Bernard Kouchner, founder of MSF, argues that "without television, contemporary humanitarianism would not exist." Television opens out the possibility of immediate relationship, of breaking through the structures of bureaucracy and immobility. Television brings the drama of distant suffering directly into the living rooms of television viewers, and as such demands and solicits a response from the viewer. Luc Boltanski explores such "distant suffering," and argues that it is possible to identify different frameworks or "topics" within which the reception of the image and the construction of the response takes place. The first takes the form of an emotional response of "indignation," where confronted with the reality of suffering, we become angry, and our attention turns away from the victim of suffering, to focus on the persecutor. Anger allows us to master the experience of embodied indignation, but at a cost of a shift in focus, from the suffering person toward abstract systems or organizations, where we proceed through states of indignation, denunciation, and accusation. Boltanski emphasizes the extent to which this viewing experience is embodied rather than simply being cognitive – we feel indignation, and this in turn is embodied as anger.

The second grammar of response explored by Boltanski takes the form of what he calls "sentiment." Here mediated suffering is experienced in terms of the intervention of a benefactor, the viewer sharing the gratitude that a sufferer expresses toward a benefactor. To illustrate this process, Boltanski examines a famous photo taken by W. Eugene Smith in *Life Magazine* in 1951, depicting a nurse-midwife helping a poor African-American woman give birth, not in a hospital, but in a temporary dispensary set up in a church, with worshippers visible in the background. The structure of the photo does not elicit indignation, anger, or accusation, but rather is focused on the gaze of the woman giving birth, who is looking up to the midwife assisting her. Within this grammar of communication, we do not feel indignation, but rather an experience of tenderness, as we look up at the benefactor from an imagined position of the recipient. This grammar of response confronts viewers of the image with their own *interiority*. It underlines the need to go beyond a superficial response to suffering, one constructed in terms of facts and figures, to reach a deeper level:

> the surface level is characterized by *superficial* relationships between people, constructed in terms of facts, illusions, the shallowness of conventions, and above all, separation and coldness. But underneath is a deeper level, that can be accessed through focusing one's attention inwards, into oneself. This is the level of the *heart*. (Boltanski 1999: 122; emphasis in original)

It is perhaps not surprising that two examples we have explored in this chapter directly refer to the question of hearts – Coluche creating the Restos du Coeur in 1987, while in Britain Princess Diana set herself the goal of becoming the Queen of Hearts. The paradigm here is one of reaching out, of touching the other, and allowing the suffering of the other to touch oneself. In an age that no longer believes in ideologies or programs, the celebrity and television combine to make this possible. This became increasingly evident in media treatments of Princess Diana. We can see this in a journalist's account of Diana's response to suffering:

> What was striking about Princess Diana was her willingness to embrace those so often shunned by our political leaders. She did not hesitate to shake (ungloved) hands with AIDS patients, to embrace a leper, or to clasp a dying child with snot running down its face to her designer-sheathed bosom. (Summers 1997)

Several powerful themes converge in this description, in much the same way as W. Eugene Smith's image in *Life Magazine*. Diana, unlike politicians, does not stay removed from those who suffer, but enters directly into contact with them. Rather than rely upon mediations such as associations or governments, she seeks out a *direct* relationship, and this is implied as morally superior to that characterizing "our political leaders." Secondy, she makes embodied contact – she shakes the hand, she embraces, she clasps. Thirdly, we are aware above all of the physical impact that *this has upon Diana*; we identify with her, even to the point where the physicality of the experience of death of a child is communicated in terms of snot on her designer dress. These are all powerful images, constructed in terms of the gratitude of the recipient. The dying child remains without a name; we do not know why he or she is dying. The viewer experiences the physicality of dying through its impact on Diana's dress.

Such experiences, Boltanski argues, elicit an embodied response on the part of the receiver of the image. Earlier we saw that the response of indignation translates into an expression of anger. In this case, Boltanski argues that the embodied experience elicited to deal with the experience is constructed in terms of *urgency*. The embodied experience of pity is one we become aware of in a cracking of the voice and a sense of imminent sobbing. Just as the frustration of denunciation can be translated into anger, so too the experience of pity can be mastered through the speed of our response, through contracting one's expression and one's entire body, "to leap in the direction of the unfortunate victim whose suffering cannot wait, to be entirely lost in the motions of action. There is not an instant to lose" (1999: 121).

CHAPTER 5
Grammars of Experience

From Organization to Event

Rather than focus on organization or community, the experiences we have explored point to a paradigm of action centered on the event and the experience. Surveying transformations in contemporary capitalism, Boltanski and Chiapello (1999) argue that there is a broad transformation occurring at the level of social patterns: just as Max Weber, a century ago, struggled to make sense of the transformation from a family-based capitalism to a bureaucratic-based capitalism, Boltanski and Chiapello argue we are today confronted with the challenge of making sense of a shift of similar importance, from a bureaucratic model to a network model. They focus primarily on changes within large organizations, where they underline the importance of new paradigms of action based on the importance of short-term projects rather than long-term commitments. Successful careers, they argue, are increasingly likely to be made up of a series of short-term projects rather than life-long service to an organization. While industrial culture is embedded in ideas of progress and focuses on the future, Boltanski and Chiapello, as Laidi (2001), underline the extent to which a culture of networks focuses on the present. Rather than living in a world structured in terms of linear causal relationships, with a culture of sequencing (projecting out into the future), network culture values immediate relationships and connection, with an emphasis on the present and simultaneity. Hence the great importance of technologies, the most obvious being the mobile phone, that intensifies the experience of simultaneity (on the social experience of the mobile phone, see Jauréguiberry 1997).

Network culture attaches primacy to the present and to connection. The sense of complexity and indeterminacy that comes with this means that it is impossible or unwise to project too far into the future: there are too many contingencies and unknowns. This is clear in the culture of the activists we have encountered, who focus on the present. The classical model of action that emerged in the twentieth century focuses on the future – the most obvious example being models of socialism and communism embraced by the labor movement, as well as other utopias of the twentieth century, all constructed in terms of the future, and to which the present could be sacrificed. The activists we have encountered refuse to allow an image of the future to determine the present. As a result they show little interest in programs or maps of the future – they refuse to construct models of the future society, much to the frustration of many commentators. It is the culture of simultaneity that drives the idea of the "global day," with its emphasis on real time uploading of images and information via the Internet.

These events are constructed within a culture of urgency and simultaneity. A constant theme that emerges in interviews I have conducted with activists is the importance of email and list serves, important examples of the "hybridity" of social and technological systems that bring with them the imperative of immediacy, the utopia of instant exchange and simultaneity. Zaki Laidi (2001: 205) discusses the emergence of a kind of network culture, embedded in the market, that celebrates the immediate and in so doing tends to break down the capacity of people to establish distance vis-à-vis themselves. This culture of the immediate is central to the Internet. Judy, an urban justice activist in New York City, speaking of her involvement in five different anti–North American Free Trade Agreement (NAFTA) list serves, recounts:

> you write an email and you expect an immediate response. If you make a phone call, if someone doesn't get back to you for a few days, that's normal. You write a letter and you don't get something back for two weeks, that's normal. You get an email and you feel you have to respond right away. Then, if you don't, somehow you are breaking the unspoken code of when you are supposed to respond to something.

Judy is concerned that this experience of immediacy breaks down the capacity to create a reflective distance from herself:

> this need to respond immediately [pause] is difficult. With so many things to respond to, the self-reflection involved in writing and thinking about communicating – I think has really been challenged.

But there is another side to this temporality: the importance of multiplicity. Judy describes her involvement in the Quebec City action against the FTA agreement in 2001:

> What we have is a bunch of people thinking, putting different ideas in to the pot so we are acting simultaneously and I don't think this is actually conscious,

that we are sitting down and saying, "OK, this is my strategy, this is your strategy and this is your strategy and we are going to do them all together and figure out how they look." I think it would be nice if it could be that way, but we're not organized that way. But organically what's happening is that many different strategies are being promoted at the same time . . . which is not something that necessarily happened or was accepted, say, even 10 years ago when we were still kind of ruled by there being one essential solution to the problems that we faced. Which is, I think, another exciting component of the movement, that there is a little more fluidity in the way we can express ourselves.

From this point of view, the event is a hub where different actors converge and where different networks and flows intersect. This is clear in the case of the camp, where people come and go, and which is connected to cultural networks such as festivals, or in the ways Reclaim The Streets flowed through networks constituted by rave music in Europe. In the case of the United States, where a first Reclaim the Streets action was initiated by Critical Mass, we encounter an example of *resonance*, where one form of urban action flows into another.

From Solidarity to Fluidarity

The patterns of action and culture that we have been exploring manifest a clear break with the paradigm of "identity correspondence" and the "civic grammar," and the understanding of the group as constituted through the act of representation. This is evident in the break with structures of representation and delegation, or modes of organizing where elections proceed "upwards" and decisions proceed "downwards." This has a number of consequences. Firstly, a significant effort has to be spent on making decisions and the processes involved. But once decisions are reached, they are not considered morally binding as in the forms of solidarity where the group acts through the individual. Affinity groups function as action groups, working on tasks ranging from communication, media, cluster liaison, blockading, theater, first-aid, puppets, cooking, and so on. The culture they are based on is one of skill sharing – this underlines what people bring to the group, as opposed to joining a group and learning about its history or philosophy. This makes an explicit reference to what each persons brings to the action – personal experiences, not collective identities, are being mobilized. The grammar of action is thus radically different from that associated with the civic/industrial paradigm. In that case, the group makes a decision, and is them implemented by its members. In the case of the affinity group:

The affinity group is a group of people that you know and that you can trust. Before things happen you talk about what you are going to do, if you are going to get arrested or not. You help each other, you watch out for each other. Each person knows what the other can do and is prepared to do. If one person intends to get arrested and another doesn't, you help each other in this. (Anne, student and ecologist, Vermont)

This is not an example of "serviceable agents," of individuals implementing the decisions of a group – the paradigm where the collective, whether the union or the class, acts through the individual. Instead, through the affinity group, each person enters into a relationship with a concrete other (people you know and trust), as opposed to relating to a totality. The paradigm is closer to one of friendship (Pahl 2000), in that each person recognizes the other as a person, as opposed to someone carrying out a function on behalf of a collectivity or organization, and at the same time is recognized as a person. There is an experience of personal recognition here that is reciprocal, as is friendship: a friendship requires mutuality. Similarly, a friendship is not based on sharing a category: a friendship is an experience of the recognition of singularity.

Actors working within a paradigm of "we-ness" publicly manifest a collective identity through flags or banners: they declare who they are. They consider themselves to be represented by the group, in the way theorized by Bourdieu. This is the basis of the spokesperson or the leader, who incarnates the collective and is able to speak on its behalf. But in the cases we have explored, the paradigm is one of fluidity rather than collectivity, and there is little sense that actors regard themselves represented by the collective, which can speak as well as act through its members. As we saw in the case of Critical Mass, action takes the form of an event, a convergence, not an identity. Hence we do not encounter many of the practices and cultures associated with membership. Rituals of joining, membership cards, life memberships, and so on, which played such an important role in organizations such as the Communist Party, are completely absent (see Ion 1997 for a discussion of such symbols and rites in the constitution of earlier activist communities). Because there is no collective that acts and speaks through its members, there is no spokesperson.

The experiences we encounter here underline French sociologist Jacques Ion's argument (1997) that contemporary forms of action involve what he calls the "end of militancy" (1997), by which he means the end of a model of action where the person is integrated into an organization, and understands himself or herself as a vehicle for the organization when acting. Recognition of a personal identity is increasingly a condition of action. Karen illustrates this when she describes being approached by a representative of a political organization immediately after a police baton charge during an occupation against the World Economic Forum:

> On the Tuesday night I ran down – because I was doing media – with a friend – down with my camera and just missed the baton charge – and got there to find 300 people completely freaked out and a couple of friends had just been taken to hospital and everyone was [pause]. It was an extreme situation [pause] and I turned and walked with the group, and as I was walking someone came up to me with a clipboard and said, "Hi! Do you want to join the [name of a political organization] ?" It was just like [pause] don't ask me to join an acronym! Least of all after [pause] I could go on for quite a while about how pissed off I am . . . (Karen, Indymedia activist, Melbourne)

While the representative of the political organization is at the protest seeking new members, they are disconnected from what is happening, because they are disconnected from the people who are involved. The organization is experienced as empty, as an acronym.

At these actions, the group is invisible, or where it is visible, it is an enigma, such as *tutti bianchi*, the "white overalls" group that began in Italy following an encounter with the Zapatistas in Mexico, who set out to be invisible. Where names are used, they describe an action, not an identity: Reclaim The Streets, or in the case of Autonomous Web Of Liberation (AWOL) in mobilization against the World Economic Forum in Melbourne in September 2000, a type of organization that, while present, is also absent. Banners and symbols proclaiming a collective identity are eschewed, and the refusal to accept that groups can represent activists means that groups will adopt a "no media" policy on the grounds that "no one can speak for anyone else" (Karen, Indymedia, Melbourne). The idea of the leader or the spokesperson who in some way incarnates the group is rejected.

A further dimension to this is evident in the ways activists use multiple names. The same person may use several names when signing emails, posting to the Internet or even writing articles, while several activists may share the same name when interacting with the media. At the Pollok Free State occupation, for example, all women involved with media used the name Theresa Green. The idea of sharing names and the use of multiple names is clearly part of an Internet culture, where the person is free from the constraints of identity. But the sharing of names points to a mode of experience that is personalized (as opposed to secretary, treasurer, etc.), but not individualized. The fluidity of names points to a context where the relationship between person and identity is fluid, both present and absent, evident, and an enigma. There is clearly something similar at stake in the importance of the Zapatista leader Marcos to these activists, who while clearly a person, does not have what we expect of an individual – a fixed name and biography.

The dominant approach to social movements, with its emphasis on organization and the state, has not significantly engaged with these emerging patterns of action and culture that clearly involve a new type of relationship between individual and collective experience. Two very different approaches attempt to make sense of emerging patterns. In the United States a number of sociologists underline what they regard as critical dimensions of new forms of *personalism*, while in Europe there has been significant interest in a quite different interpretation; namely that emerging forms of action and movement represent a new form of *postmodern tribalism*. I believe that neither of these approaches is adequate to make sense of what is at stake in contemporary forms of action and culture. Each, however, highlights important dimensions of emerging patterns, and in the process, raises important questions.

Personalized Politics?

The American sociologist Paul Lichterman explores emerging patterns of action and culture in the American environmental movement, and he argues that it is possible to detect an emerging model of action and culture that he calls "personalized politics," which he sees particularly evident in middle-class green activists. To illustrate key dimensions, Lichterman contrasts what he regards as the new "personalized politics" with models of activism that he encounters in the African-American antitoxic movement. In this latter case, activist groups are based on a strong sense of community and collective identity, and this translates into modes of acting and organizing as well, with an emphasis on formal organization (Chair, Co-chair, Executive Director, Board of Directors), committees and elections, and a model of representation and delegation where we see the key dimensions of the civic grammar of action. In this case, there is a strong sense of fighting for the community, acting on its behalf, and understanding organization as the expression of the community, representing its interests and its culture. The organization possesses a strong sense of leaders and an "unambiguous division of labor" (1996: 113) – its role is to empower the community, as opposed to empowering individual members, and, as a result, the organizational structure does not have as its major goal to facilitate individual participation. Instead, the aim is collective action for the community, and on its behalf, while the image of the community is one that emphasizes unity and its moral primacy. It is on the basis of loyalty to the community that the organization exercises forms of internal discipline; sanctioning, for example, members who fail to meet expectations in terms of commitment to the organization and its action.

Lichterman contrasts this community model of activism with the culture and forms of activism of white middle-class Greens, involving what he calls "personalized commitment." He defines personalism as "shared ways of speaking or acting that emphasize the personal self rather than its relationship to specific communities or institutions" (1996: 17). In Lichterman's account of community activism it is clear that accounts of self and commitment are structured in relation to community. Accounts of personal involvement are constructed in terms of loyalty to the community, while the authority the organization claims and mobilizes finds its origins in the community. Lichterman interprets the personalism he encounters among the Greens as consisting of ways of acting that involve a unique and personal self, evident in particular in the emphasis activists place on personal involvement in decisions and the reluctance to embrace formal hierarchy and organization.

Lichterman locates this personalism in wider patterns of cultural change, in particular the personalism he detects in contemporary American culture, evident in the increasing importance of psychology, therapy, and so on. He argues that the great importance attached to personalism by American Green activists reflects a wider culture of the middle class, in particular what he calls, following Bourdieu (1991), the activists' "cultural capital." He argues that the Green activists' high education levels generate a culture of individualized ways of doing things, an articulate style, and a concern with "self-actualization" (1996: 153). This in particular reflects educational models that emphasize personal creativity. In a context where older political traditions such as socialism have weakened or no longer respond to contemporary social problems, Lichterman argues that activists have made their shared cultural capital, one that sustains a "politics of selves," the basis of their culture (1996: 189). In something of a paradox, while setting out to contrast the community-based model of activism of the antitoxic movement with the personalized forms of action characterizing the middle-class Greens, Lichterman locates the source of activist culture and organization in community culture – in this case, the personalized culture of the American middle class. Personalism, in the terms Lichterman has described, can be seen as a community culture, reflecting the social origin and location of its members, just as other forms of community culture. As a result he opposes ideas of "new social movements" that emerged in the 1970s, associated with the idea that such movements represent a radical break with earlier forms of social movement. Personalism is an action repertoire like others, and in no way requires a rethinking about movements. Above all Lichterman emphasizes the importance of the *personal articulation of belief* in this culture, evident in the great importance that activists attach to articulating shared values. In this account talk and meetings take on an extraordinary significance.

Francesca Polletta (2002) places a similar emphasis on the discursive in her study of American social movements entitled *Freedom Is an Endless Meeting*. This approach sees social movements as essentially deliberative and discursive, and draws on important traditions in contemporary social thought. The most well known internationally is the work of Jürgen Habermas in Germany, who has attempted to develop a theory of communicative action, one that originally he attempted to ground in biological models of moral development (drawing on Kholberg 1981), and later in the philosophical structure of language itself, which he believed has within it the potential for what he calls "the ideal speech situation" (Habermas 1979). This model, which has echoes of themes we encountered before in Rousseau, proposes that it is possible for people to break free of the constraints of identities and interests and reach agreement, a process that Habermas sees as grounded in the very rationality of the structures of language itself. Polletta's study is located in an American tradition that draws heavily on the American philosopher John Dewey. Dewey believed that the "machine age" had broken down older forms of community without creating new forms to replace these. Dewey in the 1920s, just as Habermas in the 1970s, looks to the development of discursive communication and to the formation of rational consensus grounded in such communication processes to reconstruct civil society. Habermas developed a very influential argument (1991) where he affirms that the coffee houses of central Europe played a key role in the construction of the modern form of public and public opinion, the basis of modern democracy. For Habermas, the core of this activity was *discussion*, which he argues constitutes the basis of "civil society," a domain that emerges between the individual and the state.

Polletta's account of American social movements develops a similar argument. She discusses the Direct Action Network that played a key role in the mobilization in Seattle in November 1999 against the World Trade Organization, arguing that DAN is a good example of what she calls "participatory democracy." She focuses in particular on the importance of "process" in DAN meetings: the role of facilitators and "vibewatchers"; the use of symbols to indicate agreement or disagreement (wiggling fingers to indicate agreement, creating a triangle with fingers to indicate concern about process, raising a fist to indicate an intention to veto a decision); the emphasis on timekeeping and other innovations underlining the importance of personal participation in meeting process and decision making. For Polletta, the DAN represents the possibility of realizing what Habermas points to in a theoretical way, an "ideal speech community." Polletta describes the way people interact in DAN meetings:

they expected each other to provide legitimate reasons for preferring one option to another. They strove to recognize the merits of each other's reasons for favouring a particular option . . . *the goal was not unanimity, so much as discourse*. But it was a particular kind of discourse, governed by norms of openness and mutual respect. (Polletta 2002: 7; emphasis added)

Certain dimensions of the civic paradigm, however, enter into this account of these movements. Polletta argues that "unlike a Rousseauian 'general will' reflecting the wills of noncommunicating individuals, the emphasis here is on communicative give-and-take." But despite this emphasis on communicative give and take, as opposed to Rousseauian virtues, Polletta's end point is similar, her analysis combining the nineteenth-century understanding of aggregates with Rousseau's conception of the moral primacy of the group. For Polletta, discussing these American social movements,

in principle, *authority rested with the entire group*. But of course, no group makes every decision by consensus, and no group offers equal power to anyone who wants it. The critical question is whether the grounds for authority are specified and, when appropriate, reformulated. Activists in many of the organizations that I studied sought to create new kinds of legitimate power. (2002: 8; emphasis added)

Just as Lichterman, Polletta equally emphasizes continuity in her account of movements. The echoes of Rousseau are loud when she conceptualizes movements in terms of groups that possess authority, where the critical question is whether the grounds upon which this authority is based are specified, and open to reformulation. She underlines a kind of discursive reflexivity, where what is important is not so much the decision, but the possibility that the group can debate and change if necessary the ways it arrives at decisions.

Both these accounts of movements open rich ground. But at the same time both authors' work also hints that the discursive paradigm that they advocate both as a description and as the base for theorizing contemporary movements may have problems. Lichterman refers to the case of Earth First! activists who are attracted to direct actions such as blocking trucks or disabling saw motors, and who have little patience for what one calls "talk about talk about talk" (1996: 197). Francesca Polletta (2001: 25) records leaders of the Direct Action Network remarking, somewhat ruefully, that "Young people just don't find our concern with process interesting." These are hints within these authors' work that placing talk and discourse at the center of movements may not be adequate to contemporary shifts in culture and action.

Neotribes?

While Polletta (2002) and Lichterman (1996) emphasize discourse and discussion, clearly drawing on an American tradition venerating the town meeting, European attempts to rethink the relationship between individual and collective experience at stake in movements have increasingly turned to theories of ritual and performance, and with this, increasingly to the idea that older forms of social movement are being replaced by new forms of postmodern tribe.

Over the 1990s, a series of analyses attempted to make sense of new forms of movement and sociability, all drawing on the theme of "tribe" developed by the French sociologist Michel Maffesoli (1996). Andy Bennett focuses on changes in collective experiences linked to music cultures and consumption, and argues that an older model of "subculture," with its conception of coherence and boundaries, needs to be replaced by a more fluid conception that he argues is offered through the concept of tribe, or more precisely "neotribe": "groupings which have traditionally been theorized as coherent subcultures are better understood as a series of temporary gatherings characterized by fluid boundaries and floating memberships" (1999: 599). The concept of subculture, in Britain in particular, is associated with the concept of class – subcultures are understood as expressions of class and generation. The idea of "tribe" allows for a more fluid conception that reflects the weakening impact of class, locality, and gender, and the increasing importance of multiple identities and multiple foci or sites "within which the individual can live out a selected, temporal role or identity before relocating to an alternative site and assuming a different identity" (1999: 600). Above all the concept of tribe, Bennett argues, allows us to make sense of the affective and experiential, as opposed to the subculture's conceptual debt to images of social class.

While Bennett argues that the idea of tribe should replace the concept of subculture, Kevin Hetherington (1998) draws on Maffesoli to argue that the concept should replace the concept of "new social movements." For Hetherington, the concept "new social movements" is too embedded in macrotheories that see such movements as intentional actors aiming at social change. Instead Hetherington argues contemporary forms of action and culture are better understood as an "assemblage of cultural and political practices" involving identity politics, collective identification, and situated symbolic and knowledge practices (1998: 12). For Hetherington, the Weberian rational individual is in decline, and in his or her place we encounter increasing forms of affective and emotional communities, representing a process of "deindividualization" (1998: 52). Here Hetherington distances himself from authors such as Giddens, who argues that identities are increasingly rational, cognitive, and reflexive, and argues instead that cultural life and personal identity are increasingly constructed in terms of feeling and emotion. For Hetherington, the neotribe, "an affectual form of sociation through which both individual and collective identity are expressed" (1998: 53), has replaced an older form of "new social movement." Rather than look to reasoned argument and discourse as the basis for new forms of movement, as does Polletta, Hetherington conceives of movements as communities of emotion, and, to make sense of such forms of sociability and action, draws on the German word "Bund": "a small-scale, transitory and elective social grouping based on a shared emotional commitment to a particular set of values and beliefs, often, through not exclusively, focused around a charismatic leader" (1998: 17). Rather than place rational discourse and argument at the center of movements, Hetherington argues we encounter instead a "romantic structure of feeling" (1998: 62).

John Urry (2000) also draws on the concept of *Bund* to make sense of contemporary forms of movement. Urry's focus is on new forms of mobilities and the forms of sociality that develop through and in these, and which cut across the older forms of geographically bounded and located socialities that we call societies. The concept of *Bund* is attractive for Urry because it combines the ideas of belonging and traveling. The reference here is to early German youth movements, in a period before there were hotels or tourist routes, where there emerged *Bunde* made up of small groups who roamed the German forests, in the process forming a kind of "mobile communion" (Urry 2000: 142). This form of community, Urry insists, is consciously and freely chosen, based on mutual sentiment and emotional feeling; it is a form of community that is nontraditional. Urry cites Hetherington:

> Bunde are maintained symbolically through active, reflexive monitoring of group solidarity by those involved, in other words, they are highly self-referential . . . the Bund is self-enclosed and produces a code of practices and symbols . . . Bunde involve the blurring of public and private spheres of the life of their members. (Hetherington 1994: 16)

For Urry, the importance of the concept *Bund* is that it links experiences of sociability, or sociality, with the idea of movement – as opposed to conventional models of community, which are understood as embedded in place. An example Urry refers to is the peace convoy, part of the wider network of traveler culture that we discussed above. Urry underlines that such forms of sociality emerge out of networks, with dwelling spaces constituted through routes and nodes rather than place. This form of dwelling, Urry argues, is "intense, impermanent and mobile" (2000: 154). Such networks are defined culturally rather than politically or socially (2000: 143). This means that these networks are defined not by social location, nor by political belief, but by forms of practice – forms of *doing*. Rather than understand social movements in terms of talking, this opens a more complex and richer understanding of action, one that recognizes the "plurality of senses" (Crouch and Desforges 2003) that give access to the world, the self, and the other. This places the sensuous at the center of the movement experience.

The Limits of Vitalism

Because it points in the direction of the sensual and the embodied, the concept of "tribe" as proposed by Michel Maffesoli captures important dimensions of contemporary social life, such as imagination, the immediate, the sensual, and embodiment. But it frames this within a surprisingly dated philosophical framework, the vitalism that emerged in France in the early part of the twentieth century. By this Maffesoli means that social life is increasingly made up of experiences of fusion, where the rationality of the industrial paradigm gives way to a kind of fusion of the natural and the social, where collective experience becomes divine, transcending the artificial divisions created by civilization. In the place of the social, we encounter life pulsing through new forms of community, or what Maffesoli calls the "social erotic." From this point of view, rituals and experiences of emotion take on great importance, becoming the basis of new forms of fusion experience at the basis of contemporary sociality.

All this might seem rather abstract, but we can see this kind of vitalism at work in recent work attempting to make sense of the reactions following the death of Princess Diana in 1996. The British sociologist Sasha Roseneil, exploring the ritual that took place around the death and funeral of Princess Diana in August 1997, suggests that the mountains of flowers, the balloons with messages, the estimated 3 million people who participated at the funeral, combined with the 30 million in Britain who participated in it through television, represent a form of social drama, a "social movement, in the sense of social, cultural and political change," one that took the form of a "moment of moral remaking" (Roseneil 2001). Roseneil draws on the work of the cultural anthropologist Victor Turner to suggest that such rituals involve a period of "liminality," where participants step outside the social norms that regulate behaviour and interaction, and where they have the possibility to talk about new things in new ways, and to feel new things in new ways (Turner 1995). For Roseneil this is linked to the person of Princess Diana, who she suggests was experienced as someone who broke through the barriers to defend victims of AIDS, who sought to rehumanize Britain's welfare system, yet who also symbolized a love of life manifest in her interest in fashion, love of her children, parties, and so on. For Roseneil, what was constructed through the period of mourning and celebration of Diana's life was a powerful "emotional community," arguing that in this community of emotion we encounter what Maffessoli calls *puissance*, or power, the "will to live," "the affirmative quality of human life, which nourishes the social body" (Roseneil 2001: 103). Roseneil argues that this emotion community illustrates a break with an increasingly rationalized public world, and the emergence of an era increasingly shaped by Dionysian themes of pleasure-seeking, emotion, hedonism, and spontaneity, the center of a movement to embrace a new form of *communitas*. Developing themes that emerge from Maffessoli's vitalist sociology, Roseneil argues:

> There is a growing detachment from the abstract public sphere and its institutional structures, and people are drawn to the transcendent emotional community of the *tribus*; *puissance* – the vital energy and power of people – takes the place of *pouvoir* – the power of institutional politics and ruling elites. In the place of the rational project of the proletariat or the bourgeoisie, and instead of the goals and paths set forth by individual leaders, the Dionysian era places its collective energy in mythical figures. (Roseneil 2001: 104)

For Roseneil, such expressions of communitas reflect a moral awakening, one that she sees at the heart of what she calls, following Maffesoli, the "social divine." For her, Diana's death and the events following it represent

> a moment of moral remaking, which enacted a collective reaching, a yearning, for a new moral order . . . through the period of mourning ran an ethic of pleasure and a desire to celebrate life: there was a creativity and aesthetics in the response to her death which celebrated not just her life, but the beauty of life in general, and the commensuality and bonds which were forged between strangers in the public spaces of grief were a truly Durkheimian celebration of collective life, sociability and the social divine. (Roseneil 2001: 99, 111)

Life, beauty, emotion, and morality merge in this account of the awakening of the "social divine." But how can we know if this emotion is real or manufactured, whether the narrative of "death and resurrection in the heart of the people" that Roseneil recounts is any more than a case of celebrity-induced emotion, or any different from other movements of emotion, such as the World Cup or the Olympic Games, also occasions that have been analyzed in Durkheimian terms of religion and ritual. Maffesoli's work is full of valuable insights, but it is framed within a choice between a rationalized, disenchanted individualism and a fusion where nature, the social, and the divine merge, a fusion steeped in the vitalism of a century ago, which played a significant role in the birth of the authoritarian movements of that time.

What we have encountered thus far represents two attempts to rethink the relationship between individual and collective experience. On the one hand, an approach that emphasizes discursive rationality, and that privileges the dimensions of talk within movements, to the point where Polletta affirms that "freedom is an endless meeting." The importance of these analyses is that they caution against uncritically embracing images of fusion that are associated with theories of neotribes; but at the same time, they are limited by their reduction of action to talk and rationality. On the other hand, we encounter attempts to construct a more complex understanding of action, approaches that strive to deal with embodiment and the sensual. But rather than embrace the models of fusion that come with celebrating the time of the tribes (Maffesoli 1996) and the return of the "social divine," we need to return to think about the meaning of action.

Beyond Intentional Action

On August 1, 2000, 75 people were arrested in Philadelphia while making puppets in a warehouse in the period leading up to the Republican Convention. Following the arrests a trash compactor was brought in, and the puppets were destroyed over a period of three hours. An observer to the events John Tarelton (2000), quotes the Commissioner of the city's Department of Licenses and Inspections, saying he didn't know the specific fire or health code violations in the building. "We're just taking the trash out . . . We're responding to a police request." Tarelton quotes a worker for Licenses and Inspections, who was dismayed at having to destroy the puppets "I felt real bad," he said. "I could see they must have taken a lot of time to make those puppets. They musta been fighting for a cause they believe in." The police captain overseeing the operation was more serene. "I don't have any feelings," he said. "I'm a professional" (Tarleton 2000).

The charges laid against the puppeteers were later dropped or thrown out of court, leading the Philadelphia Inquirer (December 8, 2000) to editorialize that the raid was less about preventing a crime and more a tactical attempt by police to prevent a demonstration.

The classical accounts of social movements underline intentionality, organization, and what Tilly calls the deliberate formation of specialist political organizations. Action is defined in terms of its goal, embracing the new understandings of organization coming with the division of labor. This of course means that other dimensions of action, such as pleasure, feeling, doing, the embodied, and the sensual, are all pushed outside our frame of analysis. These are regarded by authors such as Tilly as premodern (in a way that also echoes some of the themes we encounter in the discussion of tribes). The modern for Tilly is the deliberate and the goal directed; since social movements emerge in the context of modernization, this defines them as well.

Contemporary sociological theory is increasingly attempting to get beyond what amounts to a very limited understanding of action, and this is absolutely critical if we are to grasp key dimensions of emerging global movements. One of the most important attempts to develop a richer account of human action is being undertaken by the German sociologist Hans Joas (1996) in his attempt to put creativity at the center of action. Joas argues that dominant models of action are based on three deeply flawed ideas. Firstly, they are framed in terms of intentionality, a means–end structure where the objective of action determines what is done. This of course emphasizes control, purpose, and cognition. Secondly, the relationship to the body is understood in instrumental terms: the body is something that is used, not experienced. This is central to Tilly's account of action, with his great emphasis on rationality, and where he constantly underlines that this means control of emotion (see Goodwin and Polletta [2001] for a discussion of the exclusion of emotion in theories of social movement). As Mouzelis (1998) argues, such an understanding of action excludes noninstrumental and noncontrolling ways of relating to the body. Joas argues that if we want to understand action, we need to understand nonintentional forms of action as well, which often involve letting go of control of the body. Joas refers to laughing or crying: "laughing and crying are specific human actions, that in their fullness cannot be accomplished through intentionality" (1996: 180). Thirdly, Joas is critical of the primacy of a model of the autonomous individual, who not only controls his or her body, but his or her self. The inner self disappears in such accounts of action. Not only do we need to develop understandings of action that recognize corporeality, but also the critical place of embodied communication, or intercorporeality. Here Joas emphasizes, drawing on Merleau Ponty, the critical place not simply of experiencing my body, but of experiencing the body of the other, in the construction of subjectivity – evident, for example, in the place of touch and intercorporeality between a mother and a child.

The case of puppets allows us to explore the forms of corporeality and intercorporeality involved in action. Puppets are *made*; they are a product of *doing*. They figure prominently in the antiglobalization action, from Seattle 1999 onwards (Levi and Murphy 2002) to the point where they took on the role as a signature of the emerging movement. But as such, they do not correspond to models of identity, as claims about the worth and unity of the protesters. Rather, puppets point to a grammar of *doing*, a form of sensual action. But they are also an expression of the grotesque. And from here, we can begin to rethink an ethic of action.

Embodied Narrative

In the three months before the World Economic Forum was to hold a regional meeting in Melbourne, Australia, in September 2000, a network of people began to make giant puppets that were to be used in the three-day blockade being planned. Construction took place each Saturday and Sunday at a warehouse in an industrial zone, echoing the warehouse where people constructed puppets in Philadelphia. At each construction session between 15 and 30 people worked on the project, which involved several puppets. Only one person in the group, a sculptor, had any real knowledge of the technical issues involved in constructing large puppets so that they could be carried safely, and not break.

The puppets were to be made from material found in industrial and domestic waste tips around the city. The first action involved scouring these sites, finding wood and other material for frames, wire for joints, and so on. These then were grouped together, and first discussions took place about what the puppets should be, and the idea of two emerged: a puppet to model the earth dominated by a huge dollar symbol, with different groups of people under its shadow, and a giant snake, a symbol of the life of the earth. The puppets were constructed over a period involving some 20 days, with a rush at the end. Over the period the composition of the group changed, with some people leaving, and others joining. As the construction progressed, people came with different materials, and the shape and ultimately the actual puppets themselves changed, the giant snake becoming a giant worm. At the end of the day's work, a meal would be held, with each day some of the people present working on preparing the food. The meal shared at the end of the day was coordinated by people involved in the group "Food Not Bombs," a group that had first emerged out of the networks that had been formed following the Clamshell Alliance action in the United States some 25 years earlier. Tables were pulled up, everyone sat down to eat, the food had been cooked slowly, inspired by the Italian "slow food" movement, which emphasizes cooking natural food as opposed to eating industrialized food.

Nick, the sculptor, describes what happened over this three-month period:

> People were there on their own terms, they were coming on their own time, they dictated their commitment to it . . . a really essential element in the whole

thing is an Indian fellow who cooks incredible food, he is an alcoholic fellow, incredibly committed activist, incredibly knowledgeable character, but he has got some – well, I don't know if the alcohol is really relevant at all – yeah, it should be totally irrelevant really – but he cooks these amazing curries and he cooked a curry every day of the puppet-making and I just think the ritual with all [pause] we would bring down guests [pause]. To be able to set up tables, chairs, and have enough plates for everyone to be able to sit around and have a food ritual every day and a cup of tea – morning and afternoon rituals – they were just essential. People really felt empowered that they were actually able to contribute. They were just able to vent some of their frustrations and angst about the situation. Not just the global economic situation but the whole community lack, of dispirited ailments of society that most people have no means of being able to address because they feel so individual and so unable to participate in some sense of change or some sense of contributing to change whatever. . . . What was important was the physical, actually making and doing. In the last month we pretty much did 7 days a week, 10 or 12 hours a day, it was awesome . . . It is really, just, you know that there is a big network of people out there who actually commit real time for when these things start happening, start prioritizing this sort of thing over work and leisure activities because, I don't know, I think it really represents an inner glow that people feel so void of. It really is quite heartening stuff, that so many people feel lacking in their essence or their substance. (Nick, sculptor and activist)

The puppet-making process expresses what we can call a "narrative ethic." Those involved in construction are able to alter the direction of where the puppet is going, building on interpreting what was done earlier, while leaving something for those who come after equally to interpret and transform. The construction does not take the form of a predetermined plan moving in a linear path toward a conclusion determined in advance. The ethic is one that flows, takes on new directions, turns about, as in the act of creating a work of art. With some 70 people involved in a large project, this is structured by an ethic and organizational form of narrative, of understanding where the construction is moving, which means also entering into the domain where one can contribute to shaping it.

Nick's account of the construction emphasizes intercorporeality – the physicality of shared experience of effort, exhaustion, and recovery. The story he recounts is one of recovery of personal wholeness, one where experiences of vulnerability and emptiness become present, and to which the intercorporeality of the action responds. The story he recounts is less about opposition to the World Economic Forum or the construction of a "collective identity" than about a recovery of interiority. The story Nick tells is one that underlines embodied subjectivity.

Nick's story is not one of a group meeting regularly, analyzing the world and its problems, and then drawing up an analysis or program to be communicated through slogans or leaflets. Rather than talk, or *discursive action*, the core of what Nick describes above is *embodied*, and one where subjectivity plays a central role. The social world Nick refers to is similar to that described by Alain Touraine, one where subjectivity appears thinned out and fragmented, one where the process of construction of the puppets can be understood as a form of struggle for subjectivity (McDonald 1999). Nick describes an experience of being "so individual" in terms of being unable to connect and act with others and being unable to construct meaning associated with this, leading to an experience of emptiness in what he describes as *essence* or *substance*. There is no separation between soul and body, mind and body – the essence of the person cannot be separated from the substance of the person; subjectivity cannot be separated from physicality. The physical exhaustion the person experiences through making the puppets serves to put the subject back in their body. Time, and the embodied experience of time, is essential for this kind of action. Such embodied time, where time is necessary for action, is opposed to the simultaneity and urgency of the network.

The origins of these puppets lie in New York and Vermont, in the German-born Peter Schumann's Bread and Puppet Theater, which emerged out of the first puppets Schumann used in the Lower East side of Manhattan in the early 1960s (see Brecht 1988 for a history). This form of puppet arose in New York City, the world's first global city, at the intersection of the child of a German immigrant family with the cultural creativity of the city. This form of puppetry spread from New York to San Francisco, to Art and Revolution and then to other groups across the country, and internationally as Schumann's puppet troupe, Bread and Puppets, traveled between the United States and Europe. But it was with the emergence of the antiglobalization movement that puppets came to take on a critical role, with groups getting together to create puppets in much the same way as I have described, from Tokyo to Melbourne to Barcelona.

The grammar of puppets is experiential: puppets emphasize action over dialogue, and go beyond the limits of language (Ryder 1995). The puppets Schumann developed are large and slow moving, and often grotesque, while not threatening, they are neither pretty nor cute. Schumann was strongly influenced by the plays of Bertold Brecht and his idea of the "estrangement effect." The puppets can be seen in the tradition of the clown, estranged symbols of humanity at once full of life and hope, but also at a loss in world they do not control, beings who connect through communicative embodiment rather than through rational discourse. James Fisher (2000) notes that the fool or the clown is a figure characterized by anarchy and sensuality, a "destroyer of worlds, oppressive structures, and the constraints of language" (Fisher 2000: 105). Schumann, influenced by the idea of estrangement developed by Brecht, understands puppets in this way as well:

Why are puppets subversive? Because the meaning of everything is so ordained and in collaboration with the general sense of everything, and they, being only puppets, are not obliged to this sense and instead take delight in the opposite sense. (Schumann 1999)

Schumann points to a form of communicative experience when he observes:

The arts are about areas that people can't even control in themselves, about things that are a little deeper-seeded than newspaper opinions and such . . . the arts have a chance of getting to people in their disturbing way that is more into their gut, that isn't so easily brushed off. (quoted in Larson, 2003)

Hence the importance of physical effort, one that Nick constantly comes back to, as an experience that not only connects one person with others, but allows the reconnection of subjectivity and physicality, a process of encounter and recovery of interiority that is slow and sustained through rituals of eating. A similar link between puppet-making, temporality, and meals was present in the period leading up to the action against the Free Trade Area of the Americas meeting in Quebec City in 2000. Judy, an urban justice activist from New York City, recounts the same theme of connection with the other and the construction of an experience of interiority:

In some ways, you can't make a puppet in a second, in the same way that you can respond to an email. So the process of coming together with people to build something and construct something that's positive, that will be used, that is inherently nonviolent and recharged, that can be used as a tool of expression. I think that process in itself is really rewarding and empowering. You know because it's like breaking bread or sharing a meal with someone, when you create something with someone, you have a connection and then I think that's what's really powerful.

All movements produce culture, but in this case, it is the production of culture that is itself the medium of action (McDonald 2002), allowing one to recognize the other as different, opening out the possibility of communication beyond the constraints of language:

puppets . . . are a shared form of expression, people who speak two different languages can come together and feel something artistic together and creative together and it's another means of communicating with each other. Which is pretty cool. It's also fun . . . martyrdom isn't what it's about . . . it's about becoming a person and growing as part of the world. I think puppets do that really well – that's why I like them so much. (Judy, NYC)

For Judy, puppets create the possibility of feeling something together, that is in some way linked to becoming a person in the world. Roselyn, also from New York, describes a similar experience, but she uses the term "magic":

> The use of theater and puppets seems like activism in its truest form. Much more effective than screaming and pushing one's ideas down the viewer's throat is this creation of magic. Imagery and theater reach a much deeper place within the psyche than something violent and forced. (Roselyn, Indymedia, July 9, 2003)

The freedom and magic of the puppet opens up a possibility for action that also involves becoming human, a space that many activists like Roselyn experience as closed down by the violence implicit in the contained worlds structured in terms of political slogans. It is hard to imagine being further removed from the model of social movements that conceptualizes the individual as a "serviceable agent of the collective."

Grief and Beauty: Encounters with the Vulnerable Self

Lulu, an American puppetista, describes her experience with puppets in the following way:

> It's like walking through a John Singer Sargent painting of a rainy day; all I see are blurry legs and slick slippery sidewalks. Sometimes I bump my head. It is hard to know how high the "head" (puppet head) is. Usually about 8.5 feet, from what I can figure. It's comical to be head-bumping in such a serious setting. We can't see our feet too well, either, so perhaps it is like being very pregnant. Peripheral vision and mobility are limited. Balance can be tricky in windy or slippery conditions. Sometimes a guide walks with the puppet-bearer, giving silent signals so that we can move and bend under obstructions. It reminds me a little of a parade (with the puppet as a mini-float), but this is a peace vigil. We are alone with our feelings inside the puppet. Fear, sadness, grief, longing. Alienation, hope. They are all with us in this wire and paper cage. The emotions transporting us are real. . . .
>
> "puppets" compelling grief and fascinating beauty have a magnetic effect. A puppet's silence and emotion are larger than a human's. Eyes are drawn to the large sculptured faces moving along on top of little human legs and bodies. Masks and puppets change the emotional dynamics. They inspire awe. They push the edge of what it means to make our thoughts and feelings publicly known, what it means to resist fear. Puppets catch the attention of people on the street, slow them down. The street becomes a theater. Whether acting or watching, you become both audience and actor. (Winslow 2002: 53)

And recall the responses to the destruction of the puppets in Philadelphia:

> "I felt real bad," said the city worker. "I could see they must have taken a lot of time to make those puppets. They musta been fighting for a cause they believe in."

> "I don't have any feelings," said the police captain. "I'm a professional." (Tarleton 2000)

In just a few years, puppets have globalized to become one of the defining features of the cluster of movements and groups that converge in different ways around opposition to neoliberal globalization. They help us understand a critical shift that this book is exploring, the transition from the social movements of industrial society (constructed in terms of aggregates and identities) to what I am suggesting can be explored in terms of "experience movements." The classical model of social movements, conceived of as aggregates, argues that social actors act "in the name of their asserted collective identity" (McAdam et al. 2001: 137). This perspective understands the type of communication that takes place during events such as demonstrations as "displays of WUNC" (worthiness, unity, numbers, and commitment) (Tilly 1997). From this point of view, demonstrations "display membership in a politically relevant population, support for some position by means of voice, print, or symbolic objects, and communicate collective determination by acting in disciplined fashion in one space and or moving through a series of spaces" (Tilly 2003) – an extraordinarily instrumental understanding of the communicating subject.

The grammar of experience involved in making and carrying puppets is radically different. The puppets are made from trash and discarded objects – they are a message that has no material value, they are without worth in the market economy. They are also made of papier mâché – they are fragile and temporary. They are in fact very vulnerable, and this is compounded by the difficulty of carrying them, because of wind, rain, and the restricted vision of those who are inside the puppet, wearing a harness or holding it up. Puppets exist only for the instant, for the event – by the end of the day they are battered and starting to fall apart. Their very fragility underscores their existence in the present. Puppets are not stored and reused across events, in the way that trade-union flags and banners will be carried year after year, eventually becoming venerated symbols of unions and their history. Puppets are constantly remade in the way described by Nick above. And puppets can in no way be understood as a "display of WUNC." Puppets are not representational, just as a painting or a poem does not represent, or "make claims about," the painter or the author. There is another kind of communication at stake here, closer to the experience of regarding a painting or listening to a poem.

Just as music can create a social space, linking together those who can hear the music, so too puppets can connect people in the way described by Judy (see http://www.foeeurope.org/biteback/pics/esf_puppets.jpg). But the experience is not one of the construction of a "we" experienced in terms of constituting a category or aggregate. The experience described by Lulu is one of an encounter with one's self, through the encounter with a strange beauty, but also a strangeness that takes the form of the grotesque. The puppet is not pretty, nor violent. The puppet is silent, but communicates emotion. The puppet is out of place, but through this can change the meaning of place – it can slow the traffic, break the functional logic of moving people and vehicles – the street becomes a theater, one where boundaries between audience and actor break down. Thinking about the history of puppets, Lulu links her involvement to the experience of Reclaim the Streets in Britain.

The words used by Lulu are important – the puppet's grief compels, its beauty fascinates. These are forms of experience that cannot be achieved through intentionality. We cannot decide to be compelled, nor fascinated. Engagement with the puppet requires of us an experience of surrender, of giving up control, in order to feel. But while not intentional, this is a form of action. The city worker in Philadelphia required to participate in destroying puppets "felt real bad." The police captain "felt nothing," linking this ability to acting "as a professional." The puppet interpolates a subjective experience, but just as a painting, we can decide to open our self to it or to shut it out.

Margrit Shildrick (1999, 2002) helps us understand what is happening here when she explores the encounter with the grotesque in contemporary social life. She doesn't consider puppets, but encounters with forms of the "monstrous," such as images of extreme deformity, as in the case of a child born with two heads. She describes the encounter with such monsters as encounters with the vulnerable self. The strangeness of the grotesque is such that it transgresses boundaries, simultaneously too close and too recognizable, but, in its very excess, incredibly other. The experience of strangeness is one that breaks down the stable binary of self–other. The encounter with such irreducible strangeness opens us to forms of vulnerability that cannot be spoken (Shildrick 1999). As such, as Schildrick argues, the encounter with the grotesque breaks down the post-Enlightenment ideal of the autonomous agent and form of subjectivity that depend on separation between self and other. But in this case, it does not lead to experiences of fusion or revulsion. The puppet is not a closed message, a political slogan that is clear and unambiguous. On the contrary, as Schumann argues, it involves an encounter that can only be achieved through an experience of giving up self-control. This is not simply a cognitive question, of attempting to work out what the puppet means, what its message is. Rather this form of openness to strangeness involves, as Shildrick argues, a form of openness that means becoming vulnerable. The physical sensual action of building the puppet represents, as we see so clearly in Nick's account, a discovery of and encounter with the vulnerable self, one grounded in what Shildrick calls "a relational economy of touch" (2002).

Almost all the accounts of making puppets involve accounts of sharing meals, and the important role of the Food Not Bombs network. There is much more at stake here than the obvious symbolism of sharing a meal. The presence of food, and the fact that the action of making puppets takes place at the same time and place as the cooking of the meal, mean that both become part of the one narrative, as we see in Nick's story. The role of food became that of heightening the sensual experience that is already at the center of making the puppets. Food, as the papier mâché material out of which the puppets are imagined, is fragile and temporary, while we engage with it at a sensual level. Smell brings with it memory, but a memory that is also fleeting and elusive (Ruins 1988, cited by Kirshenblatt-Gimblett 1999). In many ways the experience of smell and the elusive memory it brings is similar to the experience of the activists. They do not form an ongoing community, much less an organization. They join in the process of building the puppets, some leave while others come. At the end of the construction most are joined for the three-day period of the blockade, after which they disperse. Food is a performance medium; as Kirshenblatt-Gimblett argues, it plays to the senses. The important place in these accounts not only of eating, but of cooking, underlines the critical role of food in amplifying the sensual activity at the core of making puppets, and the importance of different senses in accessing the world, experiencing the other and oneself.

Vulnerability, the Senses, and Becoming

The question of vulnerability has recurred in different ways in the actions we have been exploring. One approach emphasizes what we could call instrumental vulnerability, which regards vulnerability as a strategic option, or "repertoire," such as when protestors climb tripods or bury themselves in tunnels. Doherty regards this as crucial to the strategic interaction between forces of order and protestors, allowing these actors to develop successful campaigns of resistance. While not in any way reducing the strategic significance of such "manufactured vulnerability," the experiences we have been exploring point to dimensions beyond the paradigm of instrumental action that Doherty, drawing on Tilly, uses to conceptualize what is at stake in these actions.

The actions we have explored demonstrate a break with the civic paradigm, where the collective acts through the person, and also the model where claims are made about a "collective actor." The grammar of these actions is one of *personalization* as opposed to fulfilling a role or a function on behalf of a collectivity. What we see, rather than a dichotomy between private and public or individual and collective, is what Ion and Pironi (1997) identify as a changing relationship between public experience and personalization. The paradigm is not one of the individual, defined in terms of separation; rather it is one of a communicative construction of personal experience. This involves a capacity to feel the presence of the other, which, as we saw in Philadelphia, can be accepted or rejected. As we saw Nick's account of making puppets, this involves an encounter with the vulnerable self. Margrit Shildrick offers an important insight into such experiences of vulnerability when she argues that these are not an "intrinsic quality of an existing subject," but better understood as "an inalienable condition of becoming" (2002: 85). She offers us a critical insight when she writes of the shock of recognition that she experiences when confronted with an exhibition of photographs of neonatal and still-born children with great deformities, an exhibition that confronts and compels a response:

> The shock the putative threat to my own well-being that the figures seem to offer, and the parallel feeling of recognition, both spring from the unavoidable realization that as an embodied subject, I too am fragile. Not only is my own unity of being uncertain, but what has seemed intolerable, even unthinkable, is precisely constitutive of my self. The notion of an irreducible vulnerability as the necessary condition of a fully corporeal becoming – of my self and always with others . . . calls finally for the willingness to engage in an ethics of risk. (Shildrick 2002: 86)

Shildrick uses the word "shock," again highlighting an experience that is not intentional. The vulnerability that she points to is personal, experienced at the level of selfhood. But it opens out the possibility of a corporeal becoming – of the self, with others. This is not a logic of the construction of "we"; instead it is an experience of self, lived in relation to the other. This personalization of experience is at the center of emerging grammars of action. *The puppet interpolates our private self, not our public self.* There is more at stake here than middle class "personalism," or the idea that freedom could be an endless meeting. But nor are we dealing with new forms of fusion, a merger of the divine and sociality in the return of the tribe. Rather we are witnessing the emergence of new moral grammars and new forms of corporeal action.

PART III

Global Modernities, Grammars of Action

Chapter 6

Zapatista Dreaming: Memory and the Mask

On January 1, 1994, several hundred armed indigenous men and women took control of the municipal buildings of San Cristobal de las Casas and five other townships in the Mexican state of Chiapas. Located in a remote region on the border with Guatemala, Chiapas is one of Mexico's poorest states. With a population of some 3 million, of whom 2 million are indigenous, 51 percent of houses have earth floors, as opposed to a national average of 21 percent. Over the 1980s international organizations increasingly expressed concern about the extent of brutality and police and military violence in the state. The group that captured the towns called itself the Ejército Zapatista de Liberación Nacional (EZLN), the Zapatista Army of National Liberation. A masked man calling himself Subcommandante Marcos read a declaration from the balcony of the town hall of San Cristobal de las Casas, focusing on the situation of the indigenous population of the region, calling for an uprising to take control of the federal government. The key theme was *Ya Basta!* (Enough!). The next 12 days saw intense fighting, with between 200 and 400 people killed, mostly among the insurgents, many of whom were poorly armed, some not at all. Mexican troops responded with extreme violence, including summary execution of captured insurgents. The extent of this violence sparked intense pressure on the Mexican government, with large protests in the capital, and internationally through intergovernmental and NGO networks that had been monitoring the human rights situation on the other side of the border in Guatemala. In this context the Government declared a cease fire on January 12, and peace negotiations began in February. The EZLN leaders sent an appeal to the Mexican press, calling for "civil society" to send volunteers to form a protective ring around its negotiators. This appeal circulated in Mexico as well as widely among North American academics and human rights networks, in particular through emerging Internet networks.

The negotiations that followed were unfruitful, and following the reelection of the dominant Institutional Revolutionary Party in June, a military blockade was established around the area controlled by the Zapatistas. In the following February, the government issued arrest warrants for the leaders of the rebellion, sending troops back into the zones controlled by the Zapatistas, retaking control of cities and forcing some 20,000 Zapatistas to abandon villages and retreat to the eastern regions of Chiapas. From this point the Mexican military adopted a strategy of low intensity warfare, supporting the development of paramilitary groups made up largely of landless young men, targeting individuals and groups seen as sympathetic to the Zapatistas (Eber 2001).

The elections that had returned the PRI to power yet again were widely regarded as fraudulent, and the EZLN created its own consultation process, organizing a referendum where some 1 million people voted on a series of reforms proposed by the Zapatistas, followed by two national consultations. These prevented the Zapatistas from being isolated in the mountain and jungle regions to which they had retreated. These actions significantly strengthened the Zapatistas, leading in February 1996 to the signing of the San Andres Accords recognizing indigenous cultural and economic rights. In this period the EZNL launched an appeal for a global consultation to take place in the zones it controlled, convoking an international meeting "for humanity and against neo-liberalism." This circulated widely among the solidarity networks that had developed over the year, and saw some 3,000 people converge in Chiapas in July 1996, accelerating the formation of new types of networks in both Europe and the United States.

The EZNL and its supporters believed that the Accords were not being put into practice, suspending negotiations with the government, while over 1997 continuing negotiations with the Parliament in a framework established by Monsignor Samuel Ruíz, the Catholic Bishop of San Cristobal de las Casas. In December, 45 unarmed Zapatista supporters in the Zapatista village of Acteal were massacred by a PRI-linked paramilitary group. Over the two years that followed, the government reinforced the blockade around the Zapatista zone, which consisted of some 30 indigenous communities. This situation would remain the same until the change of government at both federal and state levels, when in July 1990 for the first time in 80 years the PRI failed to win reelection. In December 2000 the new government began to demilitarize the state of Chiapas, closing a number of the military bases that had been installed in the region since 1995. Negotiations reopened, leading in February–March 2001 to 20 EZNL leaders and hundreds of supporters, including a large international contingent of mainly young people who had come to serve as shields to protect the guerrillas from the army, undertaking a caravan that would lead to the symbolic center of Mexico, the Placa del Zocalo, where they were met by some 200,000 people, and where they addressed the National Parliament on the situation of indigenous people in

Mexico. Following the extraordinary impact of the caravan, the government proposed constitutional reform in April 2001. This was rejected by the Zapatistas who considered the proposed amendments reversed gains made at the time of the San Andreas accords (the agreement for autonomous regions signed by the Mexican government on February 16, 1996; see Nash 2001: 122ff.). The EZNL leaders returned to Chiapas, while, despite their opposition, the government and the required number of states ratified the amendments. The period since has seen the continuation of the occupation, but at the same time, a silence from the Zapatistas, above all following the destruction of the Two Towers in September 2001, which lasted until January 1, 2003, the ninth anniversary of the uprising, when 20,000 Zapatistas, their faces covered with ski masks, marched once again through the central plaza of San Cristobal de las Casas.

It is widely believed that the struggle of those whom Mexican author Carlos Fuentes calls the "first post-communist guerrillas" (Fuentes 1994: 54) has radically changed Mexican society and culture, setting in motion a process of democratization that led, among other things, to the first change in the country's national government in 80 years. But at the same time the Zapatista struggle played a key role in a wider global movement. In this chapter, we begin to explore why this struggle took on such importance, and its implications for the way we think about movements, action, and globalization.

Lenin's Shadow, Defensive Communities

The masked guerrilla, his face hidden behind a black ski mask, who read the declaration from the town hall balcony in San Cristobal de las Casas on the first day of 1994 called himself Sub-Commandante Marcos. It later became widely known, and no longer denied by Marcos himself, the Sub-Commandante is, or was, a former philosophy student, Rafael Sebastian Guillén, the son of a furniture manufacturer from the city of Pampico, one of the main cities in the northern Mexican state of Tamaulipas. After his studies at a Jesuit school, Guillén completed a degree in philosophy in Mexico City, where he was influenced by the French structuralist theory that was fashionable at the time. His thesis (still available in the library in the Universidad Nacional Autónoma de México Philosophy Department) is full of references to Foucault, Althusser, and the Marxist political scientist Nicos Poulantzas. Significantly Guillén completes his thesis with an appeal to break with academic philosophy, calling for a new kind of philosophy that would be grounded in "proletarian political practice," which would make possible making "theory with politics and politics with theory" (Hohy 1995, cited in Rodriguez 1996). After completing his philosophy degree, Guillén took up a post teaching graphic arts in an experimental university in the suburbs of Mexico City. At the time he showed a strong interest in visual arts, playing a role in *Waiting for Godot*, as well as participating in several short films. His writings involve constant references to film, and film projections are frequent in La Realidad, the capital of Zapatista territory, without any attempt at political correctness or didactic instruction – one of the most popular films regularly projected being *Rambo*) (Le Bot 1997).

The origins of the EZLN lie in the Fuerzas de Liberación Nacional. The FLN had been created as a Marxist-Maoist military organization following the government's massacre of students in Tlatelolco in 1968, its aim being a strategy of armed insurrection in the countryside, similar to other guerrilla forces in the post-1968 period in South and Central America. The FLN was committed in classical Leninist style to the creation of "the dictatorship of the proletariat." The FLN was in the process of breaking up when Guillén became a sub-commandante in the southern region (Rodriguez 1996; Le Bot 1997), arriving in the Lacandona rainforest in August–September 1984, seven months after a base camp had been established, made up of some 10 guerrillas (Marcos 2003). In its beginnings the EZNL consisted of urban radicals and politicized indigenous leaders, both groups, as Yvon Le Bot (1997) underlines, deeply imbued in an authoritarian, antidemocratic Leninist political culture. Marcos admits he was unaware that the Indians of Chiapas had their own history, actions, culture, and forms of movement when he first arrived in the region in the period 1985–7:

> In the beginning, from our perspective as guerrillas, they were exploited and we had to organize them and show them the way. Put yourself in our shoes – we were the light of the world! . . . They were blind, we had to open their eyes! (Marcos, in Le Bot 1997, 128–9)

At the time Guillén arrived in the south, the *foco* model of social change embraced by guerrilla movements, where increasingly larger sections of the countryside would be liberated through armed action and eventually surround the capital city, was dying in South and Central America. This was already the case before 1989, but it is clear that the fall of the Berlin Wall and the collapse of the socialist utopia was a fatal blow to the FLN ideology. For Marcos, the first "defeat" of the EZLN was the failure of this model of mobilization. This, however, opened the possibility for a new relationship with the indigenous population, out of which Marcos recounts a "second zapatismo" being born:

After all, that had been the EZLN's fundamental origin: a group of "illumi-nati" who came from the city in order to "liberate" the exploited and who looked, when confronted with the reality of the indigenous communities, more like burnt out light bulbs than "illuminati." How long did it take us to realize that we had to learn to listen, and, afterwards, to speak? I'm not sure, not a few moons have passed now, but I calculate some two years at least. (Marcos 2003)

Indigenous Movements

While the model of socialism that inspired "proletarian political practice" was dying, important forms of indigenous movement were emerging in South and Central America, in particular in the countries of Mexico, Guatemala, Bolivia, and Ecuador. Dominant approaches to understanding these movements tends to conceive of them in terms of "primordialism," expressions of an almost timeless indigenous culture, or in terms of "instru-mentalism," where such movements mobilize identities as a resource to enter the political system (for a survey of both, see Yashar 1998). Both these analy-ses have been extensively developed in relation to the Zapatista action. The American anthropologist Gary Gossen regards the Zapatista movement as a reassertion of a primordial Mayan culture, a reassertion of "Mesoamerica's collective Indian soul" (1996: 116), while for political process theorists, the development of an ethnic identity and strategy is shaped by the political opportunity structure, in this case, one more open at the international level than the national level (Tarrow 1999).

While the Zapatista revolt of 1994 is clearly an expression of an indige-nous movement, there is little that suggests the reassertion of a timeless culture. The area where the movement emerged, Las Cañadas, a region of the Lacandona rainforest, had only been settled over the past five decades, a legacy of the Mexican revolution of 1917 that had made possible the colo-nization and exploitation of unowned land, in particular through forms of collective ownership and individual peasant plots or *ejidos*. Since the 1950s the Las Cañadas region had been populated by indigenous plantation workers moving down from the highlands (Barmeyer 2003). This led to a region where the population is indigenous, but multiethnic and often multi-lingual, with most inhabitants speaking more that one indigenous language. Because of this recent immigrant population, the area had been little studied by anthropologists interested in areas regarded as more traditional and authentic. The area was largely ignored as well by the Mexican government, possibly because of future development plans including petrol and hydroelectric development, with the colonist campesinos being left in a subsistence economy based on the traditional Maya crop of corn, and with little provision of basic services such as water, electricity, and housing (Barmeyer 2003).

The region was, however, characterized by important forms of self-organization. One that would prove most important was the tradition of armed self-defense against landowners who at different times would attempt to push villagers off their land. This tradition was very different from revolutionary armed political groups. Rather than finance weapons and infrastructure (uniforms, shortwave radio, etc.) through "revolutionary taxes" or crime, campesinos purchased weapons through pooling resources (Diaz 1995), an important source of funds being the sale of pigs (Barmeyer 2003). Guillén and the other FLN activists who arrived to live in the region between 1983 and 1985 eventually became accepted into these armed groups. At the same time the collapse of the Soviet Union and the effective end of socialism had a profound effect on many of the FLN members who had gone to the region, many giving up the idea of armed struggle in the period after 1989. The period of guerrilla warfare seemed to be over, illustrated by the peace accords between the most important of the guerrilla movements in the region, the Farabundo Marti National Liberation Front, and the government of El Salvador, signed in Mexico in January 1992 (Diaz 1995).

However, the period leading up to the 1994 uprising was one of increasing pressure on the campesinos. Increasing internal migration to the area, combined with rising demographic pressure, meant greater pressure on limited resources. The old system of patronage, integrating local elites through favors and grants, functioned less and less effectively in the context of declining resources and increasingly evident exhaustion of the Mexican state and political system. The country's admission to NAFTA foreshadowed the abrogation of Section 27 of the Constitution, which would mean an end to the form of collective title that allowed indigenous people to access the land. But while the utopia of socialism and proletarian democracy were fading as the twentieth century came to a close, from the 1970s there were clear signs of the presence of an indigenous movement emerging across South and Central America. The dominant ideology in Mexico, as throughout South and Central America as a whole, had been one of assimilation of the indigenous populations into a homogenous national identity. The Mexican Revolution of 1910 had declared its goal was to "Mexicanize the Indians, not Indianize Mexico" (Maldonado 2004), rendering the indigenous population invisible. By the 1970s signs of an indigenous movement were emerging. An important precursor had been the holding of an Indigenous Congress in San Cristobal de las Casas in 1974, out of which emerged the Union of Ejidos – Quiptic ta lecubtesl (Our force for Liberation in Tzeltale)

(Le Bot 1997: 50). While Marcos would constantly minimize their significance, it is clear that religious movements, in particular the Catholic movements constructed in relation to liberation theology, had a significant role in
the emerging indigenous consciousness and networks (Le Bot 1997; Leyva
Solano 1998). The first Indigenous Congress of 1974 was organized through
the Catholic Diocese of San Cristobal de las Casas. This emerging indigenous
movement took on increasing importance in the period leading up to the
commemoration of the five hundredth anniversary of the Spanish Conquest
in 1992. Le Bot underlines the importance of this commemoration, the
Spanish Conquest increasingly referred to as the "first globalization," reflecting an indigenous consciousness affirming 500 years of resistance. The international significance of this movement is evident in the according of the
Nobel Peace Prize to a Guatemalan indigenous woman, Rigoberta Menchu,
in the anniversary year of 1992 (Le Bot, 2003).

On the anniversary itself, October 12, 1992, several hundred indigenous
people marched to the statue of Diego de Mazariegos, founder of the colonial capital of Chiapas, in San Cristobal de las Casas. One man climbed up
and dislodged the statue with a sledge hammer, sending it falling to the
ground. The crowd then attacked it, smashing it to pieces, destroying the
statue, returning to their villages with pieces as souvenirs. The protestors'
banners declared "today we commemorate 500 years of destruction of the
Indian people," and "Damn the treaty that mistreats us!" referring to the
NAFTA (Diaz, 1995, cited in Le Bot 2003). The American historian Thomas
Benjamin (2000) argues the indigenous people who destroyed this statue had
long been considered a "people without history," portrayed as passive, inert,
or as obstacles to the march of progress at the heart of Mexican society. The
attack on the statue is, as Benjamin argues, an attack on a particular model
of history, one of monuments and commemorations that had the effect of
rendering the indigenous as a people without a history.

The Zapatista movement was born from a traditional Leninist guerrilla
merging with a movement of armed community defense (Diaz 1996). The
decision to move from the defense of village communities to take up arms
against the government was framed by the worsening conditions in Chiapas
and by the pervasive repression that saw arrest and imprisonment widely
directed at indigenous people as a strategy of intimidation and humiliation
(Diaz 1995). In the words of an indigenous leader of the EZLN:

We got to the stage where it was just so difficult, when [President] Salinas
started talking about the Agreement and free trade, about Article 27, about
the privatization of the ejido and enterprises . . . the companeros explained to
us what it would mean for our country, above all for the campesinos, that [the
repeal] of Article 27 would lead us to a situation as [before the Revolution of

1917] under Porfirio Diaz. "No, there, that's enough! We have to declare war!" We asked everyone, and that was the decision. That's why 1 January 1994 took place. (Major Moses, interviewed in Le Bot, 1997: 181)

Moses illustrates here the essentially defensive logic initiating armed conflict, pointing to the extent that the January uprising was an extension of the traditional strategy of armed defense of communities. This also explains the lack of strategy accompanying the uprising. Marcos's declaration, El Despertador Mexicano (The Mexican Awakening) reaffirmed the traditional *foco* strategy of advancing to the capital, defeating the national army, and creating new political structures in liberated zones. The model was one of top-down change within a Leninist legacy: a focus on the state, capturing political power through force of arms, and then reconstructing the society. Marcos had called upon all Mexicans to join revolutionary armed action against the army and government. But the hoped-for uprising did not eventuate. Looking back on the initial uprising, Marcos says:

> It was a hope, a dream that was hidden away at the deepest level, but nothing at all justified it. There was a part of us that hoped against all likelihood that the people would rise up with us, not only the Indians but also the students, workers, office workers, and not only in Chiapas by the rest of Mexico . . . but we didn't believe it too seriously. (Marcos, in Le Bot 1997: 176)

After the failed uprising, the Zapatistas fell back to defensive positions, ringed by some 5,000 troops. The strategy shifted to defending autonomous villages and seizing land, echoing traditional defense strategies of the indigenous communities. Le Bot underlines the risks in this strategy, with its constant temptation to communitarianism and the moral imperative of unanimity, that in the early days took the form of expelling from villages those who did not agree with decisions that were made. To the extent that the Zapatista villages became isolated, this could easily develop into a form of millenarianism, a repressive culture where to disagree is to be a traitor. This was evident, for example, in what Le Bot suggests has been the constant temptation to purity present in this movement, evident, for example, in the interdiction of alcohol within Zapatista-controlled territories, or the importance attached to ensuring that foreign volunteer supporters are controlled, and do not mix too freely with the indigenous people. There was a strong potential, therefore, after the failure of the initial uprising, that the Zapatista movement could mutate into a closed and defensive, potentially puritanical, community movement, in the sense that Castells regards ethnic movements as defensive enclosures against globalization. What happened, however, was radically different.

Dreams, Stories, and Encounters:
the Transformation of a Struggle

In attempting to make sense of the Zapatista experience, there is a strong temptation to project onto it categories that we are already familiar with. Canadians Johnston and Laxer (2003), for example, analyze the Zapatista movement through a very Canadian lens, arguing that both the Zapatistas in Mexico and Canadian mobilizations against the Multilateral Accord on Investment (MAI) in the mid-1990s reflect the same struggle; namely resisting the Canadian and Mexican states' respective "betrayal of historic legacies of economic nationalism" (2003: 78). For others the Zapatistas' increasing references to the theme of "autonomy" means their struggle is a form of anarchism, an indigenous expression of an antistate libertarianism influential in left political movements, in the United States in particular. It is clear, however, that the Zapatista struggle is neither an expression of economic nationalism nor indigenous anarchism. Right from the first march on San Cristobal de las Casas, the Zapatistas held high the Mexican flag, and they clearly want to transform, not abolish, the state and the nation. Yet the project of nation they struggle for is not a Mexican version of economic nationalism.

The defensive strategy of falling back was linked to a new kind of openness and a process of transformation that Tacho, an indigenous leader interviewed by Najman and Le Bot (1997) describes not in terms of programs and objectives, but in terms of dreams:

Commandante Tacho: *We wanted to meet the people, like when we took San Cristobal or San Andres, lots of groups came to see us, we wanted to explain our reasons, why we had to take up arms. We took up arms to live, simply . . . to live a life with dignity.*

Maurice Najman (interviewer): *But nevertheless, at the beginning you were talking about seizing power, about socialism, weren't you?*

Tacho: *At the beginning, yes. But in reality, we had already begun to change. We needed to find a way. If taking up arms had only served for people to listen to us, very good . . . if after the arms had spoken, we could speak [. . .]*

Najman: *With these changes, your way of thinking, your ideology changed as well?*

Tacho: *Yes. Every day. We would dream, and with each dream we learnt how to put them into practice. It wasn't just one dream. Only one dream would have been the path of arms. But it wasn't that, just the path of arms. Other dreams came, to the extent that we dreamt them.*

Najman: *What other dreams?*

Tacho: *There was a second dream, after the uprising, of creating a first Aguascalientes [a place constructed for dialogue, a first national democratic convention of August 1994, the site later destroyed by the military and turned into a military base] . . . One day, we dreamed of having a continental American encounter, and that dream was also realized. We dreamed of holding an intercontinental Encounter, and we were able to realize that dream as well. We didn't get trapped in the first dream, the dream of arms.* (Le Bot 1997: 189)

The defeat and militarization of Chiapas were countered by forms of action that aimed at creating openings and encounters. Much has been made of the role of the Internet, and it is clear that this played a critical role in mobilizing support networks, above all in the context of Mexico's joining the North American Free Trade Agreement (NAFTA) and the Organization for Economic Cooperation and Development (OECD). But as Marcos observes, there was more at stake than the technology. What counted was what was said. The extraordinary interest directed toward the Zapatistas is a result of their capacity to "produce meaning" (Le Bot 1997: 105). Here the role of Marcos is critical. For some observers, he is "a skilled and effective operator in public relations." But there is more than this. Marcos is a nonindigenous person who makes no pretence of being Indigenous. He serves, however, a critical role, one of a bridge between two worlds. The Zapatista struggle took the form of what le Bot calls "the strategy of a non-violent army serving the production of meaning" (Le Bot 1997: 105). Through his encounter with the indigenous struggle, Marcos became a storyteller. He recounts his encounter with Old Man Antonio, one where he describes how he learnt to ask questions, first published in *La Jornada*, a Mexican paper supporting the Zapatistas, almost a year after the failed uprising:

The cold is bone-chilling in these mountains. Ana Maria and Mario are with me on this expedition, 10 years before the dawn of January. The two have joined the guerrilla army, and I, then an infantry lieutenant, take my turn to teach them what others have taught me: to live in the mountains.

Yesterday I ran into Old Antonio for the first time. We both lied – him saying he was on his way to see his field, and me saying I was out hunting. Both of us knew we were lying and we knew we knew it. I left Ana Maria following the directions of the expedition, and I went back to the river to see if, with a clisimeter, I could locate on the map a very high hill that was up ahead. And to see if I could bump into Old Antonio again. He must have been thinking the same thing because he appeared at the same place where I found him before.

Like the day before, Old Antonio is sitting on the ground, leaning up against a hump of green moss, and beginning to roll a cigarette. I sit down in front of him and light my pipe. Old Antonio begins: "You're not hunting."

I respond: "You're not walking to your field." Something makes me speak formally – in a respectful manner – to this old man of indefinite age with a face tanned like a cedar bark who I am seeing for the second time in my life. Old Antonio smiles and adds: "I've heard of you people. In the canyons, they say you are thieves. In my village, they are worried because you are walking these trails."

"And you, do you believe we are bandits?" I ask. Old Antonio exhales a long wisp of smoke, coughs, and shakes his head. I get my courage and ask him another question. "So who do you think we are?"

"I'd rather you tell me," he says and looks me straight in the eyes.

"It's a long story," I say. And I begin to tell him about the times of Zapata and Villa and the revolution and the land and the injustice and the hunger and the ignorance and the sickness and the repression and everything. And I finish with "and thus we are the Zapatista Army of National Liberation." I wait for some sign from Old Antonio who never stopped looking at me during my speech.

"Tell me more about that Zapata," he says after another puff and a cough. I begin with Anenecuilco, then I follow with the Plan de Ayala, the military campaign, the organization of the villages, the betrayal of Chinameca. Old Antonio continues to stare at me until I finish.

"It wasn't like that," he tells me. I'm surprised and all I can do is mumble, "No?"

"No," insists Old Antonio. "I'm going to tell you the real story of this so-called Zapata."

Old Antonio takes out his tobacco and rolling paper and begins his story, a story where old and new events mix and get lost in each other, just as the smoke from his cigarette and my pipe mix and get lost in each other.

"Many stories ago, when the first gods – those who made the world were still circling through the night, there were these two other gods – Ik'al and Votán.

"The two were only one. When one was turning himself around, the other would show himself, and when the other one was turning himself around, the first one would show himself. They were opposites. One was light like a May morning at the river. The other was dark like the night of cold and cave. They were the same thing. They were one, these two, because one made the other. But they would not walk themselves, staying there always, these two gods who were one without moving.

"'What should we do then?' the two of them asked.

" 'Life is sad enough as it is,' they lamented, the two who were one in staying without moving.

" 'Night never passes,' said I'kal.

" 'Day never passes,' said Votán.

" 'Let's walk,' said the one who was two.

" 'How?' asked the other.

" 'Where?' asked the one.

"And they saw that they had moved a little, first to ask how, then to ask where. The one who was two became very happy when the one saw that they were moving themselves a little. Both of them wanted to move at the same time, but they couldn't do it themselves."

"How should we do it then?"

"And one would come around first and then the other and they would move just a little bit more and they realized that they could move if one went first, then the other. So they started walking and now no one remembers who started walking first because at the time they were so happy just to be moving.

" 'And who cares who was first since we're moving now?' said the gods who were one and the same and they laughed at each other and the first agreement they made was to dance, and they danced, one little step by one, and they danced for a long time because they were so happy that they had found each other. Then they got tired of so much dancing and they looked for something else to do . . . And they saw that the first question was, 'How do we move?' and the answer was, 'Together but separately and in agreement.' But that question wasn't important any more because they realized that they were already walking, and so another question came up when they saw that there were two roads in front of them: one road was very short and it just got over to there and they could see clearly that this road would end right away and their feet were so full of joy from walking that they said right then that the first road was too short and they didn't want to walk it and so they made an agreement to walk the long road.

"And they were going to start walking when their answer to choose the long road brought another question – 'Where does this road take us?' They took a long time to think about the answer and the two who were one got the bright idea that only by walking the long road were they going to know where the road took them. If they remained where they were, they were never going to know where the long road leads. The two who were one said to each other: 'So let's walk it then,' and they started walking, first the one and then the other. And only then and there did they realize that it was taking a long time to walk the long road, so another question came up: 'How are we going to walk for such a long time?' And they stayed thinking a good while and then Ik'al said real clearly that he didn't know how to walk by day and Votán said that he didn't know how to walk at night and they stayed there, crying for a long time.

"And when all the wailing and hollering was over, they came to an agreement and they saw that it was fine for Ik'al to walk only at night and for Votán to walk only during the day and Ik'al would walk for Votán during the night and that is how they came up with the answer for walking all the time. Since then the gods have walked with questions and they never, never stop – they never arrive and they never go away. This is how the true men and women learned that questions are for walking, not for just standing around and doing nothing. And since then, when true men and women want to walk, they ask questions. When they want to arrive, they take leave. And when they want to leave, they say hello. They are never still."

I'm left gnawing and biting at the short end of my pipe while I wait for Old Antonio to go on with his story, but it seems he no longer has any intention of doing so. Afraid to interfere with something very serious, I ask, "And Zapata?"

Old Antonio smiles: "You've already learned that to know and to walk, you have first to ask." He coughs and lights another cigarette that I didn't know he had rolled up and amid the smoke that comes out of his lips, words fall like seeds to the ground: "The one they call Zapata appeared here in the mountains. He wasn't born himself, they say. He just appeared, just like that. They say he is the Ik'al and the Votán who came here while they were on their long walk and so that they wouldn't scare the good people, they became one. Because after so much walking together, Ik'al and Votán discovered that they were one and the same and that they could make themselves one during both the day and the night. When they got there they made themselves one and gave themselves the name of Zapata . . .

"And Zapata said that this is where he had arrived – where he was going to find where the long road led to and he said he would be light at times and other times darkness, but he was one and the same, the Votán Zapata and the Ik'al Zapata, the white Zapata and the black Zapata. And these two were both the same road for all true men and women to follow."

Old Antonio took from his backpack a little bag of nylon. Inside there was a very old picture from 1910 of Emiliano Zapata. In his left hand Zapata had his sword raised to his waist. In his right hand he had a pistol, two cartridge belts of bullets crossed his chest, one from left to right, the other from right to left. His feet are positioned as though he's standing still or walking and in his gaze there is something like "here I am" or "there I go." There are two staircases. One comes out of the darkness, and there are dark-skinned Zapatistas as though they were coming out of something. The other staircase is lighted but there is no one and one can't see where it goes or where it comes from. I would be lying if I told you that I noticed all those details. It was Old Antonio who told me. Behind the picture, it said:

"Gral. Emiliano Zapata, Jefe del Ejercito Suriano.

Gen. Emiliano Zapata, Commander in Chief of the Southern Army.

Le General Emiliano Zapata, Chef de l'Armee du Sud.

C.1910. Photo by: Agustin V. Casasola."

Old Antonio says to me "I have asked a lot of questions of this picture. That is how I came to be here." He coughs and tosses the cigarette butt. He gives me the picture. "Here," he says "So that you learn how to ask questions . . . and to walk."

"It's better to say good-bye when you arrive. That way it's not so painful when you leave" he says giving me his hand as he leaves, while he tells me he is arriving. Since then, Old Antonio says hello by saying "goodbye" and leaves by saying "hello."

Old Antonio leaves. So does Beto, Tonita, Eva and Heriberto. I take out the photo of Zapata from my backpack and show it to them.

"Is he climbing up or down?" says Beto.

"Is he going or staying?" asks Eva.

"Is he taking out or putting away his sword?" asks Tonita.

"Has he finished firing his pistol or just started?" asks Heriberto.

I'm always surprised by how many questions that 84 year old photograph provokes and that Old Antonio gave me in 1984. I look at it one last time and decide to give it to Ana Maria and the picture provokes one more question: Is it our yesterday or our tomorrow?[1]

The Zapatistas not only claim the Mexican flag, but also the heritage of Emilano Zapata, the great historic figure of the Mexican revolution. But in the story told by Marcos, Zapata becomes part of Mayan dreaming – Voltán Zapata – while through the story, Mayan dreaming also claims a part of the Mexican story. Marcos's stories of his encounters with Old Antonio make constant reference to dreams and dreaming. It was through the encounter with Old Antonio that Marcos says he was able to free himself from an old ideology, and learn to dream (Le Bot 1997). The potency of dreams is recognized as particularly important by the indigenous peoples of Mexico (see Eber 2001). In the period following 1994, dreams and stories become increasingly important, Marcos sending these to sympathetic newspapers in Mexico City, from where they circulated throughout the country and internationally (later collated and translated into books). They become more important in the gradual emergence of the person of Marcos and the stories he tells, of characters such as Old Antonio and Don Durito. Old Antonio is a man, but Don Durito is a quarrelsome hard-backed beetle. He is a figure of imagination, but in the stories Marcos recounts, he takes on a life of his own, while at different times Marcos has argued that Old Antonio did exist, and did teach him in the way he recounts. These stories possess a dreamlike quality. They do not possess a linear temporal structure. They draw from the indigenous tradition, where an episode is narrated, as opposed to a structured didactic story with a beginning and an end. What is critical, in the encounter with Old Anthony, is becoming open to the possibility of dreaming. Within Mayan culture, it is dreams that make a person a human being.

Storytelling is central to Indian culture and social organization. Corando (1993, in Maldonado 2001: 142) points to its multiple significances:

> through this the understandings of individual and social life are articulated, it makes up the collective memory. It can be used to transmit their history, either legendary or mythic, or recent, to teach norms and group behaviour and its forms of social and religious organization, as a way of understanding the relationship between man and nature . . . an instrument for continuity and cohesion of social unity.

Storytelling lies at the center of Mayan memory. The kapok tree, the sacred tree of the Mayan peoples, could also be called the tree of words, because under this tree is where talking and listening take place (Maldonado 2001). With Marcos's stories we can see a shift, from the jargon and slogans of the FLN, that at this time still understood the world in terms of proletarian revolution and socialism (Womack 1999), to the way he describes the world in terms of Mayan oral culture. At first the first stories of Old Antonio were marginal, the key forms of communication remaining formal communiqués structured in traditional political language. But it was the stories of Old Antonio that captured attention and became widely circulated. They emerge from and reflect key dimensions of an oral culture and tradition; they capture the tone, the vitality and colloquial style of a speaker telling a story to a group; these stories

are an *event* constructed in terms of speaking and hearing. They also manifest the key characteristic of oral culture, repetition – through which the
stories take on the key dimensions of *rhythm* and *musicality* (Maldonado 2001:
143).

Approaches to literature often oppose the oral culture of traditional
societies, seen as expressing collective culture and reproduction, with the
modern figure of the creator and author, regarded as an expression of the
individual characterizing modern society. But this opposition breaks down in
the case of these Zapatista stories. More than transmitting information, the
stories produce a complexity that becomes charged with new meanings.
And rather than a timeless repetition of fables about the gods alone, these
stories are shaped by the subjectivity of the author, through humor, irony,
unexpected temporal transpositions (Colombres 1997: 75). They are not a
symbolic system, nor a timeless repetition: rather they are the grammar
of encounter between an embodied speaker and an embodied listener.
As Maldonado argues, place is central to these stories. In these stories, we are
in a place through the senses. The stories constantly begin with Marcos
and Old Antonio discussing the weather (rain, wind, heat), animals that
surround them (jaguars, birds, bats, deer). Place is critical: "the forest, with
its specific symbols, occupies a key role in Old Antonio's stories. The
forest is not a bulwark of Zapatista resistance, rather it is the space for the
creation of an oral literature" (Maldonado 2001: 152). Old Antonio sews
these stories together between puffs of his cigarette. These are not revolutionary discourses, with the leader on the platform. They are not stories
of heroes and public figures; they are conversations that are grounded in
place, in the forest, in person-to-person experience. Marcos's stories are
grounded in an oral tradition, but Marcos serves as a translator, where the
distinction between collective orality and individual literature breaks
down. The Zapatista action does not reject the dominant culture, falling
back on the defense of tradition; rather it opens out the possibility of "bilin-
gualism between peoples" (Maldonado 2001: 144). The stories do not call
for the construction of a unified Indian identity against the Mexican
state. Instead two themes recur: recognition of the other, and indigenous
interiority.

At the end of the first year following the defeat of the initial uprising,
Marcos would write, "Yeah, I know that writing a letter isn't exactly an assault
on the Winter Palace. But the letters made us travel so far" (*La Jornada*,
December 13, 1994).

In the Mayan tradition, to dream is to act. The stories are dreams that
succeeded in cutting through the military blockade constructed around the
Zapatista territory, first being printed by sympathetic papers in Mexico City;
then circulating globally.

The Revolt against Forgetting:
Dignity and Recognition

Some observers do not consider that it is possible for indigenous people to be the subjects of action, to produce their own meaning. This is evident in the argument developed by the political scientist Guillermo Trejo. He argues that EZLN and the wider Zapatista movement is an example of a traditional Marxist-Leninist movement, that converted into an "ethnoterritorial" movement in 1996, thanks to the efforts of external advisers who succeeded in framing "communal ethnic pride into a political program of ethnoterritorial demands." This in turn was only possible as a result of the development of ethnic pride among the indigenous population, which itself was the result of external forces as well:

> Such a radical shift by the Zapatistas, from class to ethnicity, was made possible by a long-term and a short-term factor. The long-term factor is that ethnic pride and language already existed at the communal level, mainly as the unintended outcome the processes of religious and political competition between Catholic and Protestant Churches and the state in the 1970s and 1980s. The short-term factor is that a group of social scientists and intellectuals who served as Zapatista advisers in the second round of peace negotiations helped the EZLN frame that communal ethnic pride into a political programme of ethnoterritorial demands . . . Without the advisers, communal ethnic pride would have remained buried, as in the past, under the peasant hat. (Trejo 2002: 104–5)

This perspective regards Zapatista action as the consequence of other processes. "Ethnic pride" is the unintended consequence of Catholic and Protestant churches' competition for market share, only later to be mobilized by external intellectuals, without whom it would have remained buried under the "peasant hat." This view regards the indigenous population once again as not able to produce its own experience. The indigenous people are not the subjects of their own action – rather their action is the unintended consequence of other forces. According to this view Mexico's history continues to be made by others, not the indigenous.

Very soon after the failure of the uprising, we see a very clear transformation in the form of action. But is this redefinition an expression of "ethnic pride" resulting from a redirection steered by "external advisors" and social scientists? Rather than focus on capturing territory, taking control of the government and transforming society by the state, the Zapatista action began to transform right at the point of negotiations that followed the failed uprising, in February 1994. During the "peace dialogue" that took place on February 24, Marcos describes the Zapatistas as people "without voices, without faces."

This powerfully captured the experience of being rendered invisible, being removed from the history of the country, being condemned to oblivion, which were experienced at the core of the experience of colonization (see www.casa115.com/ blog/zapatistas-thumb.jpg).

The evocative image of "those without voices, without faces" had extraordinary power, closely associated with the meaning and power of the mask. When the Zapatistas came out of the jungle to occupy San Cristobal de las Casas, they wore ski masks covering their faces. The origins of the mask lie in the very real fear of the danger of reprisals, a fear based in particular on the experiences of Guatemalan refugees who had sought refuge in Chiapas, following the reprisals and systematic policy of murder undertaken by Rios Monte in the Guatemalan areas bordering Mexico. The meanings of the mask soon changed. Wearing the mask became a powerful act, making visible the fact that the wearer has been rendered invisible. This is expressed in a Zapatista poster, "For 500 years our face was forbidden. Why do you demand to see it now?"

The mask also evokes powerful themes in indigenous culture, where it is a powerful medium of connection to sources of power. All the principal Mayan deities are represented by masks. Traditional healers and shamans would wear a mask to access a source of power and dreaming; masks play a central role in traditional dance and trance experiences, where the wearer of the mask becomes a conduit for cosmic power. This understanding of the mask is clearly present in the Zapatista action. The Zapatista fight is a "fight against forgetting" (Communiqué February 14, 2004), while the Mexican government is seen as attempting to obliterate memory. The mask is not primarily a symbol of that fact that indigenous people have been rendered silent and invisible; rather it is what we can call a tool for memory, memory as action. It produces a relationship with those who are absent:

> In our voice shall travel the voice of others, of those who have nothing, those condemned to silence and ignorance, those thrown off their land and from history by the arrogance of the powerful, of all those good men and women who walk these lands of pain and anger, of the children and aged dead of abandonment and solitude, of humiliated women, of little men. Through our voice will speak the dead, our dead, so alone and forgotten, so dead and yet so alive in our voices and in our footsteps. (Marcos, cited in Monsiváis 1997: 146)

The mask evokes important themes in Mexican popular culture, where it is a tool of the hero who fights for justice against tyranny, predating the Zapatistas. In September 1985 Mexico City was devastated by an earthquake, and the events that followed led to a profound loss of confidence in the state. Official figures stated that some 5,000 people had died, while press estimates put the figure at above 30,000. Most of the deaths occurred where buildings less than 40 years old collapsed, a sign of poor building practice flourishing under corruption. Government response was disorganized and ineffective. It was in this context that associations and emergency groups emerged, calling themselves "civil society." It was in this context as well that stories of super-human rescue efforts widely circulated. One person, "the flea," was credited with climbing into collapsed buildings and pulling out people alive, while offi-cials stood by doing nothing. In another case a man wearing a wrestler's red mask and tights, and calling himself "Superbarrio" organized soup kitchens and other relief activities, and took on the task of defending those being expelled from their houses in the aftermath of the quake. Superbarrio was not modeled on Mayan myth, but American comic book heroes, but his action attracted extraordinary media attention. He became active the Assem-bly of Barrios in Mexico City that emerged in the period following the quake. A decade later Superbarrio was still acting as a self-described "defender for justice," supporting the homeless and people being evicted, described by an American journalist in 1997 as "a flabby caped crusader in cherry red tights who traverses the streets of Mexico City, defending the lower class" (CNN, July 19, 1997) (see www.childrensworld.org/superbarrio/jolanda.asp).

Superbarrio's mask is not totally foreign to that of Marcos. It captures the sense within popular culture that the mask hides extraordinary power. Yet in both cases, this is a form of power that is self-depreciating. Superbarrio takes up the character of a wrestler, while Marcos, in the period following the first uprising, took on the character of a fighter who is not a fighter – the bullets in the belt he wears over his shoulders do not fit the gun he carries (see http://www.ezln.org/fotos/marcos.jpg).

Following the defeat of the uprising, Zapatista action focused on "civil society" – it aimed at transforming society, as opposed to capturing the power of the state. One of the key ways this was to be achieved was through encounters, where the Zapatistas called upon "civil society" to meet with them, to explore ways of bringing about a transformed society. The first encounter, the Democratic National Convention (CND), took place in La Realidad in August 1994, while four others occurred at places that were named Oventic, Morelia, Roberto Barrios, and Francisco Gómez. The first Encounter created a Front, the Zapatisata Front for National Liberation, to be a political organization. But it was a political organization that would aim at supporting the development of "civil society": it would not seek political power itself, and its leaders were not allowed to stand for political office. The first Encounter and those that followed were called "Aguascalientes," taking the name of the town where in 1910 Zapata, Villa, and other leaders of the Mexican revolution had met to decide the direction of the revolution. But in this case, the Aguascalientes were camps created for these encounters.

The first Aguascalientes was built on a place with no name, deep in the Lacandona rainforest, in the municipality of Guadalupe Tepeyac. This created place was called La Realidad (Realty), but it was profoundly shaped by imagination. Hundreds of Zapatistas had spent 28 days working on the site, nestled in a natural ampitheater between two peaks. Rough-hewn bench seats for some 8,000 people were cut and placed on one of the hills. Metal cable was stretched between the peaks, and across it stretched some 5,000 square yards of white canvas. These giant sails reproduced Fitzcarraldo's fabled ship from the film by Werner Herzog. In this film, Fitzcarraldo wants to construct an opera house in the middle of the Brazilian jungle. But almost all the land is in the hands of rubber baron landowners except one site, deep in Indian territory. To get there Fitzcarraldo has to travel by boat, but his crew abandons ship in fear, and Fitzcarraldo, increasingly obsessed with his goal, enlists the help of Indians to drag his ship over a mountain, the only path left to reach his land (see http://www.hackitectura.net/osfavelados/osfavela2002/anarchogeographies/urbanarquista/urbanarquista.html).

Before the event, it was not clear how many people would come to this first Aguascalientes, eight months after the uprising. In the end some 6,000 people came, from Mexico and internationally, in particular from the United States. They traveled in some 200 buses, passing through Mexican army checkpoints and going deep into Zapatista territory. At the beginning of the convention, participants were met by Commandante Tacho with the expression "welcome aboard." Many who came would later recount their voyage, and the constant theme is one of a journey into a magical place, a journey into the imagination. Carlos Monsivais, one of Mexico's foremost cultural critics, described the convention as a mixture of "Woodstock, Mad Max IV, the ship of the mad" (cited in Pérez de Lama, 2000). Marcos referred to the place as "Tower of Babel, Noah's Ark, Fitzcarraldo's jungle boat, a Neozapatista delirium, a pirate ship" (Pérez de Lama, 2000).

The Mask

The mask is not only a symbol; it communicates an experience of being rendered invisible, of being made a person without a face. This powerful definition became more and more articulated at the core of the Zapatista mobilization. Introducing the EZLN to the participants at the second Encounter (*encuentro*), Marcos captures this when he says:

We are the Zapatista National Liberation Army.

For ten years, we lived in these mountains, preparing to fight a war.

In these mountains, we built an army.

Below, in the cities and plantations, we did not exist.

Our lives were worth less than machines and animals.

We were like stones, like weeds in the road.

We were silenced.

We were faceless.

We were nameless.

We had no future.

We did not exist.

Then we went to the mountains to find ourselves and see if we could alleviate our pain in being forgotten stones and weeds.

Here, in the mountains of Southeastern Mexico, our dead live on. Our dead that live in the mountains know many things.

They speak to us of their death, and we hear them.

Coffins speak and tell us another story that comes from yesterday and points toward tomorrow.

The mountains spoke to us, the Macehualob, we common and ordinary people.

We are simple people, like the powerful tell us.

Every day and the following night, the powerful want us to dance the X-tol and repeat their brutal conquest.

The Kaz-Dzul, the false man, rules our lands and has giant war machines that, like the Boob, which is half puma and half horse, spread pain and death among us.

The trickster government sends us the Aluxob, the liars who fool our people and make them forgetful.

This is why we became soldiers.

This is why we remain soldiers.

Because we want no more death and trickery for our people, because we want no more forgetting.

The mountain told us to take up arms so we would have a voice.

It told us to cover our faces so we would have a face.

It told us to forget our names so we could be named.

It told us to protect our past so we would have a future.

In the mountains, the dead live: our dead.

With them live the Votan and the Ik'al, the light and the darkness, the wet and the dry, the earth and the wind, the rain and the fire.

The mountain is the home of the Halach Uinic, the real human, the big chief.

Here we learned and remembered that we are what we are, the real men and women.

We brought forth the war in the year zero, and we began to walk this path that has brought us to your hearts and today brings you to ours.

This is what we are.

The Zapatista National Liberation Army.

The voice that arms itself to be heard.

The face that hides itself to be seen.

The name that hides itself to be named.

The red star that calls out to humanity and the world to be heard, to be seen, to be named.

The tomorrow that is harvested in the past.

Behind our black mask.

Behind our armed voice.

Behind our unnamable name.

Behind what you see of us.

Behind this, we are you.

Behind this, we are the same simple and ordinary men and women that are repeated in all races, painted in all colors, speak in all languages and live in all places.

The same forgotten men and women.

The same excluded.

The same untolerated.

The same persecuted.

The same as you.

Behind this, we are you.

Behind our masks is the face of all excluded women.

Of all the forgotten native people.

Of all the persecuted homosexuals.

Of all the despised youth.

Of all the beaten migrants.

Of all those imprisoned for their words and thoughts.

Of all the humiliated workers.

Of all those dead from neglect.

Of all the simple and ordinary men and women who don't count, who aren't seen, who are nameless, who have no tomorrow. (Marcos, July 27, 1996)

Marcos's speech, and the power it evokes, is something that much social science has difficulty in making sense of: it is an expression of *myth*. Modern rationalizing society has been regarded as doing away with myth, the scientific revolution of the seventeenth century opening out a modernity where *Logos* would replace *Mythos*. This in particular was evident in the types of political organizations that emerged out of Marxism, which saw themselves as an expression of "scientific" socialism, possessing the keys to the laws of history. This conception of science framed the concept of "ideology" that emerged over the twentieth century, one that Guillén was deeply imbued with as a student. Many contemporary approaches to social movements argue that an older paradigm of ideology has been replaced by identity. But in this case, there is something different at work. The Italian sociologist Alberto Melucci (2000: 75) links myth to forms of *action*. Action, he argues, is shaped by an experience of lack or need – something that is both biological and cultural. Hunger, for example, translates into the action of eating, but this in itself is not enough. The issues at stake are more than biological, but social and cultural – leading to the creation of cooking and meals, at the center of social life and interaction. What is critical here, Melucci argues, is the fact that *action will always be inadequate* – there will be a domain of experience beyond our capacity for action, an experience of incompleteness. While ideology promises to fill this absence or gap, myth explores it.

From this point of view, myth is neither an "identity" nor a "characteristic," nor a symbolic system. This is an *event*, a story to be told; it is narrated. "It is a community event that takes shape only through narration, through words that are each time repeated revitalize the presence of the group" (Melucci 2000: 78). This points to the importance of Marcos's storytelling, and to the dreaming we constantly encounter in the Zapatista experience. A place with no name becomes a site for imagination, called Reality. This helps us understand the meaning of the mask. The mask is not a symbol of an identity. Wearers of the mask claim the memory as their own – it is a tool for remembering, and a weapon against forgetting. It extends the action that we saw take place on October 12, 1992, when indigenous men and women destroyed the statue symbolizing their oblivion.

The power of the mask was already evident at the first Aguascalientes in 1994. In the middle of his speech on the first night, Marcos asked participants if they wanted him to remove his mask – the response was a resounding no! *Through the mask, the wearer becomes part of retelling the myth* – the wearer's voice mingles with the voices of the dead, the voices of the mountain, the voices of those without voice. The power of memory is concentrated through places and events. It was at the first Aguascalientes that emerged the slogan "Everything for everyone, nothing for us!" Through wearing the mask the Zapatistas were able to proclaim, "Behind this, we are you." This would have an extraordinary power. We can see this in the events following the February 1995 decision by the Mexican government to recommence armed conflict and inflict a military defeat on the Zapatistas. The beginning of military action was greeted with massive street protests in Mexico City and other major cities. These marches affirmed something more than solidarity with the Zapatista struggle. The slogan that began on the streets of Mexico City, and which would globalize in the years that followed, was *todos somos Marcos* – we are all Marcos.

This is why Marcos has kept wearing his mask, long after his identity has become known. Guillén adopted the name "Marcos" to remember a *companero* who had been killed in the early days of the guerillas. In becoming the person whose identity is denied, the Zapatistas become everyone who has been rendered invisible, everyone who has disappeared when forgetting has triumphed over memory. And for Marcos, this is an experience of personal transformation. When asked by Nobel laureate Gabriel Garcia Marquez, "When everyone knows who you are, why keep wearing the mask?" Marcos's response is powerful: "They don't know who I am, but what is more, that shouldn't matter. What counts is who Subcommandante Marcos is, not who he was" (*Cambio*, March 25, 2001). Guillén had met Old Anthony, and learnt to dream, and in the process, learnt to hear the dreams of others.

Globalizing Zapatismo

The Zapatista action had an extraordinary impact over the decade following the 1994 uprising, in a way that helps us understand key dimensions of the paradigms of action and culture at work in global movements. Several analyses explain this movement's success in terms of the role of professionals of international solidarity. Social scientists linked to the RAND Corporation, argue that the Zapatista insurgency transformed itself into a global "netwar," above all as a result of international NGOs that "swarmed" into Mexico following the uprising, and without whom the insurgency would have remained locked in the Lacandona rainforest, likely to exhaust itself. It is clear that the initial Zapatista appeal for support was defensive. Observers were called upon to make possible negotiation following the failure of the uprising. Government repression involved summary executions of those captured (many being killed by being shot through the neck), and without the role of external observers, it is unlikely that the initial peace negotiations could have taken place. And it is clear the NGOs played an active role, at this point and later. But the RAND scholars assert that the open network structure of these NGOs played a key role in transforming the initial hierarchical structure of the EZLN.

There are problems with such an emphasis on "NGO swarming." The initial international solidarity networks were less the product of organizations than individuals. In a short period after the initial uprising, Internet sites developed to support and relay messages posted on bulletin boards. These developed among existing academic networks, often created by individuals. EZLN.org was created by a Swathmore College student, Justin Paulson. He was interested in the uprising, but was finding it increasingly difficult to get information, so decided to create a site where all the available information could be available. He was not a member of any political or solidarity group, but had created his own homepage in March 1994, and used the same skills to post EZLN declarations to the Internet, also setting up petitions for the release of prisoners. At first the declarations were faxed from *La Journada*, a leftitst newspaper close to the PRD political party, and every morning from January 1995 Paulson would put them into hypertext and post them on his college server. Within two years there were over 60 similar Internet sites where people could get information and get involved in support actions, although only one was physically based in Mexico.

Paulson's experience is more typical than the NGO netwar hypothesis. Studies of the "network architecture" involved in Zapatista action underline the role of individuals more than organizations (Olesen 2004). Following the success of the convention in 1994, "the First Intercontinental Encounter for Humanity and against Neoliberalism" was held in August 1996, this time addressing international networks that the Zapatistas regarded as involved in similar struggles. Participants from some 30 countries attended, the majority coming from the United States. At this *encuentro* we see the continued transformation of the Zapatista struggle. Marcos addressed the gathering of some 5,000 people, asking what would come after. He rejects the idea of creating an organization with positions, job descriptions, and titles, just as he rejects the idea of a world revolution. Instead he calls for an echo, one that will recognize the local and the particular, but reverberate through the intercontinental, an echo that will recognize the other, and not attempt to silence the other (Marcos 1996). In its final declaration, the *encuentro* determined to create an intercontinental network that would focus on resisting neoliberalism, a direction that specifically rejected creating an organization:

> The intercontinental resistance network, recognizing differences and similarities, will search to encounter other resistances throughout the entire world. This intercontinental resistance network will be a medium through which different resistances can support each other. This intercontinental resistance network is not an organized structure, it possesses neither directing nor decision making centre, it has no central command or hierarchy. We are the network, all of us who speak and listen. (Final Declaration 1996)

The 1996 Encountro would have an extraordinary impact on those who participated, like Justin Paulson. After the event he would write:

> Can the Zapatistas really be so inclusive in their discourse and their activities that they might awaken these others' own dreams and struggles? If so, when the latter do become active, if they claim to be supporting Zapatismo, are they avoiding the "struggle at home" in favor of solidarity with an indigenous uprising in Chiapas? Or have they perhaps come to the recognition that it is part of the same struggle? (Paulson 2001)

The power of the cry "we are all Marcos" meant a kind of action beyond supporting a distant struggle. The encounter with the Zapatistas opened a sense of myth, magic, and imagination. A number of radical critics argue that concerns with such "magical realism" detract from a scientific analysis of the class structures generating the Zapatista struggle. But I would argue the opposite, that this struggle touched a deeper place. We can see something of the power of this communication in a posting by a young American:

> Todos somos Marcos! We are all Marcos, pro-visional beings on our way to a vision, full of yearnings, hopes and visions, twisted by the corporate monoculture where greed for profit and for consumer goods fortify the growth mythology. (Batko, posted at http://www.network54.com/Forum/message?forumid=23164&messageid=998758179)

This recalls Roselyn speaking of puppets: "Much more effective than screaming and pushing one's ideas down the viewer's throat is this creation of magic. Imagery and theater reach a much deeper place within the psyche than something violent and forced" (Indymedia, July 9, 2003).

This is not a struggle articulated principally in terms of programs or principles. These are present, but there is a sense that personal subjectivity is at stake.

Echoes and Resonance

The day following the *encuentro*, a small group of North American and European participants met at San Cristobal, and decided to create a network, to be called Red Intercontinental de Comunicacion Alternativa (RICA), or International Alternative Communication Network. This increasingly became understood as a "rhizomatic," centerless network, one that would disseminate news in an unfiltered way. People who had been involved in low-power community radio, with an emphasis on local communities organizing and telling stories, began to converge with international solidarity activists. Over 1997, an increasing consciousness of a Free Media Movement became increasingly evident (Ruggiero and Duncan 1997). In a short space of time, the idea of creating a rhizomatic network had taken on urgent importance. The Intercontinental Encuentro at La Realidad had decided to hold a second *encuentro* the following year in Europe. The group that met the day after in San Cristobal played a key role in setting up this process that took place in August 1997 in Spain. It was through this that new links started to form, linking people involved in Reclaim The Streets with North American alternative media activists. So when computer science students in Sydney, Australia, developed the active code that would allow people to upload images and stories to the Internet in real time, to be used for the RTS Carnival against Capitalism in London in 1998, this flowed through networks to the Seattle mobilization against the World Trade Organization in November 1999, where people who had participated in the 1996 *Encuentro* played critical roles in establishing the Independent Media Center at Seattle.

Other echoes of the Zapatista experience traveled through the network of social centers, or Centri Sociali, that exist in almost all the major cities of Italy, bringing together alternative cultures and networks, from music, cafés, restaurants and bookstores, concerts and debates. These centers involve a break with an older form of Leinisit political culture, so important on the Italian left in the 1970s, that celebrated a "heroic" subjectivity grounded in an ethic of sacrifice. In the culture of the social centers, the experience of the person is more fragile than heroic. The singer with the Italian rap band Pecce, influential in the Social Centers, sings about creating a private space of her own rather than conquering and transforming the world (Wright 2001).

The culture of the Centers is one of networks and hubs rather that organizations and structures, it is one of poetry rather than programs, one where the legacy of ideology that devours the subjectivity of the person is constantly present, and rejected, in the memory of terrorism. One of the most innovative movements in solidarity with the Zapatistas, Ya Basta, emerged out of this context. The Ya Basta activists wore white overalls, first taken up in Milan in 1994 after the Northern League mayor of the city referred to young protestors from the Social Centers as "ghosts." The white overalls were taken up as an ironic response to this jibe (see Farro 2003). Italians were the largest European group at the 1996 *encuentro*, and the theme of the mask and being rendered invisible resonated powerfully with the meaning of the white overalls:

We have always been the invisible in society. The white overalls express the fact that the state ignores us. Look, we say, you do not recognise us but here we are. Many of us are immigrants, unemployed, workers in shit jobs, ecologists and people who work with druggies. But a lot of people are graduates, even teachers and intellectuals. Anyone can choose to put on a white overall. (Annelisa, Genoa Social Center, cited in Vidal 2001)

The action of the Ya Basta focused above all on embodied events and visibility, defensive physical confrontations aiming at solidarity with new excluded social groups such as immigrants or those in insecure employment. But we can see a significant transformation in Ya Basta in the period leading up to the G8 mobilization in Genoa in 2001. The Italian sociologist Paulo Ceri (2002) explores what he regards as a crisis of the social movement present in Ya Basta, evident in the increasing importance of the theme of violence in the discourse of the activists, breaking with the cultural themes that had been so important up to that point. Ceri draws out two dimensions of the response to inequality that we can see in this context, reflecting two understandings of globalization. One understands globalization in vertical terms, as the product of new global structures of power that have to be opposed. The other understands globalization in horizontal terms, as the opportunity for new types of networks and new experiences. Confronted with globalization, Ceri points out that action can take two forms: hostility toward the system, or action of solidarity with the weakest. In Genoa, the themes of rage and anger, evident in claims that global leaders were mass murderers, increasingly came to overshadow new grammars and experiences of solidarity.

This would eventually lead to the collapse of Ya Basta, and to the emergence of its successor, the Disobbiedienti, more and more defined in terms of opposition to an increasingly abstract and violent system of power (a form of practice theorized and articulated by Toni Negri (Hardt and Negri 2000). This form of discourse has less and less reference to culture and experience, defining the world instead as a confrontation between a system of power and the "multitudes" that are its product. But at the same time, a counterdirection has emerged, one that remains strongly linked to the Social Centers. Increasingly this has focused on direct and embodied forms of cooperation, with Italian Ya Basta activists spending the 2004–5 summer in Chiapas, working on clean-water projects, health clinics, and participating in the coffee harvest. This converges with other forms of embodied action, such as the slow-food movement and other forms of practice around growing and consuming food, such as critical wine (www.criticalwine.org). Support for the Zapatista coffee production is part of the attempt to break with the disassociation of body and subjectivity brought about by industrialized food and diet, and is one of the most significant forms of action in the Social Centers today. The search to hear and feel and be embodied has not disappeared into the abstract opposition of empires and multitudes.

NOTE

1   First published in *Questions and Swords: Folktales of the Zapatista Revolution*. Translated by David Romo. El Paso, Tex., Cinco Puntos Press, 2001. Reproduced here with permission of the publisher. Additional material translated by Cecilia Rodriguez, National Commission for Democracy in Mexico USA.

CHAPTER 7

Healing Movements, Embodied Subjects

The changes I can feel are within myself, I can
feel the physical changes inside myself . . . when
you change . . . you are not as easily affected by
the outside world. Maybe in this sense, your relationship with the outside world changes.

**"Jenny," speaking of her experience of
practicing Falun Gong**

Jenny is aged 35. She is on a temporary protection visa in a Western country,
awaiting the results of her application for refugee status. Eighteen months
earlier she had fled China, leaving behind in Beijing a son and a husband. She
is a practitioner of Falun Gong, or Law Wheel Practice, an exercise and meditation regime that emerged in China in 1992, and that was declared an illegal
cult (*xiejiao*) in 1999. Falun Gong emerged out of a broader movement of
body practice, qigong, made up of a wide range of practices combining
breathing, movement, and meditation, the term combining the concepts *qi*
(pronounced "chee"), the vital energy constituting the cosmos, and *gong*,
meaning "practice," "law," or "work." Jenny holds a masters degree in Geo-
chemistry from Beijing's elite Peking University, where she was a student
from 1984 to 1991, and before leaving China she had been employed as an
investment analyst for a major Chinese corporation. On March 25, 1999, she
was a participant in a day-long silent demonstration of some 10,000 Falun
Gong practitioners outside Zhongnanhai, the official residential compound
of senior state and Party officials adjacent to Tiananmen Square in Beijing.
In the weeks following this demonstration Falun Gong was banned and the
practice of its exercises declared illegal. Over the next months Jenny was
detained several times, and in April 2000 assigned to a year in a labor camp.
While imprisoned she was obliged to participate in special education classes,
while also working 10 hours every day assembling soft toys for a European
multinational corporation.

For someone who is not a specialist in China, the emergence and subsequent response to Falun Gong are difficult to understand. Even China scholars disagree among themselves about the nature of this movement. All agree, however, that in some way the Falun Gong points toward critical dimensions of social and cultural change in contemporary China, as that country moves out of the period defined by the revolution of 1949, and embraces key dimensions of an emerging global model of social organization. In a very short period of time, Falun Gong has also taken on critical characteristics of a global movement. Even before it was declared illegal in 1999, its center had shifted from China to the Queens area of New York City, a global center of the Chinese diaspora, while also rapidly developing among Chinese speakers in Europe and Asia. The movement began to extend beyond Chinese speakers as well, as the broader currents of qigong practice became increasingly linked to global cultural movements such as the New Age.

The term "Falun Gong" means the Great Way of the Wheel or the Law Wheel Discipline. The Falun Gong is a cultivation movement, built up around five exercises that were developed and promoted by Li Hongzhi, a former clerk in a government grain corporation, from the city of Changchun, a declining industrial town in the northeast of the country. What would become Falun Gong began in 1992, when Li took unpaid leave and traveled to Beijing, where he presented the five exercises he had developed to a conference of the Qigong Research Association of China, the officially sanctioned organization of qigong practitioners and associations. Li made his presentation to a hall of some 500 people, demonstrating five exercises and explaining the principles involved in what at that time he called "Star qigong." The exercises that Li demonstrated were accompanied by lectures drawing together themes drawn from Buddhism, Taoism, and Confucian thought. By the fourth appearance, no halls were large enough to hold the numbers of people who wanted to hear his lectures (Adams et al. 2000). From May 1992 to September 1994 Li held training seminars in Changchun, Harbin, and Beijing, with estimates suggesting that as many as 200,000 people were involved. During this period Li Hongzhi became one of the most important of the emerging generation of qigong masters. He presented his work at different forums organized through the state-sanctioned China Qigong Scientific Research Society, and was awarded the status of "qigong master of the year" at the Beijing Health Festival of 1993. His work was also taken up by influential members of the Chinese Communist Party as well as prominent leaders of the People's Liberation Army.

Over this period Li articulated a set of beliefs, known as Falun Dafa, developed in a series of best-selling books. In January 1995, *Zhuan Falun*, the main statement of his teachings, was officially published by the Chinese Radio &

Television Broadcasting Press. An indicator of Li's closeness to the Chinese regime is shown by the fact that his book was launched at the auditorium of the Ministry of Public Security (by the mid-1990s it was widely believed that his texts were outselling those of Deng Xiaopeng). Li locates the Falun Gong exercises of breathing and meditation in terms of ancient Chinese culture and traditions, drawing on Buddhism and Daoism. But at the same time his writings and lectures are peppered with postmodern themes that we would associate more with Hollywood popular culture than Chinese tradition: aliens being active on Earth, the prophecies of Nostradamus, while also drawing on Erich Von Daniken's (1970) *Chariots of the Gods*, and its suggestion that human beings are the imperfect descendants of alien beings.

Originally the Falun Gong was closely associated with the state, as were other qigong organizations. By 1995, however, the environment for qigong was changing. The state launched a wide-ranging campaign against "pseudoscience" that led to fines and arrests of a number of famous qigong masters, and by 1996 a cross-department strategy coordinated by the Ministry of Propaganda was setting up systems to ensure state control of qigong. As part of this process, the China Qigong Scientific Research Society terminated the registration of the Falun Gong Research Society (the organizational expression of Falun Gong) in November 1996 – which had the practical effect of making Falun Gong illegal. Following this, the organization sought unsuccessfully to affiliate with the National Minority Commission, and later the China Buddhist Federation.

From 1997 evidence of a changing government perception of Falun Gong began to appear publicly as well, with articles appearing in military and other newspapers that were critical of Falun Gong and its founder. One such critique, contesting the benefits and legitimacy of Falun Gong, was published in the city of Tianjin in March 1999, leading practitioners in that city to protest at the way the movement had been described in the press, and to call for the retraction of the article. Some 40 practitioners were arrested for practicing exercises outside the newspaper offices and displaying banners calling for the retraction of the offending article. It was these arrests that led to the demonstration on March 25, 1999, outside Zhongnanhai. Practitioners arrived at 4:00 a.m. and remained until 10:00 p.m., calling for a meeting with senior government leaders in order to defend the movement and its practice. Toward the end of the day Premier Zhu Rongji accorded an interview to a delegation, following which the practitioners dispersed peacefully.

In the period following this event, government opposition to the movement hardened. In late July, Falun Gong, together with a number of other qigong organizations, was declared illegal, with the Steering Committee of the National People's Congress passing a law for the suppression of heterodox religion, or more broadly, heterodox teaching (*xiejiao*). Meanwhile the Zhongnanhai protest was described in official state media as the "most serious political incident" since the Tiananmen crisis a decade earlier (*Renmin ribao*, August 13, 1999, cited in Tong 2002). Falun Gong was branded an "evil cult." By the end of the year some 35,000 people, according to official figures, had been detained while attempting to protest against the ban, with the first reported deaths in police custody dating from October in the same year. Toward the end of the following year, Amnesty International documented the deaths of some 77 people while in police custody, while the first trials held at the end of 2000 involved sentences ranging from 2 to 12 years imprisonment. The campaign of repression continued – by the middle of the following decade, at least 5,000 practitioners had been sent to labor camps; hundreds of cases of torture had been documented by Amnesty International, which noted also the increasing recourse to psychiatric hospitals to deal with detained practitioners.

Despite the extraordinary resources mobilized by the state, practitioners have continued to defend their practice. Within China, this has taken place through sporadic public displays. This is one of the main reasons for the pervasive presence of uniformed and plainclothes Public Security Bureau officers in Tiananmen Square, in order to act quickly to prevent any public manifestation of Falun Gong practice or the unfurling of banners defending the movement. There have been other more spectacular actions, such as in September 2002 and June 2003 with the hacking and taking control of Sinosat, China's principal television satellite, following the earlier successful hacking into of one of China's main cable television networks, an event that saw 15 people convicted and sentenced to up to 20 years in prison. These media actions are supported by a major Internet presence of Falun Gong websites, which have themselves been hacked by Chinese agencies seeking not only to block but to crash the sites – a clear example of what the RAND corporation calls "netwars."

In the case of Falun Gong, thousands of people have been detained, thousands of police mobilized, and different forms of protest have taken place throughout China, despite continuing and intense repression. But Falun Gong is clearly not an example of a western "social" movement, nor do its modes of organization and action correspond to western models of "civil society." How can we begin to explore what is at stake in this movement? Falun Gong emerged out of what came to be known as the *qigong re* (qigong craze) that developed in China in the 1980s. This is where we need to begin: with the embodied experience present in qigong.

Bodies and Civilizational Grammars

Qigong is a cultivation practice that combines breathing, movement, and meditation techniques, and was one of the most significant cultural movements to develop in China during the 1980s. While reference to the term "qigong" appears in some ancient texts, its current meaning is very much a modern one, the term entering into Chinese language in the context of struggles around Chinese traditional medicine in the 1950s, when medical institutes were established to train healers in qigong (Hsu 1999). This has shaped the way the term is generally translated into English – as "breathing technique" as opposed to the more accurate "self-cultivation practice." Qigong involves putting the "inner world" in order through controlling the rhythm of breathing and activating flows of qi within the body (Schipper 1993: 134).

The French historian of comparative civilizations Thierry Zarcone (2003: 50) underlines the contrast between a western philosophy of the object and Chinese philosophy of breathing. The western relationship to the body, Zarcone observes, is problematic, with the body being understood as embodying evil and sin, and not regarded as a medium for a philosophical or spiritual experience of the world. This lack of interest in the body is very evident in western sociologies of social movements, strongly influenced by Cartesian forms of mind – body opposition, with their emphasis on cognition, beliefs, and interests. Qigong opens out a complex model of embodiment, one that has important implications for the way we think about movements and action – rather than a "social movement," defined as representing a category, it opens us to the question of "healing movements" acting in and experiencing the world through the body.

Joseph Alter (1993) explores the development of a movement based on body practice that developed among wresters in postcolonial India. In the colonial period, these wrestlers lived a life centered on the akhara or gymnasium, a physical and conceptual space made up of the elements of earth, air, water, and trees. Oriented through these natural elements, the wrestler is part of a symbolic system, one emphasizing the power and harmony of their sponsoring prince and the primacy of the fluid body over the rigidity of the colonizing English body. The advent of independence, however, brought on the decline of the princes, with the wrestlers increasingly finding themselves interacting with a corrupt, disarticulated, and inefficient postcolonial state. Rather than sustaining their fluid and powerful bodies, the experience of the postcolonial world produces lethargy, weakness, and an experience where their own embodied selfhood begins to disintegrate, sapped of its efficacy, coherence, and power. In this context Alter explores the development of a movement among wrestlers responding to this postcolonial fragmentation, a movement built through body practice. In attempting to understand this movement, Alter encounters

> a utopia that is envisioned in fundamentally material and somatic terms. There is no philosophy or doctrine, only a poetics of power that is inscribed in earth, water, food, and exercise . . . the wrestlers are confronting the power of the state at its most basic level by making physical fitness a form of political protest and civic reform. (1993: 64–5)

The experience he describes cautions against understanding movements as a never-ending town meeting.

The body is a medium of being in the world. In China this is evident in particular in artistic representations. John Hay (1994) underlines the difference between the Confucian tradition, where the body is represented in terms of social insignia and ritual, and the Taoist body, where the body is understood in terms of concentrations and flows of qi. Hay's argument can be illustrated through two well-known works of art. The first is a depiction of the Qing emperor (see http://www.allempires.com/empires/qing/yongzheng.jpg).

The second is one of the most famous of Taoist works of art, Fan Quon's *Travelers among Mountains and Streams* (see http://images.google.com/imgres?imgurl=http://www.faculty.de.gcsu.edu/~dvess/ids/fap/Rox/16.jpg&imgrefurl=http://www.faculty.de.gcsu.edu/~dvess/ids/fap/taop.htm&h=211&w=300&sz=109&tbnid=gUqCYdWFV70J:&tbnh=78&tbnw=111&start=62&prev=/images%3Fq%3Dtaoism%26start%3D60%26hl%3Den%26lr%3D%26client%3Dsafari%26rls%3Den%26sa%3DN).

In the first case, the emperor's body is almost invisible. We see robes and station, signals of status and place in the social order. In the second, the people traveling are small; they are on a path, dwarfed by the natural world, above all the mountains and streams. The painting works so that the viewer's gaze is carried up from the small people to the macrocosm, evident in the form of the mountain. The Confucian tradition emphasized detailed regulation of social behavior, where each person would have a series of roles (husband, wife, father, son, daughter, teacher, student, etc.), each role possessing detailed duties to perform. The Taoist tradition can be understood in part as a reaction against such detailed regulation, and as interest in cultivation techniques so that the practitioner or adept can achieve an elevated status through a transcendent access to a tao or path, something that is inaccessible to those who have not undertaken such cultivation.

These two traditions involve ways of being in the world *through* the body illustrated in the paintings described above. Jian Xu writes:

through the clothes and ornaments it wears and its performance in rituals, the Confucian body bears certain semiotic insignia. A body's ritual actions and its movement through social ceremonies are significations that express subject positions. These signs are accordingly capable of either stabilizing hierarchical order or bringing about changed configurations of social relations. Constantly engaged in social activities, the Confucian body is very much a public body. The Taoist body, on the other hand, is one with nature, a microcosm of the universe in which one can find all the resources of that universe. Therefore that body is understood by Taoists to enfold the means of human liberation and perfection. To discover those means is to use techniques of bodily cultivation that tap into corporeal vital energy and to combine the latter with cosmic energy, since both originate from qi . . . The cultivation of the Taoist body is a private matter; it is performed by individuals in seclusion and solitude. (Xu 1999: 969)

The body of the emperor is hidden behind the social markers that adorn the surface. The bodies of the travelers are eclipsed by large mountains and rocks, understood as concentrators of qi, the vitality of the universe, which are more important than the surface of closed bodies. Hay notes that the importance of both these traditions helps us understand the absence of nude representations in Chinese art. These works of art alert us to civilizational dimensions of ways of being in the world. Above all they underline the importance of the concept of *cultivation* as a form of action. Eisenstadt (1999) emphasizes the contrast between the monotheistic civilizations – Christian, Jewish, and Islamic – all possessing strong tendencies toward the reconstruction of political and social orders, and the Confucian civilization, equally oriented toward a reconstruction of this-world, but rather than through a program of reconstruction via the political system, through a "strong emphasis on individual responsibility and on the moral cultivation of the individual" (1999: 52). While the Confucian understanding of cultivation emphasizes social context, the Taoist understanding, as Hay underlines, focuses on bodily cultivation to tap corporeal energy, and through this to combine with cosmic energy. The Confucian body is a social body, where social location is constituted through public ritual. In the case of Taoism, access to cosmic forces is obtained through going inward, into the body, where the Taoist body is "an interior body projected outward" (Xu 1999: 969). Both the Confucian and Taoist practices search for balance and coherence; they seek to ensure that the organizing principles of the mundane world conform to the principles of the cosmic world, the dynamic that Eisenstadt places at the center of civilizations. At the same time, these two modes of embodied experience underline the tensions within civilizations, and the impossibility of positing reified, holistic conceptions of tradition (Dirlik

2003). Indeed tensions between these forms of embodiment constitute a critical site of conflict around Chinese experiences of modernity.

Eisenstadt locates movements within China in the context of a Confucian "this-worldly" orientation. He contrasts this with movements that emerged within Hinduism, and the Buddhism that emerged from it. Such movements were other-worldly, comprising both a "renunciation of the mundane world and an emphasis on the reconstruction of the inner experience of the believer" (1999: 16). Such movements, however, had far-reaching impacts, not only on the religious sphere, but on wider institutional frameworks, including the organization of political and economic life, while not, however, oriented to the reconstruction of political centers. Eisenstadt underlines the difference with movements to emerge in the Confucian tradition, characterized by a strong "this-worldy" orientation, in particular looking to the state and political order to implement utopian visions. Eisenstadt links this to the fact that the principal carrier of Confucian themes was the literati, which was the social group from which intellectual, cultural, and political elites in China emerged. As a result, a potential intellectual and political movement of critique of the political order was located in the social group that in fact staffed the order. Hence in China there did not develop the clear separation between church and state, nor did this develop into religious revolutions as occurred within Europe. The Confucian tradition did, however, place a strong emphasis on individual responsibility and moral cultivation of the individual, and as Eisenstadt argues, these could become connected with strong other-worldly tendencies, at the private level. While the Confucian tradition emphasizes political authority is to be used to bring about harmony of the taos, the Taoist tradition emphasizes three different types of paths: the human (or social), the natural tao, and the great tao. The Taoist tradition involves distance from the Confucian primacy of roles and duties, while the idea of cultivation involves nonlinguistic forms of access to knowledge, early forms of Taoist practice involving breathing, fasting, hallucinogenic drugs, and, possibly, meditation (Hansen 2003) – ways of knowing opposed to the cognitive and linguistic.

Bodies and Revolution

During the 1950s a number of traditional practices of body cultivation became linked and given the official descriptor of "qigong" in the context of wider debates about the scientific status of traditional Chinese medicine. This official recognition emphasized the scientific basis and measurable physical benefits that resulted from traditional Chinese practices, and in the process redefined these as *health* practices, which thus became an end in themselves, disconnected from the wider goal of cultivation. But soon these body practices would be caught up in wider changes affecting the place of the body in post-Revolutionary China.

In his earliest writings, Mao had attached great importance to the health and vigor of the body, regarding the image of weak, emaciated bodies associated with the "sick man of Asia" as a symbol of China's decline (Xu 1999). Constructing a new body was a central objective of the regime that took power in 1949. The celebration of the vigorous and active body is a recurring theme in Mao's writings, with Mao launching the Cultural Revolution by swimming the Yangtze River. The Maoist body was a mass body, one constituted increasingly through joint exercise in public, with the state setting out to construct a body that could serve socialism, above all through labor and military service (Brownell 1995: 58). Mao deeply distrusted any attempt to withdraw from this construction, regarding this as a feudal or elitist attempt to reject the active, vigorous mass body being constructed through socialism. In Mao's China, as Xu (1999: 971) argues, individual, private bodies effectively disappeared, where under Mao's "somatic nationalism" body cultivation came to be an instrument of formation of the nation, where the private cultivation of the Taoist tradition became absorbed into ritual and public practices of exercise aiming at forming the mass body, where the subject disappears into the whole.

This attempt to obliterate the private space and experience radicalized in the Cultural Revolution, a period lasting from 1966 to 1976, involving violent and unpredictable trauma for tens of millions of Chinese. Families were broken up, millions experienced internal deportation, lifelong employment was lost. Techniques of criticism were imported from the Soviet Union and meant that individuals could be subject to brutal and sustained critique, leading to violence, corporal punishment, or torture administered by families and work colleagues, while they could equally be expected to be part of administering such criticism. Almost no one was free from the possibility that his or her world could be torn down. The Chinese sociologist Tu Wei-ming describes the experience as an "ideological holocaust," one that broke down not only forms of social organization, but the capacity to constitute interpersonal relationships: the destruction wrought by the Cultural Revolution even reached the forms of civility evident in polite expressions such as "good morning," "excuse me," or "thank you," which had to be relearnt in the period following (Wei-ming 1997).

This was a period of exemplars that were held up to the population to emulate. The anthropologist Judith Farquhar (1996) explores the case of Lei Feng, a member of the People's Liberation Army, who was born in 1940 and suffered an accidental death in 1962. The year after his death, Lei Feng was taken up as an exemplary figure by Mao. Lei was celebrated as the archetype of the selfless workers, who, during a bus trip for example, would clean the bus, read newspapers aloud to those unable to read, hold political discussions on Mao's thought, and look after children. Lei, so the story goes, had mastered Mao's work by heart, and always surpassed production quotas. He became a symbol of the collective personhood imagined by the Chinese state, the socialist everyman (Farquhar 1996) projected as a model of emulation, celebrated in books, posters, and films. Lei's objective was to be a "cog in the machine of socialism." After his death, he was turned into an exemplar of what we can call "selfless commitment." As an exemplar of virtue, as Farquhar notes, Lei did not possess a biography. Not only did he die young (an exemplar of sacrifice), but he did not marry or have children, particularly powerful markers within Chinese culture. Lei is literally selfless. Today, he has returned, this time in cyberspace, where it is possible to explore his life, now integrated into a commercial culture where "to get rich is glorious" (www.leifeng.org.cn).

The Cultural Revolution set about hunting out and destroying tradition, and during the Revolution qigong was declared a superstition (*mixin*) and its practice banned. But the period following witnessed an explosion in qigong practice, with the number of practitioners certainly reaching some 50 million by the mid-1980s. Jian Xu (1999) argues that the tensions that emerged in relation to qigong during this period are a key to understanding Chinese culture and society, not only in the period following the Cultural Revolution, and that the current conflict around Falun Gong indicates the continued importance of these tensions.

How Bodies Remember

Immediately after the Cultural Revolution followed a period of opening, characterized by an outpouring of grief and criticism, to the point that this seemed to be developing into a movement reclaiming democracy. In 1979, the Chinese government acted to close off this emerging movement, silencing the memory of the traumatic events of the Cultural Revolution through constructing an "authorized version," which apportioned blame for what amounted to a decade of trauma to the "Gang of Four." As the medical anthropologists Kleinman and Kleinman argue, this action effectively closed off the possibility of political expressions not only of critique, but grief as well. They note this political closure was soon followed by a cultural closure as well. The years immediately following the Cultural Revolution and Mao's death in 1976 had seen an explosion of literature exploring themes of trauma, as well as plays about ghosts who had returned to claim debts – cultural expressions that were closed down from late 1978.

It was in this period that Kleinman and Kleinman began a large study of illness in China, where they encountered a widespread incidence of particular forms of illness and suffering, in particular dizziness (or vertigo), exhaustion, and pain. They argue that the widespread incidence of these forms of suffering was not an accident, but needs to be understood in the context of the trauma occasioned by the Cultural Revolution. Dizziness, they argue, possesses a particular importance in Chinese society: it is an expression of loss of the balance and harmony that is constitutive of health. Dizziness also takes the form of vertigo, an experience of or fear of falling. The Cultural Revolution was a time of a loss of legitimacy of key institutions in Chinese society, a time where no one could feel safe in core institutions such as the communal work units, production brigades, Confucian morality, and even the family. Kleinman and Kleinman argue (1994) that the experience of living in what amounted to a broken moral order was for many people literally dizzying, one where the widespread incidence of dizziness represents the "embodiment of alienation," where the pervasive experience of, or the uncontrolled fear of falling was an expression of the unpredictable rises and falls that one could experience in the context of the cultural revolution. The importance of dizziness is equally underlined by more recent studies of illness in China, in the context of the demands of a rapidly modernizing society, associated with the experience of falling behind one's peers at work, of coping with new demands being placed upon women, or dealing with the increasing pressures of economic competition. In this context, Park and Hinton (2002) link dizziness to experiences of discord in interpersonal, work, or societal conditions, where external turmoil is experienced as internal disequilibrium (2002: 231). For these authors as well, dizziness is a "paradigmatic symptom" in China:

> Dizziness, a common though usually unmarked symptom of neurasthenia and other chronic fatigue syndromes in the West, carries particular salience in Chinese society, where the Chinese medical tradition emphasizes balance and harmony as constitutive and expressive of health. To be dizzy (or vitiliginous: Chinese patients do not make a distinction between the two) is to be unbalanced, to experience malaise, to be dis-eased. Dizziness was understood by our informants to be the embodiment of alienation, the felt meaning of deligitimation in their local worlds. The broken moral order of local worlds was quite literally dizzying. To experience dizziness was to live and relive the memory of trauma. (Kleinman and Kleinman 1994: 175)

Kleinman and Kleinman point to two other paradigmatic symptoms, exhaustion and pain. The widespread incidence of exhaustion and associated paralyzing weakness in the period following the Cultural Revolution, they argue, pointed to the exhaustion of vital resources, to a draining of personal and collective efficacy that was the result of endless hours of meetings spent criticizing. In traditional Chinese medical theory such experiences of loss of energy or vitality express a loss or blockage in the flow of vital energy or qi. This experience of devitalization affects not only the body – self relationship but also the ability to constitute relationship with others (*guanxi wang*). The forms of *pain* that Kleinman and Kleinman encountered in their research were typically experiences of headache, backpain, and cramp, experiences that they interpret as experiences of compression and pressure.

For Kleinman and Kleinman, these patterns of pain and physical distress are a form of social memory, one that is lived through embodied experience. In developing this argument, they draw on the work of Paul Connerton, who explores the ways that societies remember. Connerton points to three critical ways that social memory is transmitted: firstly, through inscriptions and cultural texts, such as great books or monuments; secondly, through commemorative rituals that make sense of the past as a "collective autobiography" (1989: 70); and finally, through forms of bodily practice. In developing this argument, Connerton explores the way that forms of sociality and culture are inscribed and transmitted in forms of embodiment. For example, the social roles of men and women are inscribed in the ways that men and women may sit, or walk, or in their use of touch or gesture. Power and rank are expressed in posture, such that often when we look at a group of people talking we can detect who possesses or does not possess authority by the way space is occupied (1989: 73). Thus Kleinman and Kleinman insist that we cannot explore social life in terms of a dichotomy of individual and collective. On the contrary, they argue that we need to explore social life in terms of a category of "experience," one that they define as "an assemblage of social processes that together create a medium of interaction that flows back and forth through the social spaces of institutions and the body-self" (Kelinman and Kleinman 1994: 712). From this point of view, "the great question of how to relate the body and society is also a question about the borderland between subjectivity and the symbolic order, agency and social control, experience and representation" (1994: 708). Kleinman and Kleinman are not simply arguing that social transformation or disorientation are transferred into the body. Symptoms of social suffering, they argue, are the

cultural forms of lived experience. They are lived memories. They bridge social institutions and the body-self as the trans-personal moral-somatic medium of local worlds. . . . bodies transformed by political processes not only represent those processes, they experience them as the lived memory of transformed worlds. (1994: 716)

The German anthropologist Thomas Ots explores the development of qigong as a mass cultural movement in the wake of the repression of 1979. Ots underlines the dimensions of *craze* and *fever*, both terms frequently used in China at the time to describe the extraordinary scenes associated with its development. Ots suggests that qigong needs to be understood as a form of experience of an emotional self (1994: 130), in a context where the body has been silenced. He quotes a practitioner:

I felt a stream of qi leaving the earth, lift me upwards and then turn me around in different directions. I had trained for three days, thus I felt self-assured and did not go against it. Suddenly, a force pushed me back. I stumbled forward and fell down on my knees. Now I became frightened. I wanted to finish the session, but before I could get up, another explosion of energy just whirled me around and around. Again and again, I tried to stop, but I just didn't succeed. Then, for the first time in all those years, I became aware of my sadness and shock. I started crying. What a relief. (Ots, 1994: 127)

This is a story of the body as a medium, of an encounter with embodied memory, of an experience where the body is a path to the self. Qigong involves learning to "breath" in a new way – not simply through the lungs, but through other organs as well, in a way that allows the human subject to experience the flow and power of qi. As Canguilhem argues, "respiratory rhythm is a function of our awareness of being in the world" (1989: 168); it plays a constitutive role in the "generation and experience of emotion in the social context" (Lyon 1994: 84; both cited in Chen 2003a: 8–9). Nancy Chen (1995) points to a crucial dimension of the development of qigong when she underlines the public nature of the practice. Qigong exercises involve relaxation practices, where a series of points along the body literally breathe the qi that constitutes the world. In the process, the body becomes a "tool of perception" (Chen 1995: 358) that not only experiences the world, but also creates private spaces in a social setting. Through qigong, the practitioner gets in touch with his or her own body, and

through these traditional points of energy links the body to a universe outside the immediate urban surroundings of the Chinese state . . . the self is rewritten as a personal being apart from, or disembodied from, the state. The linkages of the mind-body to a different source of power, that of a cosmological order, transgress familiar boundaries of the state. (Chen 1995: 358)

Qigong re and the emergence of Falun Gong

Falun Gong emerged out of the "Qigong fever" or "Qigong re" that began in the period immediately following the suppression of the nascent 1979 democracy movement that had emerged as a critique of the Cultural Revolution, with parks becoming full of people practicing many different forms of Qigong (Ots 1994). "Qigong masters" emerged, filling football stadiums with crowds who wanted to learn Qigong techniques, as well as to see evidence of spectacular events, if not miracles. During the late 1980s estimates suggested that there were some 60 million qigong practitioners in China – a symbolically important number, approximating the number of members of the Chinese Communist Party, with observers suggesting that the power of qigong was coming to rival that of the Party itself. During this decade qigong formed the basis of the most extensive network of popular associations and organizations in China not directly controlled by the state (Palmer 2003: 472), "possibly the greatest mass movement in modern China outside the direct control of the government" (Xiaoyang and Penny 1994).

The period following the Cultural Revolution and the suppression of the democracy movement that followed it was marked by a search in many areas of social and cultural life to reconnect with Chinese identity and culture, a movement both encouraged and steered by the Communist Party. Deng Xiaopeng warned against "foreign contamination," referring to foreign ideas as "flies" that had to be kept out. This nativist orientation was a reaction to the destruction of Chinese culture and tradition that had occurred during the Cultural Revolution. The increasing importance of the qigong movement, as well as other cultural movements that developed during this period, represented the possibility of a potential loss of state control of the process, leading to an increasing concern to regulate a wide range of practices from the arts to qigong.

During this first period, the structure of Falun Gong as an organization mirrored that of the Chinese Communist Party, largely reflecting the requirements of registration at various levels, from provinces to Beijing. This took the form of a hierarchical structure with a relatively clear and centralized command structure, made up of "main stations," "guidance stations," and practice sites, corresponding to the vertical structure of provincial, regional, and local government. And just like the Chinese state, the Beijing or central station often found it difficult to exercise effective control over the substructure of the hierarchy, via three functional committees for doctrine and method, logistics and operations, and propaganda. These committees were responsible for dissemination of what developed as doctrine, identifying followers with special abilities, organizing research on the human body, and monitoring training, education, and practice at the different levels.

Despite this impression of hierarchical integration, James Tong's (2002) detailed study of the structure of Falun Gong identifies a rather loose structure even during this first period when Falun Gong was officially registered. The organization had no system of compulsory fee payment, no institutionalized means of separating members from nonmembers, no rituals of initiation nor expulsion (Tong 2002). Nonetheless, over this first period when it was legally registered, the Falun gong developed significant organizational capacity to service the needs of the rapidly growing numbers of practitioners. In the province of Wuhan, for example, it sold some 4.3 million copies of books and over 680,000 video products (Tong 2002), requiring a degree of organization similar to that of a medium-sized publisher. Over the period of 1992 to 1995, the Falun Gong moved from a local to a national movement, while in late 1994 Li notified the China Qigong Research Society that he was disengaging from training programs, to devote himself to the study of Buddhism, and to writing the texts that would play such a critical role in the expansion of the movement.

Once it was no longer registered, the organization had no choice from 1997 but to divest itself of its offices, national administrative system, and command. However, the numbers of people practicing Falun Gong were still rapidly increasing, and so emphasis was placed on informal communications, via telephone and pager at first, followed by the Internet. Tong describes the new pattern:

> The top leadership of the Falun Gong was reduced to a board of directors without corporate divisions, a Papacy without the Roman Curia, a Politburo Standing Committee without the Party Secretariat and State Council. Central administration became minimal, its command and control functions inactive, two-way communications became scarce, while local units gained increasing doctrinal, policy and operational autonomy. (2002: 660)

As Patricia Thornton (2002) observes, many qigong masters who emerged over the 1980s and 1990s linked the perceived health problems of their followers to social problems, and this is readily understood within a cultural matrix that looks upon the body as a microcosm of the universe, understood in terms of balance and flows, as opposed to the mechanical and bounded conception of the body within classical western culture. Thornton (2002) argues that Falun Gong texts are particularly explicit in this regard, offering "a diagnosis of the Chinese body politic that assigns moral responsibility for somatized social ills to the party-state, then prescribing a course of treatment which implicitly pits the individual practitioner against the moral foundations of the regime" (2002: 674). Chronic health problems and illnesses such as depression, exhaustion, and loss of balance are interpreted as expressions of a world out of balance. The increasing inequalities being generated over the 1990s in Chinese society are explicitly addressed, Li arguing that intensified competition leads to "emotional wounds," leaving people "bitter, tired and mentally unbalanced," unable to sleep, and vulnerable to all kinds of illnesses (Li Hongzhi 1999: 128–30).

The core of Li Hongzhi's writings are the imperatives of truth, kindness, forbearance (Zhen, Shan, Ren). And while Li does not explicitly challenge the role of the Chinese Communist Party, his writings clearly contest the type of claim to power that it makes:

> The characteristic of Zhen-Shan-Ren is the criterion of the universe that determines the good from the bad ... As a practitioner, one must follow this characteristic of the universe to conduct himself instead of the standard of ordinary people. (Li Hongzhi 1999)

It is the "criterion of the universe" to which Li claims access, and which his followers can access through a regime of exercise and meditation, rather than the guidance of the Communist Party, that offers a basis for the conduct of life.

Fantasy, Desire, and Healing

Important analyses like Thornton's understand qigong as constituting a domain of experience that the state does not control. This is clearly a key dimension, but understanding qigong primarily as a form of action directed against the state largely reflects a framework that locates movements within a state-society lens. It seems to me that this model of somatic or corporeal resistance to the state neglects a key dimension of qigong, one that is particularly pronounced in the practice of Falun Gong: mysticism and magic.

We began this chapter with the story of "Jenny," whom I interviewed not long after her year in a labor camp. She participated in the student demonstrations of 1989, going to Tiananmen Square on most days of the movement, but because of a family responsibility was not present on the day the tanks invaded. She was able to get out of Beijing, and returned to recommence her studies when the universities reopened. But when telling her story leading up to her practice of Falun Gong, she makes no direct mention of the violent deaths of friends at the square. Her story of what was happening in that period is not one of the rise and destruction of the democracy movement, but of her search for esoteric forms of knowledge. She speaks of the excitement she experienced as a member of a postgraduate course exploring supernormal abilities, of the case of a boy in a remote province who can read through his ears (when paper with writing is put next to his ears, he can hear the writing). Such developments reinforce her idea of science, but at the same time point to its limits: "after that university course I believed that supernormal abilities exist, but science does not have the ability to explain them." Jenny began to explore Chinese mystical writings, in particular the Yijing (Book of Changes), reaching the point where she decided that she herself had paranormal powers: "I reached the point where I could predict quite precisely certain forms of events. I predicted, for example, that I would have a very difficult birth." The subsequent birth of her child was followed by a life threatening accident. Eventually she recovered, but describes an experience of being blocked:

> After that I was totally lost. I thought to myself, even if I can predict everything, I could not change anything. What's the use of study? So I just forgot about all this. I just struggled with my own health problems. I lost my ability to work for four years.

Jenny goes on to recount how a family member began practicing Falun Gong exercises in 1997, and how this family member had given her the books of Li Hongzhi. "I read them all twice, and then suddenly all my previous searchings had answers. In these books! So for me it was quite natural. I began practicing."

In classical Taoist thought cultivation practices were a path to immortality and to the gods. In contemporary China, such exercises are not simply a form of health practice or exercise regime. For many practitioners the occult is at their center, above all in the case of Falun Gong. In the books Jenny refers to, Li Hongzhi describes the presence of aliens and higher beings (of which he is one) on earth, he writes that evidence has been found of a nuclear reactor in Africa 2 billion years ago, which functioned for 500,000 years, demonstrating the earlier presence of such beings. In interviews Li claims the power to levitate, and suggests many other masters have similar powers, offering as an example the entertainer David Copperfield.

The importance of mysticism and the occult, above all evident in Falun Gong, underlines the extent to which qigong involves the construction of a fantasy space (Xu 1999). For many social scientists, the growth of qigong and popular interest in magic and the supernatural represents a reassertion of folk religion and superstition, and can be regarded as expressions of irrationality and social strain in the context of rapid social change. But we need to be careful of such functionalist accounts. The break with the politicized, mass body took the form of a recentering on the individual, personal body, evident in cultural movements that developed in the period after the Cultural Revolution, such as the "literature of the wounded," while mystical themes were closely associated with the language of protest, evident in the ghost plays that also developed at the same time. The intense debates in China over the 1980s saw a process where qigong was seen to point to the limits of modern science and to the type of modernizing rationality incarnated by the Chinese state. Qigong, as Xu argues, represented a fantasy, offering the possibility of cure beyond the limits of science. While offering people tools for cultivation and individuation, qigong escaped from the control of the state. In this context,

> qigong has been elevated from a medical device to the position of a special, high-powered technology of the self, situated between science and mysticism. The enigma, the magic spell, the irrational nature of qigong rather than its scientific truth have made qigong practice popular; the two corollary beliefs, that it cures where medicine fails, and that through qigong training humans have a way to improve themselves morally and biologically, conspire to produce another potent cultural identity founded on the vacuum of a "lost tradition." For the many who practice qigong because qigong fulfills their fantasy and whose belief in qigong constitutes who they are, to expose magic tricks will not make much sense. (Xu 1999: 985)

Subjectivity, Healing, Magic

Qigong and its development as Falun Gong have developed in China in the context of an explosion of healing movements and practices. One explanation for this explosion is to offer a functionalist account; namely, these movements have emerged in the context of market-led reforms in China, which have gradually dismantled its public health system. Hence the development of healing movements is a product of the end of public healthcare, in particular free hospital care, and can be understood as instrumental equivalents to the forms of healthcare being removed as a result of market reforms. But there are very significant problems with this argument. The qigong craze developed in the early 1980s, well before the dismantling of the public health system began. But more importantly, at stake is a profound transformation in the meaning of healing, which is not simply a search for a functional equivalent to the Maoist public health system.

Judith Farquhar (1996) attempts to explore this shift by contrasting two modes of healing that she conceptualizes in terms of *representation* and *embodiment.* She sees the mode of healing she describes in terms of representation evident in the figure of Lei Feng whom we discussed above, the socialist everyman serving as a powerful model of absorption into the collective person. Farquhar underlines the importance of this "selfless" mode of subjectivity, where Lei Feng is disembodied, a representation of a collective personhood imagined by the Chinese socialist state. She contrasts this with modes of healing emerging in contemporary China where she explores two examples. In the first case, Dr Wang, a woman doctor who heals through touch, using pressure to unblock flows of qi in the body of her patients; in the second, Dr Yang, a male doctor who uses divination, relying on the Book of Changes and information about the birth time of his patients to understand the cause of symptoms such as dizziness or insomnia. Both these are examples of a wide movement in contemporary China that is embracing traditional forms of healing. But rather than suggest that these simply reflect the closure of public hospitals, Farquhar underlines the ways that these forms of healing reject generalizing or collective explanations, intensifying instead the particular and the contingent, either through the unique experience of touch between a patient and healer, or through the unique configuration of each person's birth. What is at stake here, argues Farquhar, are forms of healing that involve a particular form of efficacy, involving what the Chinese call *ling* or *linghuo*, everyday words that translate as "magic" or "efficacy" (1996: 246). This term captures the skill, sensitivity, and responsiveness of a doctor that are built up over years of practice. The socialist everyman model of health involved interchangeable doctors providing services on behalf of the state – *ling* is excluded. In the emerging forms of healing Farquhar explores, *ling* is central: "*ling* accumulates at the site of an embodied personage. Its presence and expansion at a particular site is manifested in the flow of good fortune to that site" (1996: 246).

Farquhar focuses on the increasing significance of such magic or *ling* to healing practices in rural China. Rather than argue that the importance of *ling* results from the increasing difficulty in accessing medical services in contemporary China, she argues that such magic involves *ways of knowing and acting.* These persuade in part because they were so vigorously rejected by a now discredited regime, but also because their "effectiveness, their magic, reconnects ordinary people to natural sources of power" (1996: 252). What is happening here, she insists, is an experience of individuation, or "individualism under construction." But it is not, she insists, leading to the kind of individualization that we are familiar with in western terms, manifest in the "bourgeois imaginary's discreet and bounded "classical" body (Stallybrass and White 1986), bearer of a unique and unchanging biography, rational calculator of the optimum means to self-interested ends" (Farquhar 1996: 251). Instead, she argues, these healing practices, one based on touch and the response to touch, the other based on locating a sufferer in a unique position in space and time, lead to what she proposes thinking of as "intensified personhood" for both healers and patients.

Embodiment, Agency, and Movement

While original forms of Taoist self-cultivation were undertaken in private, the qigong movement that emerged in China over the 1980s took the form of exercise in public, a legacy of the Maoist exercise regime. And while Falun Gong involves one of the most developed references to the esoteric among these qigong practices, many forms of its action mirror Maoist experience. There are obvious parallels between Li Hongzhi, the Teacher, and Mao Zedong, the Helmsman: these are clearly evident in the visual representations of Li that mirror those of Mao (looking out over the mountains, benevolently regarding their followers, etc.) (Penny 2002). Mao claimed supernormal powers, as does Li. As mentioned earlier, the original structure of Falun Gong mirrored that of the Chinese Communist Party. When Falun Gong activists hacked into the television systems in 2002 and 2003, their message was "Falun Gong is good," a mirrored response to the regime's affirmation that Falun Gong is bad. Actions in Tiananmen Square have tended to mirror the presence of the state: in February 2000, protestors attempted to unfurl a Falun Gong flag next to China's national flagpole at the entry to the square, while others attempted to hang a giant portrait of Li Hongzhi over the giant portrait of Mao that overlooks the square (Perry 2001). There is no critical debate or interpretation of Li's writings; rather these are discussed in order for followers to grasp more deeply the meanings involved, just as Mao's writings were studied rather than explored and critiqued. There is a clear continuity between Mao as a higher being, and the powers claimed by Li Hongzhi. As Perry (2001 argues), in the period following the brutal repression of Falun Gong, a mimetic relationship developed between the Chinese Communist Party and Falun Gong. The Party declared Falun Gong to be heterodox as opposed to itself as orthodox, implicitly defining Falun Gong as a rival. There is a parallel to the emergence of trade unions, which in many ways embraced key dimensions of the industrial order that they were contesting, such as hierarchy and bureaucracy. But within the trade unions we also encounter a movement, one grounded in forms of solidarity and an ethic based on work. Despite its sectlike characteristics, which have accentuated in the period following its repression, is there some sort of movement present within Falun Gong?

The understanding of agency that has been most influential in theories of social movement emphasizes intentionality, increasing self-control and autonomy, and movement toward freedom (Asad 2003). The body from this perspective is either irrelevant, or something that has to be overcome, as Zarcone argues. But in the experiences we have been exploring, access to the world, to the other, to the self, and to memory, are achieved through the body. The model of "social movement," where the social is understood in terms of the "politics of large numbers," is arguably of little use to make sense of the forms of movement we have been exploring in this chapter. What we have been exploring is better understood as a "healing movement" full of tensions and contradictions. We need to recognize that there is a form of communicative embodiment here. Jenny recounts:

> When you practice, the energy inside yourself and outside, all around you, changes. And when more people practice together, their energy fields work together, so the whole energy field is stronger . . . I was once practicing with thousands of people, and you can feel the energy around you.

The aim of cultivation is not only to change the experience of embodiment in the flow of qi, but to develop the moral qualities of the person. Li Hongzhi's writings develop the Buddhist concept of kharma, which he understands as a form of black negative substance in the universe and within the body. For Li, the aim of the exercises is not only to become aware of qi, but also to physically expel this kharma from the body – the experience of pain that a practitioner feels, in particular in the early stages of exercising when holding a position for a period of time is difficult, is interpreted in terms of physically expelling such kharma. Living badly serves as a kind of attractor that draws this karma to the body, while living according to principles that Li develops in his writings, focused on Zhen, Shan, Ren (truthfulness, compassion, and forbearance), means that a practitioner or a cultivator will assimilate the nature of the universe, and progress toward the stage of becoming an enlightened being, or Buddha.

There is little ritual present in Falun Gong. Arguably this reflects the extent to which China over the twentieth century was deritualized by a series of governments fearful of symbolic systems they do not control. The temples in China were closed under the Qing regime in 1900, a decision that the Communist regime continued. Falun Gong does not have rites of initiation or rites of progression from one "stage" of cultivation to another. The basis of Falun Gong is practice. It has no temples, as we would expect in the Chinese context, instead exercises take place in public – reflecting the Maoist legacy. Nor is there in any sense a "liturgy" understood as reenacting or representing symbolic content. As Burgdoff (2003) underlines, what is important about Falun Gong exercises is what they accomplish; namely the elimination of karma from the body and accessing cosmic flows of qi. Falun Gong is a form of orthopraxis, not orthodoxy. As such, Falun Gong involves a form of embodied action that is performative – it aims at expelling karma; it is not concerned with the symbolic expression of belief (Burgdoff 2003: 341). Hence while Li's writings are discussed, Burgdoff rightly cautions against the idea that people "believe" in them, as if belief consisted of an inner state of thought that directs action (on the emergence and limits of this conception of "belief," and the problems associated with privileging orthodoxy over orthopraxis, see Asad 2003). This above all is the case within the Taoist tradition, where body practice that can be understood as "tuning" the body so that it can perform the "music of heaven" (see Schipper 1993, esp. ch. 10). Within this tradition, inner truth can only be accessed through the body rather than as a collection of intellectual propositions or creeds (Giradot 1983).

Globalizing Qigong

The globalization of Falun Gong has occurred simultaneously along different "scapes" (Appadurai 1996) or experience flows. Three are of particular importance: the ethnoscapes consisting of flows of people; the ideascapes, in particular the domains of New Age healing and new religious movements; and technoscapes, above all the Internet.

The practice of Falun Gong began to spread beyond the borders of China before the repression began, extending the model already developed within China itself, with Li Hongzhi traveling, giving talks and demonstrating his techniques to audiences consisting of Chinese diasporic networks in Europe, North America, and Australia. Li, as other qigong masters, can be seen as an entrepreneur, traveling to talk up his product. Subject to increasing scrutiny from the mid-1990s, prominent qigong masters relocated out of Beijing, either to the provinces or overseas. As Chen agues, the entrepreneurial logic driving these groups pushed for expansion. Li had thus relocated to New York by 1997, two years before the repression directed against Falun Gong.

The Chinese diaspora have played a critical role in the development of Falun Gong. New York is one of the major concentrations of Chinese population in North America, and Ma's (1999) study of Chinese communities in the United States underlines the importance of traditional understandings of health and illness, in particular a sense that Western medicine focuses on symptoms (and is efficacious in the treatment of acute disease), while Chinese traditional medicine is more efficacious as a way of understanding and responding to chronic health problems. Disease and its cure, as ways of knowing, acting, and being in the world, have been at the center of Taoism since its codification in the third century (Strickmann 2002), and as a result health practices and cultures are critical markers of Chinese cultural identity, where health is not a question of repairing the body/machine, but a way of being in the world. When Li Hongzhi arrived in New York he thus entered a community strongly shaped by what Ma (1999) calls a "culture of health" as a marker of Chineseness.

Health is one of the most obvious areas where globalization is not leading to homogenization, but to new forms of hybridization, evident in the critique of biomedicine, and the increasing use of practices such as acupuncture and qigong in cancer treatments, to the point where Frank and Stollberg (2004) argue that we are witnessing a "globalization of Asian medicine." This not only reflects an increasing awareness of the limits of the biomedical model, but a changing relationship between patient, illness, and physician in the west as well: rather than treating the disease as a category (with the patient effectively reduced to the role of observer), there is increasing recourse to personalizing treatments. Hence, while Falun Gong was being attacked in China as feudal and obscurantist, important cultural movements within Western medicine and culture were accelerating the globalization of Asian healing practices, while also "westernizing them," as we see in the words of a Chinese-trained American qigong grandmaster, "Giving individuals the power to determine and manage their own health and destinies is the secret of true healing" (Effie Poy Yew Chow 2003). The embracing of qigong becomes part of a wider cultural movement of "empowerment" of the individual.

A significant section of Falun Gong practitioners in the west consists of highly educated Chinese immigrants, from finance and scientific sectors in particular. Many of the former embrace Falun Gong as a "technology of the self." "It's way, way above qigong," said Gail Rachlin, a media relations consultant. "Qigong can help you physically but it doesn't stay with you and Falun Gong goes beyond the physical by helping you upgrade your thinking and mentality" (New York Times, October 29, 1999). Among scientists and researchers, a key crossover concept between qigong and science occurs where the Taoist ideas of vitality, music of heaven, or breath become understood as "energy," as we see in the words of a doctoral student in immunology: "qigong is based on science that we don't fully understand."

Falun Gong has shifted to the west at the time when ideas such as the "tao of physics" had become part of a background New Age culture emphasizing themes such as the unity of all things and transcending opposites, a synthetic culture incorporating Taoism, Buddhism, Zen, and "Chinese thought" into the "new physics" (Capra 1984). The Chinese government claims it is defending "scientific spirit and scientific attainment" when it attacks Falun Gong, suggesting that the interest in the practice reflects China's feudal heritage, "a kind of subconscious more noticeable in older people" (*People's Daily*, May 18, 2000). However, the contemporary blurring of science and mysticism has meant that representations of Falun Gong as feudal and antiscience (*People's Daily*, August 7, 2002) have had limited effect outside China, where, not surprisingly, a high proportion of Falun Gong web sites are located on university servers.

The Internet: Person to Person

People communicated with each other. They said, "I will go. How about you?" Then others said, "I will go as well." Because everyone benefits so much from the exercises, they felt that it was their duty or their responsibility to safeguard the principles or the practice. So it was just by people: I tell you, you tell him, he tells another, and that was it. Also that day was Sunday, so people said, "OK. it's Sunday, I can go." I was surprised to see so many people there, because we did not organize or calculate how many would come, people just said "I would like to come." I was happy because there were so many people there, I thought, "The government must pay attention: there are so many people here."

Jenny, describing how she came to participate in the demonstration of April 25, 1999, outside the Zhongnanhai government compound

Chinese official media portray Falun Gong as an integrated, hierarchical organization, piloting attempts to disrupt public order from a distance. However, to the extent that it is possible to reconstruct the events of April 25, these correspond more to the account offered by Jenny. The aim of the April 25 action was to appeal for redress following the publication of an article condemning Falun Gong, and the subsequent arrest of some 40 practitioners who had protested two days earlier in Tianjin. This form of action, petitioning government officials for the redress of collective grievances, was also the basic mode of action used by the student movement a decade earlier during the Tiananmen protest (Esherick and Wasserstrom 1991; see also Nathan 1985). Falun Gong practitioners gathered outside the same entrance to Zhongnanhai where, in 1967, the Red Guards called successfully for the sacking of President Liu Shaoqi.

Many observers of Falun Gong have underlined the importance of the Internet. However, the primary form of communication organizing the event in April 1999 was the telephone. And while it appears clear that there was a call from Beijing leaders to practitioners to appeal against the arrest of Falun Gong practitioners in Tianjin, the lines of communication were by no means vertical, with people from different areas calling each other, in much the way described by Jenny (see Tong 2002, who reconstructs the networks involved in the event through officially published accounts). However, in the period following the banning of Falun Gong, the Internet has emerged as critical to its ongoing development. The Internet allows potential practitioners to download the writings of Li Hongzhi at no const. Potentially interested people can download compressed videofiles that explain how to perform the exercises. If you want to find out about locations and times for practice sessions in your neighbourhood, the Internet details practice sites and times for hundreds of cities in Europe, North America, and Asia (offering names and phone numbers of contact people for each practice site) (http://www.falundafa.org/world.htm). The Internet and Chinese diaspora combine together to explain the rapid globalization of the movement. This is illustrated in the case of Sharon, one of the key people of the Falun Gong in Hong Kong. She works for an international finance bank, and learnt the practice of Falun Gong from her sister while living with her family in Chicago. Her family left China and emigrated to the United States in the 1980s. Her sister downloaded Li's book from the Internet, and began practicing in the United States, where Sharon began to practice as well, before taking up her high-level finance position in Hong Kong.

Goubin Yang's study of the virtual Chinese diaspora underlines the extraordinary extent of Chinese Internet networks, arguing that these constitute a "transnational public sphere" (2003) offering what Appadurai (1996: 3) refers to as "new resources and new disciplines for the construction of imagined selves and imagined worlds." Themes that we encounter elsewhere are present in this Internet experience. The culture of the Internet is personal. Users refer to each other as "net friend" rather than "net user," and the culture underlines private dimensions of experience, evident, for example, in the extraordinary importance of chat groups aiming at making friends, personal exchange, as well as matchmaking and dating. The culture of the Internet is one of personal individuals rather than constituting a public sphere of "collective actors."

Magic, Religion, and Syncretism

Qigong practice constitues a relationship between the body and subjectivity. In the case of Falun Gong, this is linked to the demand to live according to the imperatives of truth, kindness, and forbearance, which essentially translate into personal relationships. But at the same time, Li Hongzhi's texts combine themes from Buddhism and Taoism with dimensions of New Age culture such as an interest in "energies," out-of-body experiences, paranormal abilities, prediction of the future, levitation, and so on. These "paranormal" aspects reflect important dimensions of the qigong craze in China in the 1980s, where qigong masters would fill stadiums and enthrall audiences with their abilities, such as levitation, projecting qi, and so on – important dimensions of Chinese popular culture.

The globalization of qigong points to a wider transformation in grammars of religion and belief. Manuel Castells (2000) underlines the long term decline of hierarchy as a form of organization in the network society, while Chilean sociologist Cristian Parker-Gumucio (2002) underlines the implications of this process in terms of patterns of religion, where he notes the increasing deinstitutionalization of religions and the increasing importance of magical-religious syncretisms. In such emerging forms of magic, which range from Gnosticism to future prediction and the occult, the figure of the priest (as a mediation between profane and transcendent) is absent, while the "cosmovision" of such new magics is one of a universe governed by spirits and energies. Two social groups are most associated with such neomagic: those from a scientific background who live in a world of science and technology, and those from marginal groups. These two groups represent the principal carriers of Falun Gong – people involved in sciences and technologies, and older people dealing with health issues.

Falun Gong's globalization is part of a wider expansion of magic and the esoteric. Parker-Gumucio argues that this needs to be understood in the context of the shift to a network society. The rationality of industrial society is one of exclusive codes (classification in terms of A or not A), a mode of organization that involves the circulation of goods, services, and people, leading to clearly determined borders, in terms of space and symbolic systems. Parker-Gumucio argues (as did Max Weber) that institutional forms in industrial society are thus hierarchic. The shift to a network society brings with it the increasing importance of flows of communication and information, involving forms of communication code that are inclusive (rather than exclusive) and tolerant of diversity. This leads to forms of organization based on cells and networks, characterized by multiple interfaces and interpenetrations, convergence, and intersection points. This shift to network as the basis of social organization means that boundaries blur, leading to a dissolution of the clear boundaries around "religions."

Talal Asad has explored the emergence of the idea of "religion" as a specific symbolic domain in eighteenth-century Europe, part of a much wider transformation involving "a new kind of state, a new kind of science, and a new kind of legal and moral subject" (Asad 1993: 43). As Asad argues, the particular conceptualization of religion that emerged to claim the status of a universal category in fact reflects key transformations in the self-understanding of Christianity that took place within Europe over the seventeenth and eighteenth centuries, one that "emphasizes the priority of belief as a state of mind rather than as constituting activity in the world" (1993: 47). As a result, religion took the form of a recognizably delimited domain, while also being understood as universal – all societies, so it was argued, would equally possess such a delimited domain, transformations within European Christianity thus serving as the basis of a universal model of "religion."

Parker-Gumucio argues that the multitude of interfaces and convergence points is leading to a dissolution of the religious sphere that emerged in Europe over the eighteenth and nineteenth centuries. This does not mean the end of religion, but the relative dissolution of the "frontiers" once separating religion and nonreligion. In western societies this means a blurring of the once clear separation between religion and magic, evident in new forms of devotion and the search for the miraculous, and the declining significance of institutions and mediating roles such as priest. But as well as this process of weakening of frontiers, Parker-Gumucio argues that just as there was an "elective affinity" between the protestant ethic and industrial capitalism (the moral value of work, effort, saving, etc.), he suggests that there is an equal affinity between new cultures of science-technology and the increasing importance of what he calls "neo-magic" in global culture. Industrial modernity was associated with the triumph of a rationalizing model, opposed to superstition and popular knowledge and wisdoms, where modern science emerged out of traditions such as alchemy and magic (evident, for example, in the important debt that the founders of modern science such as Newton owed to alchemy); then setting out to deny these as irrational. Modern science that developed was rationalist, materialist, mechanical, empirical, and positivist, setting out to exclude the action and the experience of the knowing subject in favor of the objective status of knowledge (Prigogine and Stengers 1997). Parker-Gumucio argues that contemporary science is increasingly influenced by themes of magic, evident in a fascination with breaking limits, and the search for possibilities once associated with the occult, such as overcoming the limits of life and death. Geneticists, for example, refer to the human genome as "the Bible," the "Book of Life," or the "Holy Grail," suggesting that in DNA we encounter immortality and god (Sfez 2001). Harvard entomologist Edward O. Wilson argues that rather than see religion replaced by the rationality of science, "science is religion liberated and writ large . . . another way of satisfying religious hunger" (Wilson 1997: 7).[1]

China specialists underline a dissolution of the sphere of "religion" in that country, underlining in particular the action of the state that has historically sought to control the expansion of Buddhism and Taoism, under the Song (960–1279 CE), Ming, and Qing (1368–1911 CE) dynasties, a process that continued and intensified under the Nationalists and Communist regimes. In the twentieth century, this continued, where the closure of temples and the forbidding of local festivals aimed at destroying the practice of ancestor veneration. Historians of popular religion in China argue that the very success of this state-driven project has accelerated the emergence of "a modern religiosity expressed through individual voluntary commitment and through personal trajectories in movement" (Palmer 2003).

Embodied Grammars

In this chapter we have been attempting to grapple with what China scholars describe as "possibly the greatest mass movement in modern China outside the direct control of the government" (Xiaoyang and Penny 1994). At its center is not talk, but embodied experience, and forms of practice where the body is a path to the self, and to the other. Rather than an obstacle, the body is a form of presence in the world, a path to worlds hidden from a rationalizing science, a path that is sensual and emotional, one where understanding cannot be achieved except through embodied experience. The forms of healing that we have considered respond to experiences of loss, suffering, and grief connected with the meanings of sickness, leading to forms of practice that do not aim at the construction of "collective identities," but forms of "intensified personhood" and what we could call "intensified intercorporeal personhood."

This has globalized rapidly through several paths: the grammar of person-to-person relationships has been facilitated by the culture of the Internet; the culture of healing is one that has particular resonance in Chinese culture; meanwhile, the blurring of the esoteric and science in the form of neomagic has meant a powerful penetration of this movement among educated scientific groups, accelerating its globalization. The most powerful impression the nonspecialist of China has in attempting to make sense of this movement is the search for private space and private experience, a search that is lived through the idea of "cultivation" achieved through a form of communicative embodied practice. The esoteric and the strange play an important place in this experience, but not in the western understanding of "belief" determining "action." Instead the esoteric and the strange open a domain of the imagination, in the process perhaps opening experiences of subjectivity similar to others we are exploring in this book. This healing movement has at its center not the triumphant categories of collective identity and rational actors, but personal experiences of loss, embodiment, mystery, and magic.

NOTE

1   These trends are not only evident in the natural sciences, but in the social sciences as well. In France, for example, in 2001 the prestigious University of Paris awarded a doctorate in Sociology to a thesis defending astrology as a social science. The thesis (supervised by Michel Maffesoli) was written by one of France's best-known astrologers, who not only publishes a weekly column in that country's most widely circulated television magazine, but also served as the astrologer advising French president François Mitterrand ("Astrologer's Degree Raises Scientists' Fears," *Science* 292(5517) (April 2001): 635).

CHAPTER 8

Global Islam: Modernity's Other?

Dominant understandings of modernity have been deeply shaped by theories of modernization, involving the idea of progress, increasing individual freedom, as individuals free themselves from the constraints of tradition and community, a process generating secularization, where the domain of the religious declines, or becomes increasingly limited to personal life and private beliefs. This understanding arguably reached its peak in the 1950s, but had clearly been part of western self-understanding since the Enlightenment. Thinkers like Marx either embraced the movement of modernization, or like Tonnies regretted the passing of community. This self-understanding was also constructed in relation to the Other. Marx's understanding of historical materialism and his theory of evolution was constructed against what he called the "oriental despotism" present in the Asian mode of production, by which he meant that Asian societies were nonhistoric.

A century later Daniel Lerner published his influential *The Passing of Traditional Society* (1958) where he argued all societies are involved in the passage from tradition to modern society, and where he insists the critical process necessary for modernization to occur is the privatization of religious belief. Lerner also develops his theory in relation to the Other, focusing on the Middle East and societies with Islam as the majority religion, asserting that these societies confront a stark choice, one opposing "modernization and Mecca." While Marx had looked to the economic structure to explain the failure to modernize, Lerner argued that a society's failure to modernize could be understood by its failure to secularize. From this point of view, modernizers were by definition secularizers. This view was embraced by Bernard Lewis, the British historian and doyen of American Middle East studies, who believed that the only path to modernization in that region was the one taken by Kemalist Turkey, where the state and army together imposed a model of secular modernization on the society – evident, for example, in the shift from Arabic to western script, and in the banning of wearing headscarves in public. A similar ban was later introduced by the Shah of Iran.

It was Lewis, the admirer of secular Turkey, who coined the term "clash of civilizations," although it had been used earlier by American Protestant missionaries in the Middle East in the 1920s (Bulliet 2004), which would be taken up and popularized by Samuel Huntington (1996). Lewis extends Lerner's opposition between Mecca and modernization, popularizing a functionalist argument where he asserts that traditional social structures and mores have broken down, but nonetheless Islamic societies have failed to modernize. The collapse of the old followed by the failure of the new is the source of "Muslim rage" driving the "clash of civilizations" (Lewis 1990). Implicit in Lewis's argument is the idea that Islam is a failed civilization, one that has not succeeded in producing the separation of public and private, individual and community, religion and culture that characterize the secular west. This account of Islam as the failed Other clearly taps a deep vein in western culture, one that is by no means limited to political conservatives. The British political theorist of "global civil society," John Keane, describes Islamic history in terms of an "Islamic quest for world supremacy" (2003: 42), one that was "thwarted" by Europe, "leaving many Muslims with a forward-looking memory that remains strong until today: a vivid awareness of Islam's splendid historical achievements combined with the refusal to accept the present-day world" (2003: 42–3).

This conception of modernization has profoundly shaped the relationship between social scientists and Islamic movements. In most cases, it has meant ignoring Islamic movements and experiences all together, since most social scientists have understood social movements as modernizers and hence by definition secularizers. This appeared self-evident in a postcolonial period dominated by nationalist, secular movements and leaders, such as Nasser in Egypt, the National Liberation Front in Algeria, the Bath Party in Syria and Iraq, or the Palestine Liberation Organization (Kepel 1994: 14). A situation that remained until the crisis of Arab nationalism, made so evident by Israel's victory in the war of 1973.

The period following the crisis of these nationalist movements has been widely understood in terms of the "Islamization of dissent" (Kepel 1994). Many observers, as well as political actors, regard Islam as the equivalent of earlier expressions of nationalism, replacing the pan-Arabist themes associated with Nasser's generation. Writing within a political process perspective, Paul Lubeck argues Islamic movements "don the mantle of nationalist resistance to foreign domination without rival, thanks to the suppression of the secular left." What is more, such mobilization is easier than the task facing the political left, since

> there is no need for militants to teach the foundational concepts of Hegel, Marx or Lock. All know the vocabulary of the Islamic alternative, which they

already understand as a local culture . . . By strategically seizing the mantle of antiimperialist nationalism, a discourse formally controlled exclusively by secular nationalists and leftist movements, Islamism has become the world's most extensive and militant antisystemic social movement. (2000: 161, 163)

From this perspective, Islam is regarded as the expression of national culture and identity, and expresses a preference for the traditional instrument to achieve social change, the political party. For other observers, however, the crisis of nationalism means a crisis of the very possibility of modernization.

A widely held view thus regards religious movements as a defensive reaction against globalization, an affirmation of the particular against the universal. This is illustrated by the model of "resistance identity" Manuel Castells articulates when he argues "God, nation, family and community will provide unbreakable, eternal codes, around which a counter offensive will be mounted" (Castells 1997: 66). This analysis echoes a model that has recurred in western culture, namely the defence of community and its culture against the encroaching logic of the market, evident in the German Romantic tradition, or in Tonnies' sociology, or in Castells' earlier work on the global city (1983), where he argues where local communities will construct defensive enclaves to defend themselves from the global. In Castells' opposition between potentially universal movements (human rights, feminism, ecology), and defensive movements (ethnic, national, and religious), the defensive movements are antimodern and authoritarian, where the relationship to meaning takes a form where it "cannot be processed . . . only obeyed and followed" (Castells 2000: 22). This view is echoed by Anthony Giddens who writes:

How would you define fundamentalism? Fundamentalism is essentially embattled tradition locked into the new communication systems . . . Fundamentalism is tradition defending itself in a world where tradition can no longer be defended in a traditional way . . . fundamentalism is purified tradition. (Giddens 1999: 6–7)

Here we encounter a rehearsal of the opposition between modernity and tradition, between society and community: for Giddens, this is an opposition between "cosmopolitans" and "fundamentalists," for Castells, an opposition between "project" and "reactive" identities.

Sydney Tarrow, interestingly, suggests that Islam has in fact emerged as a global movement, yet goes on to offer what amounts to a caricature:

It is worth recalling that the most powerful global movement of the early 1990s was made up not of Western environmentalists or human rights activists linked benevolently to indigenous people's movements in the Third World but of radical Islamic fundamentalists who murdered folk singers and beat up women who went around unveiled. (1998: 242)

Civilizations: Interpenetrations, Borders, and Edges

Opposed to this dominant model of the center and its resistance, studies of comparative civilizations underline the extent to which civilizations inter-penetrate through encounters that cannot be understood uniquely or even principally in terms of conflict and clash. The historian of comparative civilizations, Thierry Zarcone (2003), underlines just how important has been such interchange, observing that it was the first "clash of civilizations" in the thirteenth century of the Common Era, through which, thanks to the Arabs and via Islam, Europeans discovered the Greek heritage of Plato and Aristotle, chemistry, arithmetic, astronomy, and medicine. The extent of this interchange goes beyond the role of Islamic civilization as a storehouse or transmitter of the Greek and classical civilization. It was in fourteenth-century Cairo, then the intellectual capital of the world, that the North African Ibn Khaldoun (1333–1406 CE), exploring the rise and decline of different Islamic societies, developed the first conception of nonreligious history, his work representing the birth of the modern understanding of history. This modern time consciousness would play a key role in the birth of modernity, as would those sections of Europe that most interacted with the Islamic experience, above all the Italian city-states. Zarcone also notes the "western" character of Islam: geographically, owing to its location vis-à-vis Asia; and culturally, as Islam emerges from a tradition that is both Abrahamic and Greek (deeply indebted to Aristotle and Greek philosophy, above all its hypothethical-deductive model that forms the architecture of Islamic law and theology). Zarcone argues that important sections of the Islamic experience develop in buffer or intermediary civilizations, among Persians, Sassanids, and the Turkish-Iranian world, whose language is Indo-European and who are culturally located in the west. Zarcone points as well to the encounter between Islam and the Eastern civilizations of China and the Hindu experience, where products of this cross-fertilization eventually make their way to the west. Important dimensions of the Islamic experience remain deeply influenced by eastern experiences as well, from the Confucian and Taoist basis of Chinese Muslims, the Hindu basis of the Indian and Indonesian Muslims, and the Buddhist, animist, and shamanist foundations of Turkish Islam – that play a key role in the mystical Sufi tradition of Islam (Zarcone 2003). These innovations spread throughout the Muslim world, from the Buddhist monastery architecture constructed around a central courtyard that gave rise to the *madrasa*, to the Buddhist origins of Persian literary aesthetic, while the Muslim Uighurs of Xinjiang in China's far west mix dimensions of Greek and Arab medicine with Chinese herbalism. Yoga entered the Islamic world in the fourteenth century, linked to chants and breathing exercises that developed in Indian sufi brotherhoods and spread through sufi practice (Zarcone 2003). This interpenetration continues to the present, and is not without contestation and conflict, as in debates about yoga in Egypt today.

The American historian Richard Bulliet develops a similar argument through introducing the theme "Islamo-Christian civilization" (2004). He argues strongly against the idea of civilization clash, suggesting that the Muslim-majority societies of the Middle East and North Africa and the Christian-majority societies of Western Europe and America are better understood as part of the same civilization. He argues that the historical development of Christianity and Islam parallel each other so closely and are so interconnected that they are best understood as two versions of a common "socioreligious system" (2004: 15). Armando Slavatore equally locates the *din* (a concept similar to religion) that Mohammed proclaimed within the "occidental mode" based on transcendence, differing from the Asian versions of the Axial civilizations not based on the transcendent. In Islam we encounter the Axial tension between cosmological order and the mundane world, leading to the idea of the "accountability" of the rulers to God or God's Law – a source of instability and tension, and generator of historical change. The followers of the Prophet were engaging with a new faith and community, based on individual deliberation to follow the one God and His Prophet – they were no longer simply members of a tribe, but also a superior Community, the *umma*, justified in terms of transcendence, where all were in principle equal, while in reality a series of hierarchies emerged based on closeness to the Prophet (Salvatore 1997: 18).

The emergence and development of Islam was a dynamic process, as in other movements that would become religions. Salvatore points to the tension within the movement founded by the Prophet, where in the Qur'an, the word *Allah* (God) appears 2,697 times, the word *din* (to behave duly before God) 92 times, while the reified term *Islam* as a noun occurs only 8 times. Much more frequent is the nonreified verb *aslama*, meaning "giving oneself in total commitment." The gradual triumph of the term "Islam" occurs much later, as the result of complex historical process, and is much more recent, mirroring the emergence of the concept "religion" within Europe, in the context of the emergence of modern science (Asad 1993), where the Axial tension between this world and the hereafter became reformulated as a tension between two spheres, the religious and the secular (Salvatore 1997: 24). It was in this context as well that the modern idea that religion consists of a series of personalized *beliefs* emerges, and where the modern generic concept of religion as a systematization of such beliefs develops – a development within Christianity that forms the basis of the modern anthropological understanding of religion as a symbolic system (Asad 1993).

Scholars of contemporary religions underline the way more recent transformations are paralleled across religious traditions. The American anthropologist Robert Hefner (1998) observes important parallels between contemporary Islamic and Hindu renewal and the renewal of Protestantism that took place early in the twentieth century. The French political scientist Olivier Roy (2004) develops a similar argument when he points to key processes at work in contemporary Islam, in particular the personalization of belief and the decline in organized forms of religious authority (a situation Bulliet describes as a crisis of religious authority) – developments and tensions equally evident within contemporary Christianity.

We can link the question of civilization to contemporary debates around globalization, which focus increasingly on global flows, emerging forms of fluidity, and complexity (Urry 2002), and the interpenetration of different forms of scapes (ethnoscapes, finance scapes, etc.). Bulliet suggests that key processes of innovation and transformation within Islam occur in what he calls "edge situations" – these are not necessarily on the geographic periphery of Islam, but in zones of encounter with other traditions or civilizations. Historically such zones have played a key role in the development of Islam, from the collection of sayings of Muhammad through to the emergence of madrassas in the frontier zone with Buddhism, or the emergence of Sufi tradition and practice in what is today Turkey.

A New Publicness

Contemporary Islam is a striking example of what Urry refers to as "global complexity," networks of flows, symbols, communications, and experiences. Eickleman underlines the extraordinary growth associated with Islam of an emerging public sphere, pointing to critical processes: the expansion of higher education, the increasing importance of travel and mobility, and the proliferation of media, new and old, throughout the Muslim-majority world and beyond – ranging from print, radio, television, music, video and audio cassettes, CDs and DVD, to the Internet. This is part of an explosion of Muslim popular culture, from music to pulp fiction, in particular romance fiction (for an overview, see Anderson and Eickelman 1999; Gole 2002). Anderson underlines the extent to which this does not correspond to the mass-media paradigm of a small number of senders and a large number of receivers, but involves new vernaculars, new voices as well as new audiences.

Eickelman argues, "a new sense of publicness is emerging throughout Muslim majority states and Muslim communities elsewhere" (2000). But we need to distinguish what is happening here from the models that have dominated social sciences. The immensely influential approach developed by the German sociologist Jürgen Habermas was based on an idealized account of the emergence of the public sphere in Europe, one that underlines the development of cafés and discussion clubs in European cities, from where Habermas argues emerged the modern conception of public sphere.

Jon Anderson suggests that we can take this idea, and drawing on Benedict Anderson's (1991) theory of imagined communities, proposes a model less based on structural characteristics of language, but instead, proposes that we focus on the concept of "creole journeys," a concept that allows us to move beyond international NGOs, as well as fixed communities, to instead explore publicness in terms of processes of circulation, or domains of communication that people enter and leave. This is a shift that we have encountered elsewhere: a shift from a paradigm of community to one of contact. This echoes Peter Mandaville's exploration of what he calls "translocal Islam." Such public spheres spread across Muslim majority countries, as well as between them and wider zones of diaspora. Anderson offers the example of a lawyer in Jordan who explains that via the Internet he can find an expression of Islam that is not available to him at his neighborhood mosque or from local *shayks* (religious scholars), a situation that applies equally whether in Virginia, Hamburg, or Cairo (Anderson 2003).

These accounts suggest we need to break free from global versus local, or cosmopolitan versus fundamentalist oppositions, free ourselves from an a priori understanding of Islamic movements as defensive tradition, and be open to explore the possibility of new and dynamic processes. This means engaging with a wider reconfiguration (Asad 1996) where Islam, as other religions, is experiencing a process of deinstitutionalization. As Bulliet underlines, the authority of Islam's formal religious leaders is weakening, just as we witness in other religions as well. The declining authority of the *ulema* (formal religious leaders) means a decisive shift, where the meanings of Islam are increasingly constructed by political actors and cultural movements rather than religious institutions (Gole 2000). And here the experience of the Salafi movement is critical to explore.

Neofundamentalism against Tradition: the Salafi Experience

Movements of religious revival and reform always occur in wider contexts of social, cultural, and political change and upheaval, as we would expect, to the extent religions and religious experience are important ways of being in the world, and are important ways through which the distance separating the world and the transcendent is experienced. The birth of European modernity is intimately linked to religious movements, where the vision of future redemption present within the Christian religion became secularized through the English, French, and American revolutions (and their precursor in the Dutch revolt against Spain) (Eisenstadt 1999). Eisenstadt suggests that the dynamics involved in Islamic renewal are different, linking this to processes of geographic expansion of Islam.

Fattah (2003) demonstrates the impact that the expansion of Wahabism leading up to the formation of Saudi Arabia in 1932 had in terms of accelerating other movements within the Islamic world, in particular reinvigorating the Salafi tradition, which had had a long presence, particularly in Iraq. This tradition was based around scholars and preachers advocating the way of the *salaf al-salih*, pious Muslims of the early Islamic period. This movement received a powerful impulsion from the writings of Jamal al-Din al-Afghani (1839–97), a scholar, philosopher and politician born in Iran and who died in Turkey, after spending a considerable time both in Paris and in Afghanistan (as his name suggests), where he became involved in the fight against British colonization. Al-Afghani believed Islamic civilization to be profoundly threatened by European imperialism, believing Islam had become weak and decadent, contaminated by local cultures and traditions. The response to European colonization, he argued, needed to be based on a reengagement with the Islam of the Prophet, and he thus called for a renewal movement returning to the religion's origins. For al-Afghani, a correct interpretation of the Qur'an and Hadith (actions and sayings attributed to the Prophet) was completely compatible with modern science and rational thought, it would encourage diligence, hard work, and frugality, facilitating the development of rational civilization, capitalism, and democracy. Al-Afghani's core conviction was that the modernization of Islam required a return to its origins – indeed that the modernization of Islam could occur only through its "fundamentalization" (Turner 2001).

This cultural and religious movement internationalized rapidly, an example of Appadurai's ethnoscape. Wahabist Islamic reform, for example, spread to Sumatra rapidly, brought to the island by religious leaders in Mecca during the period it was first occupied in 1803. On their return to Sumatra these leaders set about cleansing local Islam of its toleration of traditional customs, such as cock-fighting and use of tobacco, while men were required to wear turbans and women to cover their faces in public. As in Arabia, this drive to purify took the form of armed assaults on villages, and served to weaken the traditional social structure, in the process modernizing the society as the new outward-looking elites opened it to trade (Dobbin 1983).

A further wave of Salafi Islam developed in Java from 1900, with Arab immigration to the island. Religious movements are not defensive and locally oriented, opposed to the global cosmopolitans, and global flows did not begin with air travel.

The Western Origins of Salafi

It is important to recognize that this modernizing Islam was not simply strategy against western domination. Noah Salomon's important research in Sudan shows clearly how the British colonial regime from 1898 to 1914 wanted to remove precolonial social structures and culture, targeting in particular Sufi Islam and the form of government associated with it, the Mahdiyya based on the power of the *mahadi* ("divinely guided one"). The colonial administrators set about creating a distinction between orthodox and heterodox Islam, banning visits to the tomb of the *mahadi* (in fact destroying the tomb and scattering the bones), and persecuting other practices associated with the Sufi tradition. The British administrators saw Sufi practices as cruel, uncivilized, and sensual, while regarding the Salafi reform movement, present in Sudan through the Egyptian and collaborator of Al-Afghani, Muhammad 'Abdu, as based on jurisprudential interpretation of scriptures. Salomon demonstrates that Lord Cromer, governor of Egypt from 1883 to 1707, actively supported the development of the Salafi movement as the version of Islam most adapted to the demands of modernization. The impact of colonization did not seek either to secularize, nor to impose Christianity, but to govern through religion:

> the establishment of a secular state necessitated not that religion retreat into the private sphere, but that religion enter the public sphere in a very different manner than it had previously. Though religion was not the foundation of law and government any longer, as it was in the Mahadist theocracy, religion was made into an important arm of disciplinary governance. It was precisely the privatization of religion that the British feared, for that meant an Islam beyond their control. Instead, the British attempted to create a new Islamic public to supplant that of the Sufi and Messianic orders popular in the Sudan. (Salomon 2003: 29)

Colonial government and transformation of Sudanese society in significant ways was exercised *through* Islam by fostering Salafi reform.

Overall the Salafi movement took the form of a pietistic movement, and did not aim at transformation of political systems. Over the twentieth century, however, key transformations took place that led to the constitution of contemporary political Islamism. Two key authors play a key role, each located in critical contexts. Sayyid Abul A'la Mawdudi (1903–79), an Islamic cleric in the region of Hyderabad, one of the principal Muslim majority regions of India at the time of the partition, wrote and preached about what he called the decline of the Islamic population when confronted with the Hindu experience. Mawdudi insists on the importance of political action and called for the end of mixing with other religions. As the Tunisian author Abdelwahab Meddeb (2003) underlines, Mawdudi performs a radical transformation in reading of the Qu'ran, introducing the modern political concept of sovereignty, arguing that "sovereignty belongs to none but Allah." The consequences are a radical rupture: a modern understanding of the political sphere enters Islamic thought, and in the process, the political becomes defined in terms of the sacred. This innovation was developed further by an Egyptian intellectual and member of the Muslim Brotherhood, Sayyid Qutb (1906–66). Writing in what he experienced as a crisis situation, namely the triumph of Nasser's secular Arab nationalist ideology in Egypt, Qutb considered the current world to be so corrupt that it represents a state of *jahili*, the state that the world existed in before the revelation of God through Islam. As such Qutb radically transforms one of the core conceptual structures of Islam, the before and the after revelation to the Prophet. This division, a marker of a radical shift in ways of being in the world, was transferred from the seventh century to the present.

Qutb was as a school inspector, westernized, and was born into a small village that he later came to regard as steeped in ignorance due to superstition. His early writings, as those of al-Afghani, are steeped in the kind of Romanticism and vitalism out of which emerged European fascism. In *Islam and Social Justice*, he creates a vision of an organically fused world, held together by the divine category, Will:

> all creation issuing as it does from one absolute, universal, and active Will, forms an all-embracing unity in which each individual part is in harmonious order with the remainder . . . Thus, then, all creation is a unity comprising different parts; it has a common origin, a common providence and purpose, because it was produced by a single, absolute, and comprehensive Will. (1970: 19, 49)

Aziz Al-Azmeh (1996) underlines the debt this political Islamism owes to European culture and ideologies. Afghani developed his key themes not as a religious scholar in the holy city of Qom, but in Cairo, Istanbul, and Paris, drawing heavily on the European Romantic tradition: Herder's vitalist Romanticism and Rousseau's general will. He draws on the Darwinist conception of struggle for existence, arguing that one nation can grow strong only through weakening another, and seeing the decline of societies as the result of being weakened by internal sects. Thus, he argues, the classical civilization of the Muslim Arabs was weakened by esoteric sects, allowing its defeat by the Crusaders and Mongols, while the Ottoman Empire was weakened internally by westernizing reformists. Al-Azmeh points to the similarities between this organicist, vitalist conception of the nation and the model of political action it inspired, and the development of European fascism emerging out of the same intellectual matrix.

The debt to European political theory is equally evident in the work of Qutb. He theorizes the role of a vanguard drawing on Leninism. His writing is full of references to healthy values, degenerate nations and weakness, infertile values – all expressions of his fascination with the writing of the French fascist, Alexis Carrel, the author whom he cites most frequently, and from whom he adopts an overarching framework of analysis (see Al-Azmeh 1993: 30). Carrel's "laws of life" that must be followed become the law of God, interpreted in terms of the *Shari'a*. As Al-Azmeh notes (1993: 12), the *Shari'a* is not a code, but a general concept of "good order" similar in meaning to *nomos* or *dharma*. Qutb reframes the Sharia, Europeanizing it by conceiving it as a code to be applied, and locating it within the tradition of European Romantic thought, where it becomes the equivalent of the "laws of life" (a nineteenth-century conception of vitalism and eugenism). The importance of this debt to European fascism is also evident in the place of anti-Semitism in contemporary Islamist thought, equally a product of European right-wing Romantic thought.[1] Qutb does not seek a return to a premodern utopia. His writings about his time in America show how he is deeply affected by the extraordinary technological power of the west, just as al-Afghani. He wants to separate that technological power from western culture, and harness it to serve the transformation of the social order he envisages.

The extent of this interchange underlines just how much the idea of separate civilizational development is a myth. But this myth is powerfully supported in countries shaped by Islamist ideologies. The Tunisian Abdelwahab Meddeb (2002) explores the enforced amnesia sweeping contemporary Islamic societies. He recounts stories of doctoral students in the humanities who are completely unaware of the degree of interpenetration of Islamic and western cultures. Not only is the extensive interchange between the Islamic world and the west being removed from educational curricula, but so too are centuries of history and culture. Poetry on the body, sensuality and beauty, one of the great cultural achievements of eleventh-century Baghdad and once a source of scandal to the west, are now burnt or destroyed. One of the greatest stories of the first millennium, *The Thousand and One Nights*, is a collection of stories, written in Arabic and set in India, where the newly married Princess Scheherazade seeks to keep her husband, the king (who marries a virgin every day and then kills her so he can remarry), from killing her by entertaining him with a tale every evening. The book is full of stories of good and tyrannical rulers, good and bad genies, sex, violence, and spiritual quests. While some characters were added during its translation into French in the eighteenth century, most of the stories are Persian, Indian, and Arabic folk tales. Regarded as one of the treasures of human history, the book is banned in Saudi Arabia and Egypt. This amnesia extends to pre-Islamic history as well, evident in the destruction of the Buddhas at Bamiyan in Afghanistan, while in Saudi Arabia, archaeological remains that predate the Islamization of the country are regularly covered over with concrete (Meddeb 2003). Saudi funds for *madrasas* in Indonesia come with curriculum changes, which involve removing Indonesian history and culture from the school curriculum. Here we encounter another form of homogenous time.

There are obvious parallels between political Islamism and the Cultural Revolution in China, evident in the way the Red Guards set about destroying historical monuments and wanted to obliterate China's Confucian past. Far from being a cultural movement seeking to reinstate local traditions, political Islamism is an antitraditional modernization movement: it wants to replace customs with law (just as the British in Sudan), a dimension that has strengthened over the twentieth century. Its founders Jamal and his Egyptian collaborator Abduh were clearly open to wider dimensions of the Islamic experience, such as Sufi mysticism, evidenced by the extensive correspondence between them couched in Sufi language (Reid, in Wuthnow 1998). As the Salafi movement sought increasingly over the twentieth century to purge itself of cultural impurities, paradoxically it has come more and more to rely upon western intellectual sources. There is a parallel in the way Maoism embraced another European tradition, Leninism, to modernize and purge China of its Confucian past.

Uncivil Society

Qutb returned to Egypt from the United States and joined the Muslim Brotherhood. The Brotherhood was an example of a classical modernist organization, hierarchically structured and functioning as a bureaucracy made up of a complex structure of branches, delegates, and representation. Founded in Egypt in 1928 by Hassan al-Banna to oppose British imperialism, the Brotherhood was deeply influenced by modernist culture. At first it was closer to a youth club, emphasizing health and fitness, but gradually it developed a wider range of organizations and came to focus on political action and on using the state to overcome British imperialism and connect with Egypt's Islamic heritage. The Brotherhood swiftly extended to other countries of the Middle East, and for a half century remained the paradigmatic reference point and model for Islamic political projects: a bureaucratic organization aiming at social transformation through taking control of the state, combining extensive charitable activities, presence in professional associations (above all labor unions), as well as local organizing, combined with the development of a political party. Wiktorowicz (2000) notes that studies of social movements in Middle East countries have largely focused on formally organized groups, with the Muslim Brotherhood as an exemplar. This, he suggests, because the Brotherhood corresponds closely to the classical models of Social Movement Organization that were important in American sociology of resource mobilization, appearing to confirm William Gamson's (1975) argument that movement success depends above all on organization.

Diane Singerman notes that such a focus on formally organized groups, central to the "contentious politics" approach to movements, with its emphasis on "public" actors and issues and detecting the presence of movements through "episodic, public, collective interaction" (Singerman 2004: 149) directed toward public space, has the effect of narrowing the way we understand movement and action in the context of Muslim majority countries. Asef Bayat's (1997) study on what he calls "uncivil society" or the politics of the "informal people" in the Middle East, exploring Iran after the 1979 revolution and Egypt, illustrates the same point. In Iran after the Revolution, while revolutionaries were marching in the streets, important movements of squatters developed among the urban poor, with families taking over half-finished apartment blocks, refurbishing them, and when they were unable to have a service such as water supply provided by the state, setting about using "do-it-yourself" mechanisms to establish roads, open health clinics, build mosques and libraries and set up consumer cooperatives. For Bayat, around issues of day-to-day survival, "a new and a more autonomous way of living, functioning and organizing the community was in the making" (1997: 54). He notes a similar trend at work, relating to access to employment in the postrevolutionary period in Iran. Initially the unemployed poor and the middle-class jobless undertook "impressive collective action to demand work, maintenance and compensation" (Bayat 1997: 54). While this brought about significant change, mass unemployment and underemployment remained. From here, Bayat notes a shift in forms of action:

> Having exhausted collective action, the unemployed poor turned to family, kin and friends for support. But many more poured into the streets of big cities to establish autonomous subsistence activities, engaging in street vending, peddling, street services ad industries. They set up stalls, drove pushcarts, set up kiosks. Businesses were lit by connecting wires to the main electrical poles. Their collective operation converted the street sidewalks into vibrant and colorful shopping places . . . These kind of urban practices are not extraordinary. They occur in many urban centers of the developing world on a daily basis. (1997: 54)

Bayat notes that Cairo in the 1990s, for example, contained over 100 spontaneous communities of the kind he describes. These forms of action and movement simply do not correspond to the emphasis on NGOs, associations, and organizations that has become so dominant in the literature on "civil society." This literature privileges the place of associations in civil society, and as a result "tends to belittle or totally ignore the vast arrays of often uninstitutionalized and hybrid activities which have dominated urban politics in many developing countries" (Bayat 1997: 55). What we encounter here is not the organization, but forms of embodied co-presence coming from being in the same streets or occupying the same footpaths.

Quintan Wiktorwicz's (2000) study of the Salafi movement in Jordan echoes similar themes. While the Muslim Brotherhood has gone into a slow decline, the Salafi movement has undergone significant growth since the 1960s. As a form of mobilization it is embedded in informal networks, Wiktorowicz's research underlining the extent to which Salafi spreads through personal conversion, mediated by personal networks. In that sense, the structure of the Salafi movement is decentralized and segmented, developing through fluid networks of personal ties, with no formal hierarchy or organization, structured instead in terms of overlapping clusters around different teachers who serve as network hubs. While different teachers clearly possess differing prestige and power, no teacher can speak "on behalf" of the movement, because while a movement exists, it is not one that acts collectively through individuals. The culture of the Salafi movement is one that emphasizes personal study and search, the seeking out of a teacher, the frequenting of lectures of different teachers to find those who are exploring questions that the student considers important. Wiktorwicz suggests that this structure is the result of "strategic choice informed by evaluations about the tactical efficacy of formal organizations" (2000: 236). This pattern seems to me, however, to point to more significant transformations in grammars of experience that become evident once we grapple with the most significant global movement occurring within Islam, the movement of personal piety.

NOTE

1   The Hamas homepage offers a copy of the "Protocols of the Learned Elders of Zion," a document purporting to uncover a Jewish plot to control the world, written by the secret police in czarist Russia. For a wider exploration of the relationship between anti-Semitism and Islamism, see Wieviorka 2005b.

CHAPTER 9

Islamic Makings of the Self

Studies of contemporary Islamic movements emphasize two moments. Kepel points to a first period reaching a peak with the Iranian revolution of 1979, focusing on mass mobilizations, Islamic militancy, and the search for Islamic collective identity, followed by what he calls a period of "Islamization from below." While alerting us to a shift in paradigm of action, the metaphor of "from above" and "from below" is deceptive, suggesting two directions along the same path of "re-Islamization." Bayat (2002) notes a similar shift from earlier forms of action focusing on an Islamist polity to emerging forms of action focusing on personal piety and ethics. For him, these new movements around practices of piety involve a "thinning" of politics. Opposed to this, Turkish sociologist Nilufer Gole argues such shifts in grammars of action involve a focus on what she calls "Islamic makings of the self and the micropolitics associated with it." She emphasizes language styles, corporeal experience, and spatial practices (Gole 2002: 174), which she suggests open new social imaginaries transforming the public sphere in a nonwestern context. This stark opposition in frameworks of interpretation is central when exploring Islamic movements in the context of globalization. It is particularly at stake in one of the most important of such movements, the practice of veiling. Engaging with this confronts us with questions of embodiment, corporeal experience and action, and with the nature of public experience. In the process, questions are raised about the universality of the western, autonomous subject and the model of freedom within which this is constructed that go to the center of the way we think about movements.

Veiling: Resistance, Tradition, and Modernity?

Practices of veiling exist in many societies, having very different meanings, from the exercise of power in China, to the exposure of the poor to the regard of the Other in Yemen (see El Guindi 1999 for an overview). Veiling, and its relationship with the place of women in society, has been a critical marker of the relationship between Islamic majority societies and modernity. For secularizing, modernizing, and westernizing regimes, veiling has been a sign of backwardness and the inability to modernize. In Turkey, the westernizing Kehmalist government in the 1920s banned the traditional fez worn by men as well as the veil worn by women – both regarded as symbols of Ottoman backwardness, and attempted to introduce a straw hat for men and a bonnet for women. Turkey is one of the few countries to legislate around appropriate headwear for men, the European hat being introduced to replace the fez. In a similar way, in Iran the veil was declared illegal in 1936, the authoritarian modernizing regime introducing the Pahlavi hat in 1927 (similar to a French kepi). The Khemalist banning of the traditional fez continued practices of regulation that predated it from the Ottoman period, where *firman*, "decrees," were issued regulating women's dress in public (Gole 1996: 72). The fight against the veil was not only initiated by authoritarian modernizing states. In Egypt in 1923 a movement of upper-class women involved in the nationalist struggle against British colonial power initiated a movement against veiling. For Huda Shaarawi, founder of the Egyptian Feminist Union in the 1920s, nationalism, secularism, and the opening of public space to women all combined in the struggle against the veil. The success of this movement was such that over most of the twentieth century, the dress of middle-class women in Cairo and Egyptian urban centers was western (MacLeod 1992).

Nilufer Gole (1996) argues there is more at stake here than a simple symbol of western modernization. Turkey's Khemalist government was aiming at a radical cultural transformation shaping embodied subjectivity as such. The introduction of the straw hat and the bonnet may not have been successful, but the Khemalist reforms saw the introduction not only of hats and bonnets, but the idea of fashion as such, which as the German sociologist Georg Simmel underlined at the beginning of the twentieth century, is a celebration of the new, of change, of the ephemeral. With this came a transformation of embodiment, of ways of being in the world, in particular linked with the widespread adoption of the corset. Nora Seni underlines the shift from forms of clothing associated with modes of embodiment of the Ottoman period, soft, curved, round, and full, associated with cushions and a reclining body, which were replaced in a short time by a new body, one that was straight, thin, tall, and angular – the impression of height being emphasized by a belt at the now narrowed waist, emphasized further by holding a long umbrella vertically, close to the body (Seni 1995). But how to be in the world and communicate through this body was not yet clear: Gole quotes a participant at a dance in the early 1930s in the Turkish capital Ankara: "No-one yet knew how to behave, how to go out, how to dance, nor what to do with their eyes, their hands, their head" (Gole 1996: 66). This was overlaid with issues of class and geography. Westernizing elites embraced modern forms of clothing and embodiment, while women in rural regions continued with the practice of wearing the headscarf. The issue of the headscarf appeared to be framed within a wider debate about the relationship between tradition and modernization, religion and secularization, city and provinces, elites and popular classes. From the 1980s, however, the question of veiling has reemerged. In Turkey, as in many other countries, its social base is urban rather that rural, made up of young professional women and university students. In 1999, Nuray Canan Bezirgan, a 23-year-old woman, was removed by police from an examination at a prestigious Turkish university, and charged with "obstructing the education of others." She had attended her final examinations wearing an Islamic headscarf, which she refused to remove. She was tried, convicted, and sentenced to six months in jail, the penalty later being amended on appeal to a fine. The impact of this event in Turkey set off a boycott of examinations with similarities to the impact on American life of the action of Rosa Parks, an African-American seamstress, who in October 1955 refused to give up her seat on a bus in Montgomery, Alabama, when directed to do so for a boarding white passenger.

Arlene MacLeod's (1992) influential study of "new veiling" among lower-middle-class women in Cairo in the 1980s explores the decision to veil made by office workers in a city where veiling had not been widely practiced for decades. She argues that these women are largely located in dead-end jobs in a bloated and inefficient public sector, torn between the economic imperatives of paid employment, and a culture that regards the home as the appropriate place for women. MacLeod argues that they are in a "double bind." They make relatively limited economic gains through work, while being subjected to disapproving comments from neighbors or harassment by men in public or at work. Adopting the veil, she argues, represents a strategy to reinstate their position as valued centers of family and domestic life (the veil affirming that they are in paid employment for their family's sake, not their own), without compromising their ability to leave home and earn an income. They are thus able to reclaim the respect accorded to women in traditional Egyptian society, while at the same time participate in employment. This analysis echoes sociological studies of populations that are "in-between" tradition and modernity, evident in particular in immigrant experiences, where a group, excluded from the benefits of the mainstream, will reconstruct traditional forms of social organization.[1] MacLeod proposes that the veil is neither a rejection of modern society nor a wholesale embrace of tradition, but "a highly selective attempt to revitalize and emphasize some of the old ideals" (1992: 555). This selective appropriation of tradition serves as a resource to allow women to participate in modern society. MacLeod underlines the ambiguity of the strategy, one that implies acceptance that women are trespassing in men's public domain.

There are similarities between this attempt to identify a limited and ambiguous form of agency in "new veiling" and the argument of social psychiatrist Mervat Nasser (1999). Nasser argues there are parallels between the type of agency evident in veiling and the agency she sees present in anorexia. Both anorexia and the "new veil" can be understood as forming systems of messages that are conveyed through the body, in both cases combining obedience and protest through conformity, moral discipline, and ambivalence/refusal of the opportunities open to women. From this perspective, veiling, as anorexia, consists of

> substituting self-control for effective control of the world in which women exist . . . Both anorexia and the veil reflect inner conflict and convey distress, symbolic of struggle that looks like resignation, rebellion that takes the shape of conformity and resistance that is dressed in complicity . . . The moral crusade of the anorexic and her strive for purity are mirrored in the young woman's voluntary return to the veil. Each pursues her externally different but psychologically analogous and culturally approved objective with fanatical and compulsive devotion. Both are symbolic of woman's self-denial, self-control as well as her search for self-validation . . . They are forms of veiled resistance adopted by women who are torn between tradition and modernity. (1999: 410–11)

Conversion stories posted to the Internet, in particular in western societies (where the majority of converts to Islam are women), in fact often attach importance to *hijab* and to the change in relationship between men and women that it produces. Although a small number, they possess considerable importance. One young woman offers the following personal account:

> Before Islam, I had experimented with the headscarf out of town to see what people's reaction would be. To my surprise I found the whole experience very positive – men would be shy and respectful and I felt at ease in not competing with other women. I decided to wear *hijab* (headscarf) immediately. 8 months later I took my Shahadah (became a Muslim). (Kareema http://www.leedsnewmuslims.org.uk/new_muslims/personal.asp)

In her conversion story, Naheed from Canada describes her prior experience of constant preoccupation with weight and appearance. The decision to wear the *hijab* or headscarf frees her from this:

> Wearing the hijab has given me freedom from constant attention to my physical self. Because my appearance is not subjected to public scrutiny, my beauty,

or perhaps lack of it, has been removed from the realm that can be legitimately discussed. No one knows whether my hair looks as if I just stepped out of a salon, whether or not I can pinch an inch, or even if I have unsightly stretch marks. And because no one knows, no one cares. Feeling that one has to meet the impossible male standards of beauty is tiring and often humiliating. I should know, I spent my entire teenage years trying to do it. I was a border-line bulimic and spent a lot of money I didn't have on potions and lotions in hopes of becoming the next Cindy Crawford . . . Women are not going to achieve equality with the right to bare their breasts in public, as some people would like you to believe. True equality will be had only when women don't need to display themselves to get attention and won't need to defend their deci-sion to keep their bodies to themselves. (Naheed Mustafa, *Globe and Mail*, June 29, 1993)

The constant theme running through these accounts is one where the *hijab* is understood as an instrument to resist male domination. It creates access to cultural resources: either tradition in the case of Egypt, or some-what paradoxically as a means to achieve a modern form of equality where men and women access the public sphere on the same terms. These accounts construct stories of *hijab* in terms of a type of agency that can be understood as resistance to masculine domination. They imply that a world that was not shaped by such domination would have no need of *hijab*. In the process, the religious meaning of this practice is marginalized – religion is understood uniquely as a repository of traditional values (in the way understood by Giddens) that can be selectively mobilized to negotiate the new forms of domination characterizing modernity, in a context where "the hijab operates as a symbol within a system" (MacLeod 1992: 556).

These approaches to veiling movements are important, in that they attempt to recognize a form of agency present, contrasting with accounts that see such movements uniquely in terms of the absorption of a convert into a group, where they gradually become resocialized and (in a phrase rem-iniscent of currents in social movement literature we have explored) become its deployable agents. The frameworks of tradition versus modernity, or fem-inine versus masculine, locate the *hijab* within a secular identity paradigm, and as a result do not consider any significance of *hijab* as a religious prac-tice. These analyses embrace a "resistance" paradigm that we are largely familiar with, one where the practice of piety poses no new questions.

Piety and Inwardness: Western Legacies

At different points in this book we have encountered the influential work of the sociologist Jürgen Habermas, in particular his understanding of the construction of the public sphere in European societies. We have seen he privileges discussion or talk to the detriment of sensual, embodied dimensions of social life. He places such an emphasis on this because he locates this at the center of what he calls communicative rationality, which he, as the Enlightenment philosopher Kant, regards as the basis of modern autonomous individuals, ones who have freed themselves from the constraints of tradition and religion. From this point of view, the modern public sphere and the modern autonomous individual both emerge out of a struggle to free societies and individuals from the constraints of religion. This analysis, first published in German in 1962, was path-breaking in the way it attempted to understand the construction of a public sphere in Europe. But historical work in the period since has underlined the extent to which Habermas's account overemphasizes not only Kantian rational discussion, but also the secular basis of this movement. As the American historian Margaret Jacob emphasizes, what has become the Habermasian orthodox understanding of the emergence of the public sphere ignores the central place of the religiosity of the actors involved. She argues that the Western culture out of which the Enlightenment emerged was deeply shaped by a new spirituality, shown in new forms of religious experience evident in Methodism in Britain, Pietism in Germany, and in the emergence of Freemasonry – all focusing on the individual and seeking to revitalize personal commitment to Christianity (Jacob 1991, 1992). Habermas's individuals, writes Jacob, are "far too secularized . . . the by-product of an idealized, Kantian version of the Enlightenment." She insists that rather than embrace this vision of the secular autonomous individual, we need to understand the "centrality of the religious transformation at work in the creation of modernity" (1992: 77). Jacob explores the intensity of these religious movements: dialoguing with science and the new rationality; constructing new forms of sociability such as Freemasonry, which emerged in the context of the collapse of older, restrictive guilds; interpenetrating with other cultural movements such as the emergence of the novel and its new way of addressing the inner person; combining themes from paganism with Christianity (in ways reminiscent of contemporary New Age movements). Edmund Leites (1986) underlines the central place of the body, sensuality, and sexuality in the Puritan movements that emerged in this context. The British historian E. P. Thompson (1963) underlines the critical role of Methodism in the cultural shifts leading to a new ethic of the dignity of work, which played a decisive role in the emergence of the English labor movement. These analyses all underline the importance of attempting to understand religious movements as a process of social, cultural, and ethical creativity, rather than simply the product of some other factor. In the case of European modernity, these religious movements are not expressions of "tradition," defensive reactions against modernity. They engaged with science, were often fascinated by rationality, at times blurring boundaries, most famously in the work of Newton, who explored alchemy and believed that gravitation was the expression of the will of God at work in the universe. These religious movements, as Charles Taylor (1989) demonstrates, played a critical role in constructing ways of being in the world, acting as "sources of the self," constructing new forms of inwardness that had a critical role in bringing into life new forms of public culture. Such piety movements and the forms of inner experience produced through them are critical to the emergence of western modernity.

What is striking, in the light of this, is the way that many contemporary analyses of Islamic piety movements reduce these either to secular expressions of resistance, a defence of tradition against modernity, or the experience of being dominated by brutal regimes such as the Taliban in Afghanistan. This reflects a political and intellectual context dominated by a consensus stretching from conservatives such as Bernard Lewis or Samuel Huntington (2004) to radical democrats such as John Keane, which regards Islam either as a "failed civilization" or as an expression of embattled tradition. What is clear, however, is the extraordinary limitations of this approach, above all in a globalizing world, where religions are not communities defending themselves, but are increasingly porous flows of experience and meaning. From this perspective, inner experience can reshape public spheres. Two cases point to critical dimensions of such an emerging paradigm: the first from one of the poorest countries in the world, Senegal (declared by the United Nations to be one of the world's Least Developed Countries in 1991); the second from a center of global flows, Cairo.

Globalized Fundamentalism, Personal Experience

In the West African country of Senegal, social structure is deeply entwined with Sufi Islamic orders, structured around religious teachers who claim their position through inheritance (Villalón 1999). Since the 1980s the country has witnessed an important movement of Islamic piety, in particular based among students and urban populations, embracing Sunni Islam, critical of the dominant Sufi tradition and culture. One of its most important expressions has been the movement of young women taking up the practice of veiling (Villalón 1999). But while one of the poorest countries on the planet, life in the geographic space of Senegal is increasingly shaped by global flows. Commodity flows penetrate, opening up forms of practice constructed in terms of the possibility of life elsewhere, beyond the borders: from "hindi" music and videos to rap and hip-hop. Internet cafés open possibility and practices of imagination, as does the circulation of books, cassettes, and other forms of media. The movement of young women taking up the veil is equally shaped in terms of such flows, from imaginations and yearnings for more authentic forms of life in Arab countries to clothing, from the lace-edged veil from South-East Asia to the Iranian *tchador* (Augis 2002). Imagination is central to social practice, and this is increasingly framed in references beyond the border.

Erin Augis's (2002) careful ethnographic study of young Islamist women in Dakar, Senegal, reconstructs the path taken in adopting the veil. Her interviews underline just how much this involves anxiety, uncertainty, a deep sensitivity to the opposition of friends, family, and, in many cases, religious leaders, and a real awareness of the costs involved such as ceasing to play certain sports, being made fun of by school friends. Rather than reflect a community culture defending its tradition, these young women clearly embrace forms of Sunni Islam in opposition to both Senegalese nationalism and traditional forms of Sufi Islam. They are part of a global culture of pan-Islam, associated with flows of goods, ideas, and people originating outside Senegal, in particular from Arab countries. This underlines the extent to which globalization involves cultural flows emerging from different locations, in this case India and Arab countries, not just the centers of global capitalism. Augis argues it is not possible to understand the action young women take through veiling as simply the product of one or more causes, whether the decline of nationalism, the economic crisis, and so on. Despite the importance of these wider processes, her study underlines the importance of practices of piety themselves – cultivating modesty, regular prayer, and Qur'anic literacy – all of which lead these young women to oppose parents, peers, and teachers at school and university, friends, and community. The accounts of these young women underline individual hesitation and struggle, grammars of personal sacrifice. Augis's account corresponds to Alain Touraine's model of "subjectivation": subjective experience constructed against community, and against the market.

This piety movement, just as the European piety movements at the birth of modernity, produce new forms of inner experience. While taking place within a context of social networks, the conversion experience of these young women is a highly individualized process, requiring both "reflection and resolve" (Augis 2002: 165). The young women whom Augis encounters are critical of a corrupt and stalled political regime, just as much as the Maraboutic model of Sufi Islam. They are critical of what we can call an "identity paradigm," powerfully represented in Senegal in the legacy of President Senghor and his themes of "negritude," or the search for an authentic African culture and identity. The key reference points of these young women are outside Senegal. This is neither a "community" nor a "traditional" movement, but a form of global movement that has as its center the construction of forms of personal experience.

Embodied Piety, Embodied Subjectivity

Similar themes emerge in the contemporary mosque movement among women in Cairo (Haenni 2002; Bayat 2002; Salvatore 2000). This movement is built around embodied micropractices: prayer, observing rituals, negotiating public spaces modestly, recitation and study sessions, discussion of the meaning of religious texts. It is located within a wider process within Islam, of the decline of traditional forms of authority centered on the formally trained religious scholars, and the emergence of new, often self-taught, leaders and teachers. In this case, the leaders of the piety movement among women in Cairo are women themselves, most of whom do not possess formally recognized Islamic qualifications.

Saba Mahmood (2001b, 2003, 2004) explores practices of veiling, prayer, and moral cultivation emerging within this movement. Her core argument, one that is of great importance to the task of rethinking movements today, is that such practices of piety cannot be reduced to a symbol or identity logic, as if in some way veiling is to be understood as representing the culture or identity of a group or a community. Nationalist and Islamist parties attempt in fact to transform the veil into a symbol of collective or national identity. Mahmood quotes Adil Hussein, until recently a leader in the Islamist Labor Party (Hizb al 'Amal), who attempts such an construction of veiling:

> In this period of [Islamic] Revival and renewed pride in ourselves and our past, why should be not take pride in the symbols that distinguish us from other countries [like the veil]? So we say that the first condition is that clothing should be modest. But why can't we add a second condition that we would like this dress to be a continuation of what we have created in this region, like the Indian sari? . . . Why can't we have our own dress which expresses decency, a requirement of Islam, as well as the special beauty that would be the mark of our society which has excelled in the arts and civilization? (York 1992, in Mahmood 2004: 52)

Thus described, this grammar of identity is familiar to us: the veil is a symbol; it represents and is a secular claim to recognition of a national community. But, Mahmood argues, this is an understanding imposed from the outside, which fails to capture the critical dimension of this practice of piety. What is at stake, she argues, is not veiling as a *symbol*, as representing identity, but veiling as a form of *embodied action*, part of a wider embodied process through which a pious subject is constructed, in particular through practices of prayer, recitation of the Qu'ran and modest behavior. These practices, evident in particular through veiling, center on the body; they are practices where corporeal experience is central, constituted through prayer, through movements in public, and other forms of embodiment such as learning to cry while praying. Such forms of corporeal practice, Mahmood argues, do "not simply *express* the self but also *shape* the self that they are supposed to signify" (2003: 842; emphasis in original).

This is captured by Amal when she recounts her experience of veiling, not in terms of representing an identity, but as a way of producing a subjectivity that is "shy" or modest:

> I used to think that even though shyness [al-haya] was required of us by God, if I acted shyly it would be hypocritical [nifaq] because I didn't actually feel it inside of me. Then one day, in reading verse 25 in Surat al-Qasas ["The Story"] I realised that al-hya was among the good deeds, and given my natural lack of shyness, *I had to make or create it* first. I realised that making it in yourself is not hypocrisy, and that *eventually your inside learns to have al-haya* too . . . It means making yourself shy, even if it means creating it . . . And finally I understood that once you do this, the sense of shyness eventually imprints itself on your inside. (Mahmood 2004: 156–7; emphasis added)

Namma, another of Mahmood's interlocutors, describes what is at stake in a similar way:

> In the beginning when you wear it [Hijab], you're embarrassed and don't want to wear it because people will say you look older and unattractive, that you won't get married, and will never find a husband. But you must wear the veil, first because it is God's command, and then, with time, because your inside learns to feel shy without the veil, and if you take it off, your entire being feels uncomfortable without it. (Mahmood 2004: 157)

Mona, a third interlocutor, speaks of prayer and the rituals involved in the same way. She speaks of the difficulties involved in rising early for morning prayer, arguing that overcoming these difficulties can in turn shape other areas of life, in this case, mundane areas such as avoiding getting angry with one's sister or using bad language. Praying, including developing the ability to rise at sunrise for first prayers, is understood in terms of

> securing and honing particular moral capacities . . . religious and worldly acts performed repeatedly, with the right kind of intention, eventually root the behaviour with one's senses so much that one's ability to obey God is not a matter of exercising one's will, but issues forth almost spontaneously and

effortlessly from a pious disposition. In this understanding, intention, something that we associate with interiority, is conjoined with outward bodily acts in a manner that the two cannot be conceptually separated. (Mahmood 2003: 850)

Mahmood attempts to think about what is involved in these forms of body practices by drawing on Pierre Hadot's exploration of spiritual exercises, which he describes as "practices which could be physical, as in dietary regimes, or discursive, as in dialogue and meditation, or intuitive, as in contemplation, but which were all intended to effect a modification and transformation of the subject who practiced them" (Hadot 2002: 6, in Mahmood 2004: 122). This understanding of body practice involves a break with the paradigm of representation; body practices are not primarily to be understood as manifesting an identity, but as forms of work that aim at constructing or cultivating a moral or ethical self. As Mahmood argues, this understanding *"reverses the usual routing from interiority to exteriority* in which the unconscious manifests itself in somatic forms" (2004: 122; emphasis added).

Talal Asad underlines the centrality of the body as a "living materiality," as opposed to a body that is to be "overcome" or controlled by a subject. From this perspective this form of practice can be understood as the self becoming the body, and through transforming the body, transforming the self: the

> living body's materiality is regarded as an essential means for cultivating what such traditions define as virtuous conduct and for discouraging what they consider as vice. The role of fear and hope, of felicity and pain, is central to such practices. According to this view of the living body, the more one exercises a virtue the easier it becomes . . . the more one gives into vice, the harder it is to act virtuously. (2003: 89–90)

In that sense, there is an embodied memory constituted through corporeal practice, while such corporeal practice creates moral potential. For Asad the place of pain and agency in both Christian and Islamic traditions illustrates this point. Rather than accept an understanding of embodiment where the subject avoids pain and seeks pleasure (an instrumental relationship to the body), Asad argues that in forms of practice associated with these religious traditions actors can

> use pain to create a space for moral action that articulates this-world-in-the-next. . . . pain does not simply constitute irrefutable evidence of the corporeal

ground of experience, it is also a way of constituting the epistemological status of "the body". As well as its moral potentialities. (2003: 91)

As Zarcone notes, a whole tradition of western scholarship has regarded the body as an obstacle to be overcome, placing importance on the disembodied mind rather than on the body. Regarding the piety movement as a form of "representing" identity or "claiming recognition" fails to understand what is at stake in such corporeal practice. There is clearly a form of agency involved here, a form of action on the self that passes through action upon the body and its place in the world. In this case, as Mahmood argues, action does not issue from natural feelings (a personalist model), but is better understood as creating them. Outward embodied behavior is not understood as representing or expressing innerness – rather, embodied behavior is understood as an instrument to cultivate and transform forms of inner experience. This is not based on the separation of body and mind, where inner states are represented by outer action or appearance. Nor does this form of agency fundamentally aim at "belief," in the cognitive conception of religion as a system of beliefs. Instead this is a form of action that aims at producing a form of embodied subjectivity, a way of being in the world through the body that is understood as ethical and according to the will of God, and to be able to reach the point where to deviate from this makes the entire being *feel* uncomfortable, in a process Mahmood describes as

a mutually constitutive relationship between body learning and body sense . . . [a form of embodied practice] in which the outward behaviour of the body constitutes both the potentiality and the means through which interiority is realized . . . a modest bodily form (the veiled body) [does] not simply express the self's interiority but [is] the means by which it [is] acquired . . . The mosque participants do not understand the body as a sign of the self's interiority but as a means of developing the self's potentiality . . . the mosque participants treat the body as a medium for, rather than a sign of, the self. (Mahmood 2004: 158–66)

Mahmood, in exploring forms of corporeality involved in the women's piety movement, argues that what is critical is "the *work* bodily practices perform in crafting a subject – rather than the *meanings* they signify" (2004: 122; emphasis in original). While this might be interesting to the anthropologist, does it have implications beyond debates among specialists? In the context of the movements and grammars of action we are exploring, it does. It pushes us to rethink our understandings of action, the embodied subject, and the forms and grammars of public experience that emerge as a consequence.

Embodiment, Subject, and Ways of Knowing: beyond Representation

Western culture and history attach a primacy to the mind and the action of the mind over the body, understood as "inert, passive and static" (Csordas 1993: 136). Thomas Csordas argues that this has led to the dominance of what he calls a "textualist and representationalist" paradigm, evident in particular in understandings of culture as a symbolic system or "text," where the action of knowing takes the form of understanding such signs – a paradigm that shapes the way western forms of knowledge have sought to understand the world, from Levi-Strauss and Geertz to Derrida and Foucault. This semiotic/ textualist paradigm is at the heart of the understanding of action as the power to represent, becoming a monolithic grammar of being-in-the-world. We encounter this paradigm at the center of contemporary understanding of social movement, where the action of movement is understood as "public display" that represents a population or a category (Tilly 1997) or as the performance of identity (Hetherington), the action of representation bringing the category into existence (Bourdieu). This understanding of action as symbolic representation is at the core of the identity paradigm of social movements. Just as Bourdieu, and earlier Hobbes, for sociologist Ron Eyerman, social movements are constituted through the action of representation, where empathy and belonging, for example, are "represented and reinforced through markers and symbols, buttons, pieces of clothing, flags, placards and so on, infused with symbolic value. *These represent 'us'*, to participants, as well as marking off this group for and against 'others'" (Eyerman 2002: 8; emphasis added). Such "performance of identity" involves the "construction of the persona of the Other," where at the center of social movements we encounter what Hetherington considers "symbolic forms of resistance to the instrumentality rationality of modern life" (1998: 103).

This representational paradigm profoundly shapes the way we think about movements and action, and just like the foundations of a building, it is often unseen. As an invisible foundation, we do not focus a great deal of attention on it, presuming that action as representation is a nonproblematic, universal category. Asad traces the emergence of this modern concept of "symbolic action" through reconstructing the way ritual, in particular in modern anthropology, has come to be understood as "a species of representational behaviour" (Asad 1993: 60). He does this through exploring the practice of ritual in the medieval Christian tradition of religious orders, where ritual was a form of action understood in terms of moral discipline, where rituals such as prayer, fasting, or liturgy were not symbols to be interpreted, "but abilities to be acquired according to rules sanctioned by those in authority." In this religious context, the Ritual was a rule of behavior, consisting of "all pre-scribed practices, whether they had to do with the proper ways of eating, sleeping, working, and praying or with proper moral dispositions and spiri-tual aptitudes," the aim being developing virtues put "to the service of God." This involved learning essentially through imitation, above all of forms of embodied practice. In this context, ritual was not understood in terms of "representative behaviour," but as cultivating the "moral structures of the self" (1993: 63).

The emergence of a modern form of self involves an increasing aware-ness of the difference and tension between an inner self and what came to be understood as its outer manifestations. Norbert Elias (1994) places this at the heart of what he calls the "civilizing process," emphasizing a shift in forms of social control, where these shift from the absolutist order and create a new culture and awareness of self-control. Elias in particular emphasizes the importance of the development of manners and rules of etiquette, in particular in the French Court, which he argues are expressions of new forms of self-control. Asad points to changes occurring in Renaissance England, increasingly shaped by an awareness of the tension between inner self and outer person. Asad sees this at work in particular in the drama of the time, while Greenblatt underlines the increasing place in the Elizabethan court of manuals and other forms of instruction that emphasize the importance of "dissimulation" and "feigning" (1980: 163, in Asad 1993: 67). In this context, the "self now depended on the maintenance of moral distance between public forms of behaviour and private thoughts and feelings" (Asad 1993: 67). Representation became something that could be learnt and manipulated. This is not to suggest that intrigue and deception were absent before the Renaissance. Rather, on the basis of a new understanding of the tension between inner self and outer self, "practices of representation (and misrep-resentation) were now becoming the objects of systematic knowledge at the service of power" (Asad 1993: 68). This understanding of representation, which formed the basis of the new manuals, is at the center of Niccoló Macchiavelli's understanding of the meaning of power.

The important point here is to recognize that what we today consider to be "representational behaviour," above all associated with the idea of ritual, is the product of a trajectory. The Renaissance period can be understood as a transition period. The Renaissance masque, the Court dance of the Eliza-bethan period, was a display of power, but it was not what we now under-stand as "representational behaviour." King and courtiers participated, the dance an assertion of power more than its simulation (Asad 1993: 69). But in this period we encounter not only the birth of guides to "representational behaviour" but also handbooks of symbolic imagery that were "relentlessly explicated": "this process of explication did not simply provide authoritative meanings, it defined things as symbols" (1993: 69). This understanding of meaning in terms of the representational did not emerge only in the context of court society; Asad suggests it lies in new ways of approaching Christian biblical exegesis emerging at the time, in the context of wider religious movements that increasingly sought to understand religious texts in terms of different systems of meaning.

This points to a new understanding of ritual emerging with the birth of modernity, from ritual as embodied action aimed at moral cultivation to ritual as symbolic expression that can be read and made intelligible. In this process religion emerges as a generic category, understood by western thinkers in terms of belief rather than action. Asad traces the genealogy of this process from Kant's articulation of the generic concept of "religion" to Clifford Geertz's (1973) argument that "religion is a system of symbols" – reaffirming the view proposed by Durkheim and Freud, that religions are to be understood as collective representations. For Geertz, the task of the anthropologist becomes deciphering or "reading" these symbols. For Asad this parallels transformations occurring in western culture involving the new understanding of inner experience and outer representation. Despite the claims to universality that extend from Kant, he argues that this understanding of the religious as symbolic systems and belief is "a modern, privatized Christian one because and to the extent that it emphasizes the priority of belief as a state of mind rather than as constituting activity in the world" (1993: 47).

This understanding of symbolic representation would have a major impact in British anthropology.[2] Key figures argued that it is through ritual that community could be constructed and defended against the inroads of instrumental rationality: Victor Turner affirmed the place of ritual in the struggle of *communitas* against instrumental order, an analysis reworked today by Hetherington when he affirms the role of the "romantic structure of feeling" in contemporary movements, which "seeks some sort of holism of everyday life and challenges the instrumental that lies behind its fragmentation" (1998: 109). It is through symbolic representation, or identity, that such holism is achieved. Hence the great importance the social movement literature attaches to "collective identity."

The textualist or representationalist paradigm understands action in terms of the symbolic, the power to represent, through which the social is instituted. It is very important to understand how deeply this penetrates Western understandings of modernity and its other. Durkheim studied the embodied rituals of what he regarded as primitive societies, and saw these as expressions of effervescence, of people becoming carried away by an avalanche of passion, dissolved into some sort of crowd experience of disorder and excitation, and emerging transformed. For Durkheim, the embodied and the representational were on a path where the movement from the primitive to the modern took the form of a kind of Kantian freedom, arguing, "the more emancipated we are from our senses . . . the more we are persons" (Durkheim 1912/1995: 275). The primacy of the representational that Csordas underlines within paradigms of action is one that asserts the evolutionary primacy of the representational over the embodied, and the secular over the religious. Equally for Freud, the cognitive and the symbolic stand above the embodied, which he understands in terms of forces, energies, and the "pneumatic": embodied practice understood as inferior to the more superior conceptual and representational practice. Starrett (1995: 953) notes that Freud's view of the relationship between thought and action drew on his understanding of the "lower orders," where he understood action as evolving (at the level of the personal subject and societal types) and proceeding toward progressively greater capacities of symbolization, an argument developed in *Totem and Taboo*. From this point of view, both societies and children act first through embodiment, and progressively develop a capacity for symbolization.

Starrett (1995: 953) underlines the impact of this conceptual framework in the colonial encounter. Colonial administrators and educators, when confronted with Egyptian practices of learning, were dismayed at the extent to which this involved a form of embodiment and corporeal experience, contrasting this with the European, conceptual mode of learning. Hence they were dismayed when confronted with what they regarded as meaningless bodily oscillation and noise present in classroom experiences of teaching, when compared with the stillness, order and, morality of the European subject learner; the religious system was regarded as one of dogma and taboo as opposed to the reason and morality of Christianity, emphasizing a corporeal understanding of sin as opposed to abstract ethical concepts. These administrators saw themselves fighting a culture of intoxication and sensuality, as opposed to their own, which they understood in terms of inner asceticism and silent attentiveness. These differences were understood as manifesting an evolutionary path, from embodiment to the conceptual, paralleling Freud's worldview. Societies were understood to evolve from the embodied and active to the contemplative and symbolic, as too was the process of individuation and biological growth: the child first acting through embodiment, later developing the capacity for symbolization. The forms of embodied action that the colonial administrators encountered in Egypt were regarded not simply as different, but as primitive on an evolutionary path moving from the embodied to symbolic. Freud believed that such passions and emotions could ultimately be mastered by observation and interpretation, "thereby giving rationality primacy in the constitution of the modern, secular subject" (Asad 2003: 69). This proposition has deeply shaped the way we have thought about social movements. Tilly's contrast between direct action (riots, blockades, etc.) and the association mirrors this evolutionary understanding of the relationship between the embodied and the rational. One of these involves a practice of representation; the other does not.

The Embodied Listener

The tradition extending from Kant, via Durkheim and Freud, through to Habermas emphasizes rational deliberation, where the abstraction of deliberation is the source of its potential universality. This gives rise to the accounts of a public sphere defined in terms of a delocalized, secular discussion, which in turn shapes the way we think of what constitutes a social movement, where freedom as such is defined in terms of the exercise of reason, eloquently expressed in Polletta's image of freedom as an endless meeting. This attaches a conceptual primacy to the reasoning subject in the public sphere. It is important to recognize that this understanding of language is disembodied. Habermas goes so far as to attempt to understand communicative action through a logical reconstruction of the theory of language, drawing on the work of linguists such as Chomsky, where language is understood as a system of symbols. What is striking in this account of the public sphere is the lack of interest in, and conceptualization of, the experience of listening.

It is this experience of listening that is at the heart of Charles Hirschkind's (2001a, 2001b, 2004) exploration of the piety movement's practice of *da 'wa* or calling. But rather than focus on preachers, Hirschkind focuses on the experience of listening, where he argues there is an important form of ethical, embodied action at stake – one at the basis of a form of public sphere. His focus is in the listening practices that are part of the piety movement, above all linked to the cassette-recorded sermons of popular Islamic preachers (*kitaba*; singular *khatib*) that have become one of the most widely used media by the middle and lower-middle classes in Cairo since the 1970s (produced by some six licensed companies, and reproduced countless times so that the number of copies circulating number in the millions), and broadcast from shops, workplaces, public transport, cafés, and taxis. Hirschkind focuses on the experience of *listening* to these sermons. A good preacher, or *khatib*, must succeed in waking his audience from a state of lassitude, must get them to focus on the way they are living and the threat and promise of the afterlife, must weave Qur'anic narratives into the daily lives of the listeners. But the action of listening is not simply one of absorption, much less one of deliberation in the Kantian/Habermasian sense of the exercise of a potentially universal reason. Rather the listeners have to respond emotionally through hearing; they have to experience fear, dread, longing, peace, and closeness to God, described in terms of stillness or inner peace. But this requires active forms of response to the sermon, involving a range of illocutionary acts – calling for prayers upon the Prophet each time his name is mentioned, imploring forgiveness. At times these responses are out loud; at others these involve a silent moving of the lips or whispers. This listening in turn requires training in forms of comportment and concentration associated with Qur'anic audition, memorization, and recitation (Hirschkind 2001b: 631). What is at stake here is not, insists Hirschkind, a psychophysiological process of catharsis (where internal, and potentially dangerous emotions, are released in a kind of Freudian pneumatic understanding of pressure and release), but instead involves a form of embodied action, where listening involves more than the ability to recall a text or a story, but where

> knowledge of these Islamic narrative forms consists not simply in the ability to recite a given text, but also in performing its emotional, gestural, and kinaesthetic contours, the bodily condition of the text as memory . . . beyond its referential content, the sermon can be seen as a technique for training the body's gestures and affects, its physiological textures and colorations, its rhythms and styles of expression . . . the stories impart ethical habits and the organization of sensory and motor skills necessary for inhabiting the world in a manner considered to be appropriate for Muslims. (Hirschkind 2001: 636–7)

This is an understanding of listening that is not reducible to mental state, nor are the gestures, movements, and illocutions that are central to such listening representative of an inner state; rather this form of listening is action to shape inner experience.

This listening, argues Hirschkind, is a form of sensory experience that is *learnt*, just as we learn to listen to music (to distinguish color, timbre, rhythm, to understand a piece of music in terms of what is coming and what has come in a way that creates a space defined in terms of memory and anticipation). The experience of listening to music, experiences of movement, color, touch, and emotion, cannot be produced cognitively, but instead is "grounded in the actual sensual experience of the body as a complex of culturally honed perceptual capacities" (Hirschkind 2001b: 629). In a similar way, the action of sermon audition needs to be understood as practice, or forms of work, cultivating the self.

Islam, Citizenship, and the Public Sphere

The Kantian/Habermasian understanding grounds the public sphere in rational, and hence potentially universalizable, communication – an approach that has been very influential in theories of deliberative democracy (Dryzek 2002) where we encounter "the Enlightenment dream of creating a pure field of politics governed by a discourse of reason mediated in the public sphere" (Salvatore 2004: 1028). This disembodied reason is framed in terms of representation and the superiority of the symbolic/representational over the corporeal. The universality of this reason can only be achieved on the basis of its abstraction, its disembodied state. Hirschkind notes the ways that the formation of the modern Egyptian state and the conception of citizenship associated with it involve such a disembodiment of the ethical listener. Within the Islamic tradition the Qur'an is not only regarded as an authoritative source; it is a source of beauty and wonder, to which access is gained through recitation and hearing – physically, not only or even primarily through cognition.

There are parallels here in terms of the ways we can access a painting as a work of art that must be experienced. To do otherwise would be to equate listening to a song with reading its lyrics. As Hirschkind argues, this means that the Islamic tradition places much less importance on the art of rhetoric and persuasion (rules and techniques that a speaker might employ to move an audience), giving priority instead to the activity of listening (2004), emphasizing cultivating ways of listening that allow the subject to experience what we could call the poetic aspects of the text. Listening thus involves the human heart and whole body, as opposed to the consideration of the rational merits of an argument. Within this tradition, "listening is privileged as the sensory activity most essential to moral conduct" (2004: 136). While the Christian tradition from Augustine came to understand rhetoric as instrumental, where there is no necessary relationship between eloquence and veracity, the Islamic tradition has been premised on a "fundamental unity of the aesthetic and the true" (Hirschkind 2004: 136). Access to the truth cannot be achieved without an experience of the beauty of message – hence the importance of the agency of the listener and the corporeal experience of listening.

What are the implications in terms of public space? Hirschkind notes the transformation of preaching and listening that accompanied the development of the Egyptian state over the twentieth century has involved the state seeking increasingly to control preaching, and where it increasingly became influenced by models emerging in western communications programs, with a new focus on the *khatib* employing "a morally neutral art of rhetorical manipulation, instilling in his listeners the opinions and attitudes that will constitute modern Egyptians" (2004: 140). At the center of this process is a changing experience of listening. In the classical model of preaching, both the preacher and the listener submit to the discipline, power and beauty of the word: the *khatib's* "relationship to his speech" is not purely an instrumental one. "Instead, he submits to its discipline, fashioning his voice in accord with the demands of the words he recites, giving them their 'due' (haqqihi), their natural pronunciation. This achieved, his task ends, while that of the listener begins" (2004: 141).

The rise of the modern Egyptian state and the mode of citizenship associated with it involves, Hisrschkind argues, a new kind of public communication – one where the *khatib* develops an instrumental relationship with his words (influenced in particular by communication and public relations theory) and seeks to inform and manipulate an audience, while the audience is stripped of its agency. As Islamic discourses became increasingly integrated into state formation, this has sought to strip listening of its corporeal-ethical agency. The state has sought to create a new type of listener, one understood as the passive receptor of public communications. Hirschkind writes:

> Today, articles in the government-controlled national press frequently bemoan the ongoing practice of traditions that cultivate a "reverence for the sacred word" and an attention to the sonic qualities of language over and above the symbolic. Hearing bypasses the rational facilities, it is claimed, penetrating directly to the vulnerable emotional core of the untutored peasant. Reading, in contrast, encourages reasoned reflection and reasoned assent. The nineteenth-century European critique of the superficiality and artificiality of Muslim practices has found new purchase in this context: tradition-bound Muslims, it is said, are too involved with surface and externalities – the sound of reciting voices, the prescribed movements of the body at prayers, rules of fasting and ablutions – all of which define a kind of life incompatible with more refined and developed modes of reason, understanding, and piety. (Hirschkind, 2004: 176)

The colonial perspective, that of the administrators or that of Freud, attaches primacy to the symbolic, understood as a stage in social and personal evolution that progresses beyond the embodied, where one mode of listening is destined to supersede another. Hirschkind argues that rather than represent stages in social evolution, what is at stake here is a "politics of hearing":

> one of the axes around which contemporary divisions in Egyptian society position themselves concerns precisely the question of whether the Quar'an's divine aspect lies in the material word itself or only in its symbolic meaning, as discovered through the operation of human understanding. The two models of language authorize very different interpretive regimes, structures of power linked to contrasting social and political projects. (2004: 146)

Hirschkind insists that what is at stake here is not an opposition between "literalist" and "symbolic" modes of interpretation. Rather contrasting modes of agency. On the one hand, a mode of listening where sound lies at the center of "practices by which the self acquires the virtues that enable moral action"; on the other, "an expressivist understanding of language whereby speech is conceived of as a material apparatus for the externalization of a nonmaterial meaning" (2004: 148).

Rather than understand the current development of da 'wa and the wider piety movement in terms of the collapse or thinning of public culture, Hirschkind's exploration opens out what he calls the "politics of hearing," the basis of an "Islamic counterpublic." Egypt's modernization over the twentieth century saw nationalists adopt a western understanding of communication, with mosques integrated into constituting a public based on opinion manipulation, where the relationship between the speaker and voice is essentially instrumental. Hirschkind argues that the contemporary development of da 'wa and piety practices do not so much represent a thinning of politics, as the emergence of a countermodel of communication embedded in education centers, preaching associations, the expanding number of private mosques (see Gaffney 1994), publishing houses, and exponentially growing communication practices built up around the circulation of audio cassettes of preachers. This form of communication also takes place in conversations among friends, from discussions about whether it is appropriate to pray at tombs or send donations to Bosnia.

This counter public does not mediate *between* state and society, as does "civil society" conceptualized on the basis of central European history. As Hirschkind argues

> the practice of da 'wa does not take place within, or serve to uphold, that domain of associational life referred to as civil society. Rather, the da'iya's narrative locates itself within the temporal frame of an Islamic umma and in relation to the succession of events that characterizes its mode of historicity. (2001: 17)

On the one hand, there is a focus on the life world: local community, self-help initiatives, dress, and modesty as ways of mediating relationships, attendance at mosque and prayer. On the other, a reference to the *umma*, a community experience that transcends the homogenous time and borders of the nation. Not only does this kind of counterpublic not function as a mediation between state and society, the state is not a mediation between local and global. There is no sense of levels (micro, meso, macro), nor of one level being represented by another.

Rethinking Autonomy and Agency

The modern understanding of agency, Talal Asad argues, needs to be understood within what he calls an "anthropology of the secular," the new awareness of the sovereignty of the human subject that emerged out of religious reform movements in Europe, in particular the understanding of the "communion of saints." This leads to an understanding of agency where the natural sovereignty and freedom of modern subjects will lead them to strive to empower themselves and to seek freedom (2003: 71). This understanding of agency translates into the understanding of the public sphere as one of rational deliberation where the critical faculty of reason is exercised. This understanding of agency plays a foundational role in the way we have understood movements, as part of this process of secular modernization leading toward increased freedom.

This alerts us to the extent to which the way we experience time is a social product, shaping both the way we understand both agency and the concept of movement. German philosopher Reinhart Koselleck (1985) explores the emergence of what we now experience as "historical time," describing the experience of time in premodern Europe as essentially "additive." History from this perspective was understood as a chronicle of events. This "additive" experience of time was uniform and static, one focused on the novelty of event to event, with a tendency to look elsewhere than one's own time to find what was new (Koselleck 1985: 240). From the eighteenth century in Europe a new time consciousness begins to develop, one that begins to interpret past, present, and future in terms of progression, and begins to locate societies and cultures on a continuum. This made possible a new sense of the present, as a location defined between past and future, a place where it was possible to register new experiences, while by the mid-eighteenth century a sense of historical acceleration shaped time-consciousness. This understanding of progress and simultaneity converges with new understandings of the politics of large numbers to give rise to understandings not only of historical change, but to the modern idea of movement. But, as Charles Taylor underlines, this new experience of time was "homogenous"; modernity could have only one temporal architecture, one that is exclusively secular.

It is possible to include piety movements within this temporality. They can be understood as "resistance" (hence located *within* modern time), a type of analysis that as Karin Werner (1998: 39) observes, universalizes fundamentalism and locates it within modernity as a form of antimodernity; or they can be framed within British anthropology's opposition of the expressive and the instrumental (the holist and the fragmented), thus defined as expressions of "collective identity." In different ways both these approaches appeal to the concept of "resistance," which locates the actor "within a secular history of freedom from all coercive control" (Asad 2003: 72–3). Such analyses locate piety movements within the borderless world and its temporal homogeneity. To include these movements within universal time we have to understand them within the model of agency upon which this is constructed, a secular movement toward freedom (they become expressions of collective identity, ways of managing the tension between tradition and modernization, or expressions of holism against fragmentation).

Saba Mahmood engages with this question directly. Firstly, this movement cannot be understood within the "flat language" of resistance to domination. Nor can this movement be analyzed in terms of the categories of rights, representation, and recognition – the grammar of identity movements. This is not a form of movement involved in "making claims on the state in particular, and the social collectivity in general, on the basis of certain shared characteristics that the participants consider essential to their self-definition as a group" (Mahmood 2004: 192). The impact of the mosque movement opens out a vision where politics is not simply about rational argumentation and moral principles, but issues forth from intersubjective levels of being and acting (2004: 152). This is not a movement of collective identity, proclaiming and demanding rights for a social category. To take categories of autonomous rational individual versus community and its culture is to fail to recognize that at the center of this movement are "practices of subjectivation" (Mahmood 2004: 194) that are not intelligible within a narrative of a secular history of the sovereign, free subject constantly seeking empowerment. Here we encounter a form of subjectivation, but not framed within a grammar of secular sovereignty.

Complex Space, Complex Time

To explore this question, Talal Asad suggests opening ourselves to think in terms of "complex space" and "complex time." To do so, he draws on the work of theologian John Milbank, and suggests that both medieval Christian and Islamic traditions recognized that complex space exists before the more simple space of the nation-state, and that as a result the "sovereign state cannot (never could) contain all the practices, relations, and loyalties of its citizens" (Asad 2003: 179). Asad links two propositions:

> Unlike the modern, secular world of nation-states, medieval Christendom and Islam recognized a multiplicity of overlapping bonds and identities. People were not always expected to subject themselves to one sovereign authority, *nor were they themselves sovereign moral subjects*. (2003: 179; emphasis added)

The emergence of the modern understanding of sovereignty was linked to the Calvinist conception of the "community of saints," secularized by Locke. While the understanding of "identity politics" can be understood as extending this logic, the Islamic experiences we are exploring here cut across it: they make a break with the type of exclusivity that Charles Taylor points to. Limiting the autonomy of the subject, they limit the autonomy of the state.

This suggests a break with an understanding of public spheres constructed in terms of rationality, discursivity, and autonomy. Just as the embodied listener enters into tension with the new understanding of symbolic communication in Egypt's public sphere, the time of the body enters into tension with the simultaneity of the nation. As Asad argues,

> the temporality of many tradition-rooted practices (that is, the time each embodied practice requires to complete and to perfect itself, the past into which it reaches, that it re-encounters, re-imagines, and extends) cannot be translated into the homogenous time of national politics. The body's memories, feelings and desires necessarily escape the rational/instrumental orientation of such politics. (Asad 2003: 179–80)

Personalization, Globalization

This understanding of da 'wa is linked to the concept of umma, the Islamic community. Historically and today, the umma does not correspond to the borders of the nation-state, nor does it correspond to the European experience where a new form of public emerged at the same time as the modern state, understood as between state and society. As a form of practice, da 'wa is both personalized and globalized. Globalization is linked to the movements of population and technologies of communication, evident in the way cassettes circulate from Bosnia to Jordan to the United States. But at the same time, it is grounded in micropractices, forms of charity or doing good aimed at one's neighbor or the place and context where one lives and interacts with others – in the neighborhood, while traveling. As Salvatore argues,

> theologically, the Islamic umma includes all Muslims but it retains some degree of concreteness in that the "other" is first of all one's neighbour whom the faithful consider, or, if necessary help to become, a good Muslim. *It is through this micro-link*, which often takes the form of moral discourse, that the *umma* is instituted. (Salvatore 2004: 1015; emphasis added)

This cuts across separations: the public and the private, the religious and the secular, and in the process, the boundaries of nation-states. Questions of modesty, the relationship between men and women in public, the practice of prayer, rather than remaining in the private sphere, become politicized and as the object of public debate, an obstacle to the modern state's separation of domains of private and public (Hirschkind 2001a). This movement opens new forms of public argument about ways of life characterized by the relative equality of those involved (women and men are both called to be involved in *da 'wa*), and cannot be understood within a liberal trajectory of traditional to modern, or resistance to this. This movement, Mahmood underlines, is "outside the bounds of a liberal progressive imaginary," yet she argues it is a valuable form of human flourishing, one that should not be approached in a way that domesticates or assimilates (in the way that the modernity versus antimodernity analysis does), nor looked upon as a lifeworld that is provisional, destined for extinction (2004: 199).

NOTES

1   In urban contexts, for example, excluded immigrant populations will instrumentalize tradition, in particular forms of honor and patronage, to counter disorganization in immigrant neighborhoods. This is the basis of classical forms of urban gang (McDonald 1999).

2   Not necessarily without some difficulty. Asad offers as an example the work of British anthropologist Alfred Gell, who attempts to apply Claude Levi-Strauss's understanding of symbolic system to the ritual practice of the Umeda people of New Guinea. Gell complains, "Among my Umeda informants I found none willing to discuss the meaning of their symbols as symbols 'standing for' some other thing or idea, rather than as concrete things in themselves. In fact, I found it impossible to even pose the question of meaning in Umeda, since I could not discover any corresponding Umeda word for English 'mean', 'stand for' etc." (Gell 1975: 211).

PART IV

Paradigms of Action and Culture

CHAPTER 10

Rethinking Movements

This book sets out to explore shifting forms of action and culture in movements that are globalizing today. Its hope is not only to address researchers and students, but people involved in creating, experiencing and living such experiences. What are the implications for the way we think about movements? Are there themes here that can help us understand action and globalization in new ways?

Beyond "Social Movements"?

The movements we have explored all point to a radical shift in paradigm from the dominant types of movement that emerged and consolidated in Europe and North America over the nineteenth and twentieth centuries, and which we commonly call "social movements." These movements emerged in the context of new understandings about generality and functional equivalence, new understandings of large numbers and forms of inclusion, and new ways of thinking about the relationship between individual and collective experience. These transformations combined to make it possible to think in new ways about categories, organization, and action. Out of this emerged what we now understand as the "social movement." The new understandings of generality, large numbers, and functional equivalents made it possible to think of collectives acting in new ways, and as Charles Tilly and Pierre Bourdieu underline, these forms of action were embedded in a new historicity of representation. We can see this in Tilly's emphasis on the historical novelty of the association and Bourdieu's emphasis on the symbolic act of representation creating new social groups such as classes. Talal Asad's analysis of the genealogy of this understanding takes us back to the birth of modernity, and to new practices in the European Renaissance that began to separate the inner beings of persons and their public representation, which led to a new understanding of symbolic action that Hobbes places at the center of the creation of the first modern collective being, the nation-state. At the center of this new modern understanding of action we encounter "the power to represent." This has been at the center of ways of thinking about social movements, where *the group constitutes itself through the act of representation*.

We can see this new understanding playing out in the industrial age, in particular in the paradigms of collective action we encounter in the trade unions that developed over the nineteenth and twentieth centuries. The structure of movements was understood in terms of vertical relationships of representation and delegation, which could go from local to regional to national to international. What was important was public, shared identity. Any person playing a role could in principle be replaced by any other in an attempt to desingularize involvement. The collective acted through the individual through a culture of solidarity. Members relate to "the totality" brought into being through congresses, declarations, and symbols. Horizontal person-to-person relationships represent a potential threat, to the extent they cut across the core relationship, the one linking the member to the totality. Action is understood above all in intentional terms.

What is striking in the extent to which the way we think about contemporary movements has largely remained embedded in this paradigm. Tarrow emphasizes a layered hierarchy in his model of "scale shift." Tilly's earlier understanding of the association, with his insistence on its deliberate formation, underlined that the association represented, or spoke on behalf of, some other group. Over the 1980s and into the 1990s we witnessed a shift in dominant approaches to social movements, moving away from organization and emphasizing instead collective identity and community. But action is still thought of in the same terms: movements act "in the name of identities," action is the "power to represent." Some authors argue movements primarily represent interests, and therefore can be understood in terms of opportunity structures and strategies. Others argue that they represent communities and identities, and so they emphasize symbolic action and "expressions of identity." Arguably what is known as the "political process" approach to social movements has achieved the influence it possesses not only because of the undoubted scholarship of its key figures, but because it combines these two dimensions of representation. Movements, these authors argue, represent their identities strategically; they make claims to worthiness, commitment, and unity, in order to be more successful players in the political system. Throughout these different approaches, the same theme recurs. Expressing the identity constructs the community (Hetherington). The association and the claim create what Tilly calls "the constituency." In both the instrumental theories (opportunities and strategies) and the expressive theories (communities and symbols), *the group is brought into being through the act of representation.* This is the heart of the idea of "social movement."

If in this book we have engaged, even briefly, with thinkers like Hobbes or taken the time to think about the new understandings of representation that emerged at the birth of European modernity, or began to explore the idea of civilizations, it has been to draw out an awareness of the social processes involved in the construction of fundamental categories of experience. These are ways-of-being in the world, but also, ways-of-being in the body: where we experience our self as having a body, or being "in" a body. Where primacy is attached to the symbolic and the representational, either within a grammar of evolution from the embodied to the symbolic, or within a cathartic understanding of embodiment, where the body represents disorder that needs to be converted into symbols to be processed. What we unselfconsciously universalize as "the social" is the product of the western trajectory. Originating from the Latin *socialis* or *socius*, Mary Poovey (2002: 127) notes that "social" entered the English language in the mid-sixteenth century, understood in 1562 as a *capacity* possessed by the individual to form relationships. This, she argues, reflects a changing understanding of the human subject, no longer understood as part of a larger whole, but as a monad possessing the capability to relate to other monads. Poovey's historical reconstruction of the origins and transformation of the term underlines just how much the new understanding mirrored an awareness of the new individualism and the new ethical burden that came with it. Originally this understanding of a social capacity was understood in religious terms, as a dimension of human nature that had its origins in God. Poovey traces over the 1700s its gradual secularization, evolving from a dimension of human nature originating in the divine, to become what the British philosopher Thomas Reid articulated in 1785 as the "operations of the mind." This had the effect not only of naturalizing what had once been understood in theological terms, but also lay the basis for an understanding of the social which privileges a grammar of signs, with Reid arguing that sensations needed to be understood as "signs" of external objects (Clarke 1987). While critical of much of the philosophy of Descartes, this shared the same understandings of the separation of the body and subjectivity. Talal Asad traces in this context the emergence of the idea of "character" as a notion of an essential identity unique to each individual (1993: 70), in an emerging society of individuals understood as both increasingly public and increasingly private, both "interchangeable and newly unique" (Poovey 2002: 137). It is out of this trajectory that we encounter a western paradigm of action as representation, one that emphasizes the primacy of the symbolic, stretching from Descartes to Kant and Reid, Durkheim, and Freud, and to the theorists of symbolic systems and their successors, from Levi-Strauss, the English anthropologists,

Habermas, and Derrida. These are not theorists of social movements, but their work has played a decisive role in constructing the categories through which we understand acting and being in the world.

Embodiment, Action, and Subject

Each of the movements we have explored cuts across the primacy of the symbolic, the idea that action represents an interest or expresses an identity, and through this, constitutes a group. Each underlines in a different way the importance of embodied, experiential grammars of action. The exploration of the "antiglobalization" movements underlined the importance of embodiment, of the multiple senses giving access to the world, to the self, and to the other. The movement of qigong that we explored cannot be understood in terms of action to represent a category – rather it is better understood as a "healing movement." The Zapatistas are not involved in ethnonational action where they represent a community identity; rather we encounter forms of openness to the other, a culture of indeterminacy, forms of embodied communication evident in narrative rhythm; it is movement built through the musicality of embodied intersubjectivity. The Islamic piety movement is not expressing an identity nor constituting a constituency, but is involved in forms of embodied makings of the self, where we encounter an understanding of language not framed in terms of the of the primacy of the symbol, but one that gives importance to sound, hearing, and the ethic of the embodied listener.

None of these movements is constructed around structures of representation and delegation, and none is an expression of a process of rational deliberation. What constantly recurs is the fact that these movements are involved in *doing*, where the senses are at the heart of action. The visual encounter with puppets involves an encounter with beauty and grief. The practices of qigong construct experiences of communicative interiority and embodied memory; practices of piety construct experiences of innerness and forms of self-making that do not correspond to the western, autonomous self. The Zapatista stories are the product of a speaker and a listener, not a recurring, timeless symbolic system. Each story evokes a sense of place – the sound, the smell, the feel of time, the touch of the wind, the smell of the earth, themes that are also at the center of the antiroads action we explored.

These forms of action underline the importance of embodiment as practice, where embodied experience is a "mode of presence and engagement" (Csordas 1993: 135) in the world. To understand the nature of movement here, we need to break with paradigms of group, community, or category, where the group constitutes itself through the action of representation. Rather than the paradigm of group or community, these movements are better understood in terms of a paradigm of embodied intersubjectivity (Csordas 1993), where we encounter hearing, feeling, touching, tasting, where time is in the body through the place of rhythm in these actions.

What is striking is the extent to which dominant theories of social movements exclude the senses. This is most obvious in instrumental accounts of movements, with their focus on strategy, rationality, calculation, and opportunity. We need to be very clear: once we introduce the senses, we limit the domain of intentional action. This is not simply the idea, one that we are familiar with, that our body is an obstacle that limits us. Rather it is to underline that while we can shape the senses (and many forms of body practice aim at this), the body remains as Nadia Seremetakis (1994: 9) argues, a meaning-generating apparatus that operates beyond both consciousness and intention. The senses open the body to memory of things forgotten, beyond the domain of intentional action. We cannot decide to remember something we have forgotten; this cannot be achieved through will or cognition. This is powerfully illustrated through the development of the qigong movement in the period following the Cultural Revolution. It is not through will and representation (Bourdieu's understanding of action) that a new sense of embodied subjectivity can be constituted after a period of trauma. Such embodiment places involuntary experience at the center of action – body practices having a significant dimension of learning to relinquish control of the body.

It is relatively easy to understand that the instrumental paradigm, with its understanding of action as strategy and maximizing opportunity, would tend to exclude the body and the senses. But isn't this at the heart of the identity paradigm, with its argument that movements are, as Hetherington argues, "expressions of identity"? Such approaches draw in particular on Durkheim, and via Victor Turner, on Freud, and attach a great importance to ritual, as we saw in Sasha Roseneil's account of ritual surrounding the funeral of Princess Diana in Britain, or Kevin Hetherington's argument that movements are "intensely affectual identifications," experiences of "communitas" which oppose the fragmentation that results from the instrumental domination of modern society (reworking, as we have seen, British anthropology's understanding of ritual) (1998: 113). The core idea, powerfully expressed by Hetherington, is that movements generate holism in response to fragmentation. Ron Eyerman, for example, echoes Durkheim when he insists that "most of all, movement refers to an experience of moving and being moved by forces greater than one's self, individual will or rational choices" (2002: 2): the choice at stake in movement is presented either as rational choice or being moved by "something greater." These approaches to ritual and communitas as experiences of undifferentiated emotion understand the "something greater" in terms of experiences of "deindividualation" (Marshall 2002), the dissolution of the individual into the unstructured collective, the *communitas*. Hetherington's account of "ecstasy," one that he places at the center of movement experiences of affect, mirrors Durkheim's discussion of ecstasy that he believes defines religious experience. These are understood as experiences of disorder and excitation through which the individual emerges transformed. When the senses enter, the subject disappears. We are offered the choice between a rational, instrumental subject, or the senses and passion of the communitas. This opposition is powerfully expressed by Durkheim when he writes "we are more personal the more we are freed from our senses" (1915: 272).

The instrumental (strategy and opportunity) accounts and the identity (expressive, community, *communitas*) theories mirror each other. The instrumental theories exclude the body in order to focus on the rational actor. The expressive theories introduce the body, but within a theory where the person is dissolved into categories of holism. This opposition between the instrumental and the expressive of course plays a key role in western experience, evident, for example, in Parsons' theory of gender roles, where he believed that men were instrumental and rational while women were emotional and expressive. It is now widely understood that this is an impoverished way of thinking about gender, sexuality, maleness, and femaleness. But we encounter this same opposition between the "instrumental" and the "expressive" constantly rehearsed in debates about movements, framed in terms of "strategy" and "identity." To begin to make sense of what is at stake in the grammars of embodiment we have encountered in this book, we need to break with these theories of catharsis, of order and disorder, of holistic ritual opposing the fragmentation of the modern world – all dating from the late nineteenth century, and all reflecting in different ways the primacy of the representational over the embodied.

Talal Asad's exploration of pain and agency opens other ways to think about embodied practice than as holistic expressions of identity. He considers the pain experienced in childbirth, engaging with the argument developed by the American anthropologist Pamela Kassen, who argues "perhaps in late-twentieth-century America, where women are taught to be critics of their own bodies from outside, the pain of childbirth puts women back *in* their bodies" (cited in Asad 2003: 87). Asad notes that in intentional understandings of action, as proposed by modernist feminists such as Simone de Beauvoir, childbirth is passive and dehumanizing, an experience that keeps women "mired in imminence" (Susan Brison, in Asad 2003: 87). Here pain and embodiment are understood as loss of agency, as passivity. But Asad argues that it is possible to understand the experience of pain present in childbirth as active, underlining the ways that experience and action are "sited in a material body": "Although the living body is the object of sensations (and in that sense passive), its ability to suffer, to respond perceptually and emotionally to external and internal causes, to use its own pain in unique ways in particular social relationships, makes it active" (Asad 2003: 89). The issue here is not what pain symbolizes, represents, or expresses. Rather Asad argues that the embodied act of birth produces a transformation:

> the becoming and being a "mother" by means of the practical methods employed in various traditions. For the act of birthing doesn't merely produce another living body, it also creates a vital relationship that is imbued with sensitivity to pain, the relationship that binds mother and child actively together. (2003: 88)

This is a form of action that is not understandable as expressing identity. But nor is it a form of action that seeks to respond to the opportunity present in its environment. As Asad argues, there are forms of experience where we connect to the world through our bodies that involve a "desire to allow one's self to be controlled by the world in certain ways" (Asad 2003: 73).

Something similar occurs in the experience of constructing puppets described by Nick. He underlines the physicality of the process of construction, the exhaustion experienced in making and building, the effort involved. There is a kind of experience of suffering present in his account, in some ways similar to the pain involved in birth. The physical difficulty experienced building the puppets constantly recurs in his account: the tiredness, the wearing effect resulting from long hours. The body is at the center of this construction, and this is heightened through the importance of food, smell, and taste. This is not an instrumental form of action – it is not governed by efficiency or cost-benefit calculations. Neither is it a case of sacrifice, of suffering so that others will suffer less. Nor is this a case of holism or communitas, where those involved transcend their individual subjectivity and become moved by something larger than themselves. Instead, through the action of building, the person can reconnect body and self, and in the process not fuse with the other, but encounter the other as another. The body is a medium of experience of the self and encounter with the other.

What we need to recognize here is not only the presence of the body, but the importance of the body's experience of time. Such embodied time is experienced in terms of rhythm, of activity followed by rest. Judy, whom I interviewed in New York, made the same point – "you can't build a puppet in an instant," juxtaposing the time experienced in building a puppet with the demand for an instant response to emails and discussion boards. In these accounts, time, experienced through the body as rhythm, is constitutive of practice. We can see how this experience of embodied time, of the time required for embodied practice, contrasts with the utopia of the network expressed in Bill Gates's celebration of simultaneity and his understanding of time as "friction." The utopia of simultaneity is one where the disembodied network is characterized by constant and instant exchange. The forms of embodied practice we have encountered open not only movement, but *stillness*. Here again we come to the limits of action understood either as representing interests through *claims* or representing identities through *expressions*.

The stories of action recounted by Judy or Nick, the experience of puppets, the experience of grief through qigong, point to something going beyond the opposition of instrumental to expressive. *To experience beauty, wonder, or grief, we have to open ourselves to something happening to us, we have to make ourselves vulnerable.* This is not a form of fusion into a collective expression or a claim that our identity be recognized. Rather it is a dimension of *subjectivation*, how we become a self that can be open to the experience of the other. This places the experience of embodied subjectivity at the center of our understanding of action. It has practical implications about the ways we think about collective action. Above all, it underscores the limits of the network paradigm.

Beyond Networks

The model of the organization, with its structure of representation and delegation, where the member relates to the totality, is clearly unable to capture the movements we have explored. But neither, I think, can the increasingly influential idea of "network." The network is a theory of structure that is disembodied, profoundly shaped by the utopia of homogenous time and borderless world. Networks, as Bill Gates underlines, seek simultaneity. The image of the network may well capture the grammar of new forms of domination at work in a globalizing world, as in the "network capitalism" analyzed by Boltanski and Chiapello, with its demands for movement and constant reinvention, the importance of the short term over the long term. And given the extraordinary impact of the idea of "network" in contemporary global culture, it is not surprising that many people involved in movements attempt to make sense of emerging patterns in terms of this metaphor. But it is not obvious that what is important in the movements we have explored is a result of their network structure. The network is silent. It can achieve simultaneity through expelling time, while the forms of embodied subjectivity we have encountered are impossible without time. The image of network expels the senses and the body, it is a flow of abstracted information.

At the heart of the movements we have explored we encounter embodied subjectivity, and with it forms of action that are nonintentional, experiences of communicative vulnerability and the limits of the autonomous subject. While the image of network allows us to break with the understandings of totality and vertical flows that were so important in the industrial age, they do not allow us to place embodied subjectivity at the center of the way we think about movements. Indeed Bill Gates is correct – the network excludes time, and as such it excludes embodied subjects. For that reason, while "network" has served to free us from industrial conceptions of organization, it does not allow us to think creatively about contemporary movements and action.

Law and Urry (2004) invite us to think about social experience in new ways, suggesting the possibility of metaphor. In the light of the experiences we have encountered, I think the metaphors of rhythm and music are more helpful than the disembodied silence of the network. Music and rhythm open us to structures of presence and absence, of movement and stillness, of fullness and emptiness, of pulse and rhythm (Cooper and Meyer 1960). Rhythm and music require time and the sensing body in a way that the network does not. Rhythm and music help us think about forms of agency that are not representational, while underlining the embodied intersubjectivity that must be central to any attempt to rethink movements. Music has structure, but unlike the network, it is constituted through embodied experience.

Rhythm

One metaphor that can help us think in new ways about movements is offered in Phillip Turetzky's (2002) analysis of rhythm as assemblage and event, where he explores the *haka* or traditional dance of the Maori, the indigenous people of New Zealand. The *haka* is an event. As such, each *haka* possesses individuality, similar to other events such as going for a walk, experiencing a wound on one's body, or a season. The *haka*, Turetzky argues, is an event produced through "rhythmic assemblage."

A rhythm is an event structured through presence, absence, and repetition. Rhythm cannot exist without time, as opposed to the network, which seeks to obliterate time. As a result, the *haka* offers no characteristics of a network at all. Instead it is an "event assembled through rhythmic relations of movement and rest," where rhythms are the ways "purely temporal intervals become grouped together by distributing accented and unaccented moments," regardless of the actual elements that are deployed. There are two sides to a rhythm: a complex connection of formed matters (people, objects), and a "distribution of accents marking off an abstract organization of temporal events" (Turetzky 2002: 125). Thus rhythmic organization articulates two things: matter into a single body, and groups of abstract intervals into a single event.

Turetzky distinguishes three moments of syntheses in the *haka*. The first involves an experience of entrainment or synchronization, where forms of rhythm that are independent of each other become rhythmically connected:

> Elements that get organized in a rhythmic assemblage usually occur independently of one another until they become rhythmically organized. There need be no particular material or causal connections inherent in these elements so long as they become coincident . . . In a highly regular rhythmic assembly like a haka, where strict time is kept, parallels of movement and rest occur predominantly because of their temporal coincidence. This coincidence happens when earlier and later occurring elements become connected by correspondent temporal intervals: where the intervals of the sequence of movement and rest come to stand in some definite relation and to resonate with other sequences which may occur within the same duration. The rates of passage of movements and rest will continue in their correspondence so long as an assemblage can maintain the connections between earlier and later movements. *Achieving connections between successive moments produces a centre around which chaotic elements may become stabilized*, the beginnings of order may crystallize, and from which the growing assemblage may be given a direction. (2002: 126; emphasis added)

Thus the first moment of the *haka* involves different and independent rhythms forming a relationship with each other, where sequences begin to resonate, elements begin to stabilize, and through these connections, a center forms. This center can flow and move as well, as in the case where drummers begin to form rhythms, and where they take pleasure in experiencing the center flow in different and unpredictable ways through their assembly. Rhythm is not a matter of fusion, but is constructed through accented and unaccented beats. Rhythm organizes the material through which it is constituted, while it is at the same time the product of those materials – in that sense, rhythm is reflexive, but not through cognitive "self-monitoring." Through rhythmic organization, Turetzky argues, synthesis forms matters into a single body, and groups of intervals into a single event, so that materials and temporalities become articulated. In this first moment, rhythms resonate, syntheses form and flow, bodies are connected and a living present is created. The *haka* creates a temporal experience of "now." This is the temporal experience that makes movements possible.

But there is a second moment to the *haka*. The experience as constituted stands in potential relationship to larger rhythmic structures and virtual states of resonance. Rhythms as constructed can produce joy, anger, sadness; they can invite or repel. But to do so, the rhythm relates to these wider rhythmic structures and experience:

> each embodied rhythm stands in virtual states of resonance with a multiplicity of architectonic levels of other rhythmic structures. A new motif cannot emerge without a continuous modulation of its entire preceding structure; so that the emergence of every motif is already retrospectively incorporated into and unified with proceeding structures. (Turetzky 2002: 130)

This is not a linear path – it is not possible to predict in advance in what direction it will flow, just as drummers cannot predict where the center will flow when they form a rhythmic assembly. It is only after that it is possible to recognize what potentiality was realized. As the rhythm proceeds, as its center flows from one point to another, it opens different potentialities in terms of what it will become, and through this, the rhythm that has occurred up to that point can take on different significations. The rhythm of the first period has multiple potentials; but what these will become depend upon a second moment.

Rhythm, Turetzky argues, not only creates synthesis, it also requires individuation: "experiencing periodic accented and unaccented moments is insufficient for rhythm. The experience of rhythm requires memory." In the first moment, rhythm involves a synthesis where bodies are connected, where through repetition a living now is constituted. But rhythm also requires memory, in a process that "individuates bodies, makes them expressive, and constitutes an a priori past." The action of rhythm in the present makes possible the act of memory:

> Memory depends on habit, but habit is not sufficient to constitute it. Memory operates according to the laws of association on former presents contiguous with and resembling the present one . . . memory must not only represent the past, it must represent the past along with its present present, and along with those representations it must represent its own act of representation. For to count as memory an act must situate its past, as past, relative to its own act of reproduction, and situate it as such an act. The act of memory takes place in a present, which must therefore contain an extra reflective dimension in which it represents itself and a former present. Memory, then, preforms an active synthesis combining acts of reproduction, reflection, and recognition. (2002: 128)

Here Turetzky evokes the idea of memory as act, and opens the "complex time" explored by Talal Asad. The *haka* as a form of embodied practice requires time to prefect itself, but it is also a form of embodied memory action that reencounters, reimagines, and extends pasts (Asad 2003: 179). This form of memory is present also within western experience, as Mary Carruthers (1990) underlines when she explores memory as *praxis* rather than *doxis* in European medieval culture. These memory acts, memory as *praxis*, break with the homogenous time of globalization, one of simultaneity of exchange, the time of the market and consumption, the network. Memory as *praxis* is only possible where action is constituted through time. This kind of memory is excluded through the utopia of the network.

For Henara Teowai, the renowned *haka* master, when performing the *haka*, "the whole body should speak" (Karetu 1993: 22, cited in Turetzky 2002: 128). In the light of Hirshkind's exploration of embodied listening, we could also add that in the *haka*, the whole body listens, the rhythmic pattern constituting a communicative experience. The second moment of the *haka* is similar to the experience Hirschkind highlights when he explores the agency of embodied listening, or where music or other body practices open an experience that has been forgotten. Such forgotten memories can only be made part of the present through an embodied memory act. Here the *haka* is a form of action that makes the past part of the present – it is a collective act of memory. Such memory acts, memory as praxis, play a critical role in the grammars of action we have explored: from qigong to the rhythm of the story in the Zapatista experience, to the place of music in the antiglobalization action, in the way music constitutes experience, in the presence of rhythm in action, from drumming through to the relationship of presence and absence in movement and stillness, noise and silence.

The first moment of the *haka* is one of entrainment and oscillation, the creation of a center. In a second moment, this center takes on meaning in relation to wider rhythmic structures, evoking wider musical structures that serve as a form of embodied memory. But the *haka* is not a ritual of commemoration. It is a rhythmic event with an open structure, it is an event that is constituted in its singularity. This singularity points to the third moment: as rhythmic assemblage takes place, the *haka* undergoes a metamorphosis. Through establishing a relationship to wider rhythmic structures and achieving memory, the *haka* creates for itself the possibility of creating the new. Turetzky explores the way the *haka* goes beyond repetition, and proceeds to a third synthesis through introducing a rhythmic rupture or *caesura*. Such breaks in rhythm play an important role in poetry, which also have to be read aloud and heard by the body, as opposed to consisting a collection of words as signs. This break is an interruption that disrupts the cycle, it brings with it the *possibility of becoming*, of a new assemblage:

> dislodging the agency of habit, changing and disrupting its cycle . . . this becoming constitutes the event in which the assemblage becomes capable of changing, when it comes into its power of acting. *This moment is precarious,*

always in danger of collapsing into incoherence or falling back into the past, into the same old forms . . . the coherence of a new assemblage belongs only to the future, to a moment after its transformation. Relative to past forms, [this] synthesis creates something formless, a difference which is extreme and excessive. It prolongs an intensive line that, as such, can continue only by changing its nature. (2002: 134; emphasis added)

If this succeeds, a new *haka* can be produced, new meaning constituted that transforms not only the participants, but also the audience, who become drawn into and part of the experience.

Experience Movements

The *haka* is not an example of a movement, but a close reading of the different syntheses it involves points to critical moments in the constitution of movements, and to ways of thinking about the shift from movements defined in terms of social categories to movements defined in terms of action. This is the shift from the social movements of industrial society to what I suggest calling "experience movements." In an important argument exploring what he calls "cultural pragmatics," the American sociologist Jeffrey Alexander argues that "politically emancipatory theory must be supported by aesthetically compelling practice" (2003: 26). Working within a Durkheimian tradition that underlines collective representations, Alexander seeks to do so through the idea of "cultural performance" that has its origins in theater studies. By cultural performance Alexander means "the social process by which actors, individually or in concert, display for others the meaning of their social situation" (2004: 529). Successful social performances, he argues, are "ritual-like," by which he means they succeed in creating a "re-fusion" between the increasingly differentiated roles in modern society and personal subjectivity. He argues that in successful performances, social actors can achieve "flow," the authenticity achieved when role and subjectivity become one: "the actor seems to be Hamlet; the man who takes the oath of office seems to be the President" (2004: 549). So understood, successful social performance achieves grace.

The grammars of action I have been exploring in this book contrast with this account of representation, "flow," and grace. Rather than integration, what constantly appears is the importance of experiences of alterity, of the in-between. We can see this in the tension between travel and emplacement, between speed and stillness, between the virtual and the embodied. An aesthetic of the strange occupies an important place, from the Aguascalientes at La Realidad to experiences of qigong or the experiential grammar of puppets. Nor is it evident that the aim of action is a fusion of subject and role. In the case of Marcos, for example, we do not encounter an attempt to create a fusion between Rafael Guillén and guerrilla leader. The whole logic of this action rejects such a fusion. This is most obvious in the use of the mask, but in other ways as well. The bullets that Marcos wears in the two belts slung over his shoulders cannot be fired with the gun that he carries. Marcos is not the fusion of Guillén and guerrilla, he is neither Guillén nor guerrilla. Rather than fusion, we encounter indeterminacy and the freedom that comes with this.

Similar themes emerge in the place of music. Exploring contemporary social movements, Eyerman and Jamison argue that music and song play a key role in "collective identity formation" through "supplying actors with the sources of meaning and identity out of which they collectively construct social action" (1998: 161–2). They take as a model the American social movements of the 1960s, where the protest songs allowed activists to link their action with what had gone before, affirming "tradition, that past in the present, is vital to our understanding of who we are and what we are meant to do" (1998: 161). Eyerman explores contemporary movements, emphasizing the didactic role of music where lyrics have replaced political speeches, where "songs as collective performance become texts" (2002: 450). The problem with generalizing this argument is the extent to which we have encountered forms of music closer to rave or dance music, where sound and sensual experience are more central than lyrics. In this case, as Jowers (1999) suggests, music does not evoke conscious memory. Drawing on Grayck (1996), he underlines instead the importance of timbre in music. Timbre differs from pitch or intensity, in that it is the quality of sound of any one instrument that makes it unique from any other, involving a "complex and protean situation, where timbre exists in fragile relationships and continua with frequency, spectral content, sonic identity and source recognition" (Smalley 1994). This has importance in terms of the place of music in movements, and music as action: "timbre has an expressive impact in direct experience that will be absent in our memories of it" (Grayck 1996: 60, cited in Jowers 1999: 392). This musical experience is very different from the didactic protest song or "performance as text," where behind the sound lies a sign. Instead we encounter a grammar of experience captured by Jowers when he argues, "we experience the thrill of the unexpected when we re-hear specific timbres form an uncanny zone between memory and forgetfulness. We are reminded of something forgotten" (1999: 392). In this case, sounds do not represent. Being reminded of something forgotten is only possible when we can free ourselves from the domination of intentional action, and become open to things happening to us.

These grammars of experience are closer to contemporary dance, where we encounter forms of embodiment as experiences of dislocation and defamiliarization rather than fusion, the creation of tensions between strength and vulnerability rather than a unified subjectivity represented by grace (Briginshaw 2001), and where place is experienced through the body (Nast and Pile 1998). This form of action does not seek to display "worthiness, unity, numbers and commitment" (Tilly 2004), but instead constructs spaces of experience where strength and vulnerability encounter each other.

We can regard movements as disembodied messages, as systems of signs, as text. Or we can think of movements as closer to music. This means introducing sound, rhythm, and sonic experience to our understandings of modernity, excluded within a paradigm of representation, and beginning to listen to modernity (see Erlmann 2004). In this case, Charles Hirschkind's analysis of the agency of hearing is important to the way we understand contemporary movements. He argues that hearing is a form of embodied, ethical agency. In a sense, the social sciences are confronted with something similar. Should we approach the music of movements uniquely as the words of a song, to be analyzed as a text, as the modernist Egyptian state has sought to silence hearing and sound and assert the primacy of the symbol and the representational?

This has implications for the way we conceive of public space, movements, and action. The public space of rational discourse is one where language is disembodied, made up of symbols rather than sound and music. Yet it is more in terms of music, rhythm, and presence that we can usefully think of movements functioning through experiences of resonance. This is what the Zapatista encounters called for – echoes and resonance. Resonance is a sensual experience, and is achieved where differences do not merge into sameness, but mutually intensify in the presence of the other, as when colors or different notes resonate. The social sciences today are confronted with the task of constructing ways of knowing that are able to understand grammars of human experience and public spheres, not as disembodied systems of signs, but as embodied experiences of resonance. In the process, we will be able to shift from the model of "social" movements of the last two centuries, with its logic of "us" and "community," to begin to understand forms of encounter based on difference and grammars of resonance. Rather than communities and categories, we will begin instead to explore grammars of practice.

The grammars of action we have encountered in this book are all different from each other. But they all point to a core proposition advanced by Talal Asad, who, when exploring the difference between ritual as action making the self and its later understanding as ritual as symbol, argues, "learning to develop moral capabilities is not the same thing as learning to invent representations" (1993: 79). As part of western modernity's self-understanding, the sociology of social movements has privileged an understanding where the action of movements is understood as representing inter-ests or identities, and at times representing interests through identities. When globalization is understood as one world, this social imaginary, just as much as the economic, is regarded as extending, eventually, to encompass the borderless space of the planet as a whole.

Rather than focus on action as representation and the processes consti-tuting groups and categories, this book has sought to explore forms of "doing" in movements that do not correspond to inventing representations. These are above all at work at the level of personal experience, from gram-mars of the Internet and practices of healing to the action of memory. But rather than the isolation of the liberal monad and his capacity for sociality, the forms of personal experience we have encountered can only be con-structed through traditions, cultures, memory, and religious subjectivities. In turn these experiences make our understanding of western modernities more complex; we are forced to go beyond the simplistic account of a radical rupture that is being extended to the planet, and to begin to explore experi-ences from piety to embodiment to memory excluded from dominant accounts of a universalizing process constituted through its own creative power. Rather than generalize a dominant social imaginary from one society to all the societies on earth, where action either projects or resists this process, these movements offer insight into globalization as an experience of shared worlds rather than one world, of borders traversing individual sub-jectivities rather than constituting closed communities and identities. In the grammars of action and culture we have explored, we glimpse more complex accounts of action and modernities, where, as Touraine suggests, the key to understanding societies lies paradoxically at the level of the personal subject. And where at the heart of struggles for freedom lie experiences of encounter and the vulnerability necessary to feel, suffer, wonder, and create.

Bibliography

Adams, I., Adams, R., and Galati, R. (2000). *Power of the Wheel: The Falun Gong Revolution*. New York: Stoddart.

Aguiton, C. (1996) "Un mouvement social en plein renouvellement." *Les Inrockuptibles* (May): 6.

Aguiton, C., and Bensaïd, D. (1997). *Le retour de la question sociale*. Paris: Page Deux.

Alexander, J. (2003). "Cultural pragmatics: a new model of social performance." Working paper, July 2003, Centre for Cultural Sociology, Yale University.

Alexander, J. (2004). "Cultural pragmatics: social performance between ritual and strategy." *Sociological Theory* 22(4): 527–3.

Alexander, J., and Jacobs, R. (1998). "Mass communication, ritual and civil society." *Media, Ritual and Identity*. T. Leibes and J. Curran (eds.). London: Routledge.

Alter, J. (1993). "The body of one color: Indian wrestling, the Indian state, and utopian somatics." *Cultural Anthropology* 8(1): 49–72.

Amnesty International (2000). "The crackdown on Falun Gong and other so-called "heretical organizations." Amnesty International, March 23, 2000 <http://web.amnesty.org/library/index/ENGASA170112000>.

Ancelovici, M. (2002). "Organizing against Globalization: The Case of ATTAC in France." *Politics and Society* 30(3): 427–3.

Anderson, B. (1991). *Imagined Communities: Reflections on the Origin and Spread of Nationalism*. London: Verso.

Anderson, J. (2003). "New media, new publics: reconfiguring the public space of Islam." *Social Research* 70(3): 887–906.

Anderson, J., and Eickelman, D. F. (eds.) (1999). *New Media in the Muslim World: The Emerging Public Sphere*. Bloomington: Indiana University Press.

Appadurai, A. (1996). *Modernity at Large: Cultural Dimensions of Globalization*. Minneapolis, University of Minnesota Press.

Arendt, H. (1973). *On Revolution*. Harmondsworth: Penguin.

Arthurs, A. (2003). "Social imaginaries and global realities." *Public Culture* 15(3): 579–86.

Asad, T. (1993). *Genealogies of Religion: Discipline and Reasons of Power in Christianity and Islam*. Baltimore: Johns Hopkins University Press.

Asad, T. (1996). "Modern power and the reconfiguration of religious traditions – interview with S. Mahmood." *Stanford Electronic Humanities Review* 5(1).

Asad, T. (2003). *Formations of the Secular: Christianity, Islam, modernity*. Stanford, Calif.: Stanford University Press.

Augis, E. (2002). *Dakar's Sunnite Women: The Politics of Person*. Ph.D. Dissertation, Department of Sociology, University of Chicago.

Al-Azmeh, A. (1996). *Islams and Modernities*. New York: Verso.

Barber, B. R. (1996). *Jihad vs. McWorld*. New York: Ballantine.

Barmeyer, N. (2003). "The Guerilla movement as a project: an assessment of community involvement in the EZLN." *Latin American Perspectives* 30(1): 122–38.

Bayat, A. (1997). "Un-civil society: the politics of the 'informal people'." *Third World Quarterly* 18(1): 53–72.

Bayat, A. (2002). "Piety, privilege and Egyptian youth." *ISIM Newsletter* 10(2): 23.

Beck, U. (2000). *The Brave New World of Work*. Malden, Mass.: Polity.

Bell, D. (1973). *The Coming of Post-Industrial Society: Venture in Social Forecasting*. New York: Basic.

Bell, D. (2003). "Mythscapes: memory, mythology, and national identity." *British Journal of Sociology* 54(1): 63–81.

Bell, J. E. (2001). *Puppets, Masks, and Performing Objects*. Cambridge: Mass.: MIT Press.

Benford, R., and Hunt, S. (1995). "Dramaturgy and social movements: the social construction and communication of power." *Social Movements: Critiques, Concepts, Case-Studies*. S. Lyman (ed.). London: Macmillan.

Benjamin, T. (2000). "A time of reconquest: history, the Maya revival and the Zapatista rebellion in Chiapas. *American Historical Review* 105(2): 417–50.

Bennett, A. (1999). "Subcultures or neo-tribes? Rethinking the relationship between youth, style and musical taste." *Sociology* 33(3): 599–617.

Berbrier, M. (2002). "Making minorities: cultural space, stigma transformation frames, and the categorical status claims of deaf, gay, and white supremacist activists in late twentieth century America." *Sociological Forum* 17(4): 553–91.

Bettelheim, B. (1976). *The Uses of Enchantment: The Meaning and Importance of Fairy Tales*. New York: Knopf.

Boltanski, L. (1999). *Distant Suffering: Morality, Media and Politics*. Translated by Graham Burchell. Cambridge: Cambridge University Press.

Boltanski, L., and Chiapello, E. (1999). *Le nouvel esprit du capitalisme*. Paris: Gallimard.

Boltanski, L., and Thévenot, L. (1991). *De la justification: Les économies de la grandeur*. Paris: Gallimard.

Boltanski, L., and Thévenot, L. (1999). "The sociology of critical capacity." *European Journal of Social Theory* 2(3): 359–77.

Bourdieu, P. (1984). *Distinction: A Social Critique of the Judgement of Taste*. Translated by Richard Nice. Cambridge: Mass.: Harvard University Press.

Bourdieu, P. (1985). "The social space and the genesis of groups." *Theory and Society* 14(6): 723–44.

Bourdieu, P. (1991). "Delegation and political fetishism." *Language and Symbolic Power*. J. Thompson (ed.). Cambridge: Mass.: Harvard University Press.

Bourdieu, P. (2004). "The mystery of the ministry: from particular wills to general will." *Constellations* 11(1): 37–43.

Bowen, J. (2004). "Beyond migration: Islam as a transnational public space." *Journal of Ethnic and Migration Studies* 30(5): 879–94.

Brauman, R. (1993). "The Médecins Sans Frontières experience." *A Framework for Survival: Health, Human Rights and Humanitarian Assistance in Conflicts and Disasters.* K. Cahill (ed.). New York: Basic.

Brecht, S. (1988). *The Bread and Puppet Theatre*, 2 vols. London: Methuen.

Briginshaw, V. (2001). *Dance, Space and Subjectivity.* London: Palgrave.

Brook, T., and Frolic, B. (eds.) (1997). *Civil Society in China.* Armonk, N.Y.: Sharpe.

Brownell, S. (1995). *Training the Body for China: Sports in the Moral Order of the People's Republic.* Chicago: University of Chicago Press.

Buechler, S. (2000). *Social Movements in Advanced Capitalism: The Political Economy and Cultural Construction of Social Activism.* New York: Oxford University Press.

Bulliet, R. W. (2004). *The Case for Islamo-Christian Civilization.* New York: Columbia University Press.

Burgdoff, C. (2003). "How Falun Gong practice undermines Li Hongzhi's totalistic rhetoric." *Nova Religio* 6(2): 332–47.

Butler, J. P. (1997). *Excitable Speech: A Politics of the Performative.* New York: Routledge.

Canguilhem, G. (1989). *The Normal and the Pathological.* Cambridge: MIT Press.

Castells, M. (1983). *The City and the Grassroots: A Cross-Cultural Theory of Urban Social Movements.* London: Arnold.

Castells, M. (1997). *The Power of Identity.* Malden, Mass.: Blackwell.

Castells, M. (2000). "Materials for an exploratory theory of the network society." *British Journal of Sociology* 51(1): 5–24.

Ceri, P. (2002). *Movimenti globali. La protesta nel XXI secolo.* Rome: Laterza.

Chan, C. (2004). "The Falun Gong in China: a sociological perspective." *China Quarterly*: 665–83.

Chen, N. (1995). "Urban spaces and experiences of Qigong." *Urban Spaces in Contemporary China.* D. S. Davis (ed.). Cambridge: Cambridge University Press.

Chen, N. (2003a). *Breathing Spaces: Qigong, Psychiartry and Healing in China.* New York: Columbia University Press.

Chen, N. (2003b). "Healing sects and anti-cult campaigns." *China Quarterly*: 505–20.

Chomsky, N. (2001). *September 11.* Crows Nest, Australia: Allen & Unwin.

Chomsky (2003). *Hegemony or Survival: America's Quest for Global Dominance.* New York: Holt.

Chow, Effie Poy Yew (2003). "Chow medical qigong: a holistic body/mind/spirit approach to rehabilitation and total health." Science of the Whole Person Healing Conference, Washington, D.C., March 28–30, 2003. Paper available at <http://www.holisticjunction.com/displayarticle.cfm?ID=1900>.

Clarke, D. (1987). "Whithead and contemporary analytic philosohpy." *Process Studies* 16(1): 26–34.

Cohen, J. (1985). "Strategy or identity: new theoretical paradigms and contemporary social movements." *Social Research* 52(4): 663–716.

Cohen, R., and Rai, S. (eds.) (2000). *Global Social Movements*. London: Athlone.

Colombres, A. (1997). *Celebración del lenguaje: Hacia una teoría intercultural de la literatura*. Buenos Aires: Ediciones del sol.

Connerton, P. (1989). *How Societies Remember*. Cambridge: Cambridge University Press.

Cooper, G., and Meyer, L. (1960). *The Rhythmic Structure of Music*. Chicago: University of Chicago Press.

Crouch, C., and Pizzorno, A. (eds.) (1978). *The Resurgence of Class Conflict in Western Europe Since 1968*. London: Macmillan.

Crouch, D., and Desforges, L. (2003). "The sensous in the tourist encounter." *Tourist studies* 3(1): 5–22.

Csordas, T. (1993). "Somatic modes of attention." *Cultural Anthropology* 8(2): 135–56.

D'Alisera, J. (2001). "I love Islam: popular religious commodities, sites of inscription, and transnational Sierra Leonean Identity." *Journal of Material Culture* 6(1): 91–110.

Daniken, E. von (1970). *Chariots of the Gods*. New York: Putnam.

Davis, J. E. (1991). *The Earth First! Reader: Ten Years of Radical Environmentalism*. Salt Lake City: Peregrine Smith.

De Nora, T. (2000). *Music's Social Powers: Soundtrack, Self and Embodiment in Everyday Life*. Cambridge: Cambridge University Press.

Dearling, A. (1998). *No Boundaries: Britain's New Travellers on the Road Outside Britain*. Dorset: Enabler.

Debrix, F. (1998). "Deterritorialised territories, borderless borders: the new geography of medical assistance." *Third World Quarterly* 19(5): 827–46.

DeChaine, R. (2002). "Humanitarian space and the social imaginary: Médecins Sans Frontières/Doctors Without Borders and the rhetoric of the global community." *Journal of Communication Inquiry* 26(4): 354–69.

Della Porta, D., and Tarrow, S. (eds.) (2005). *Transnational Protest and Global Activism*. Lanham: Rowman & Littlefield.

Della Porta, D., and Diani, M. (1999). *Social Movements: An Introduction*. Malden, Mass.: Blackwell.

Della Porta, D., Kriesi, H., and Rucht, D. (eds.) (1999). *Social Movements in a Globalizing World*. New York: St. Martin's Press.

Desrosières, A. (1998). *The Politics of Large Numbers: A History Of Statistical Reasoning*. Translated by Camille Naish. Cambridge, Mass.: Harvard University Press.

Diani, M. (1995). *Green Networks: A Structural Analysis of the Italian Environmental Movement*. Edinburgh: Edinburgh University Press.

Diani, M., and McAdam, D. (eds.) (2002). *Social Movements and Networks: Relational Approaches to Collective Action*. New York: Oxford University Press.

Diaz, C. (1995). *La Rebelion de las Cañadas*. Mexico City: Cal y Arena.

Dirlik, A. (2003). "Global modernity? Modernity in an age of global capitalism." *European Journal of Social Theory* 6(3): 275–92.

Dobbin, C. (1983). *Islamic Revivalism in a Changing Peasant Economy, Central Sumatra 1784–1847*. London: Curzon.

Doherty, B. (1999). "Paving the way: the rise of direct action against road-building and the changing character of British environmentalism." *Political Studies* 57: 275–91.

Dryzek, J. (2002). *Deliberative Democracy and Beyond*. Oxford: Oxford University Press.

Durkheim, E. (1912/1995). *Elementary Forms of Religious Life*. Trans. K. Fields. New York: The Free Press.

Eber, C. (2001). "Buscando una nueva vida: Liberation through autonomy in San Pedro Chenalhó, 1970–1998." *Latin American Perspectives* 28(117): 45–72.

Eickelman, D. (2000). "Islam and the languages of modernity." *Daedalus* 129(1):119–35.

Eisenstadt, S. N. (1999). *Fundamentalism, Sectarianism, and Revolution: The Jacobin Dimension of Modernity*. Cambridge: Cambridge University Press.

Eisenstadt, S. N. (2000a). "Multiple modernities." *Daedalus* 29(1): 1–29.

Eisenstadt, S. N. (2000b). "The civilizational dimension in sociological analysis." *Thesis Eleven* (62): 1–21.

El Guindi, F. (1999). *Veil: Modesty, Privacy and Resistance*. Oxford: Berg.

Elias, N. (1994). *The Civilizing Process: The History of Manners, and State Formation and Civilization*. Trans. E. Jephcott. Oxford: Blackwell.

Entwistle, J. (2000). *The Fashioned Body: Fashion, Dress, and Modern Social Theory*. Malden, Mass.: Polity.

Epstein, B. (1991). *Political Protest and Cultural Revolution: Nonviolent Direct Action in the 1970s and 1980s*. Berkeley: University of California Press.

Erlmann, V. (ed.) (2004). *Hearing Cultures: Essays on Sound, Listening and Modernity*. Oxford: Berg.

Esherick, J., and Wasserstrom, J. (1991). "Acting out democracy: popular theater in modern China." *Popular Protest and Political Culture in Modern China*. J. Wasserstrom and E. Perry (eds.). Boulder: Westview.

Eyerman, R., and Jamison, A. (1991). *Social Movements: A Cognitive Approach*. Cambridge: Polity.

Eyerman, R., and Jamison, A. (1998). *Music and Social Movements: Mobilizing Traditions in the Twentieth Century*. Cambridge: Cambridge University Press.

Eyerman, R. (2002). "Music in movement: cultural politics and the old and new social movements." *Qualitative Sociology* 25(3): 443–58.

Farquhar, J. (1996). "Market magic: getting rich and getting personal in medicine after Mao." *American Ethnologist* 23(2): 239–57.

Farro, A. (2003). "Le tournant italien." *Un autre monde: contestations, dérives et surprises dans l'antimondialisation*. M. Wieviorka (ed.). Paris: Balland.

Fattah, H. (2003). "Wahhabi influences, Salafi responses: Shaikh Mahmud Shukri and the Iraqi Salafi movement, 1745–1930," *Journal of Islamic Studies* 14(2): 127–48.

Favre, P. (1999). "Les manifestations de rue entre espace privé et espaces publics." *Espaces publics mosaïques*. B. François and E. Neveu (eds.). Rennes: Presses Universitaires de Rennes.

Final Declaration (1996). "2nd Declaration of La Realidad." First published in *La Jornada*, September 4, 1996. English translation available at <http://www.ezln.org/documentos/1996/19960803.en.htm>.

Fisher, J. (2000). "Images of the fool in Italian theater from Pirandello and Fo." *New England Theater Journal* 11: 103–35.

Ford, H. (1929). *My Philosophy of Industry*. London: Harrap.

François, B., and Neveu, E. (1999). *Espaces Publics Mosaïques. Arènes, rhétoriques et des débats publics contemporains*. Rennes: Presses Universitaires de Rennes.

Frank, R., and Stollberg, G. (2004). "Conceptualizing hybridization: on the diffusion of Asian medical knowledge to Germany." *International Sociology* 19(1): 71–88.

Frazer, N. (2003). "Rethinking recognition: overcoming displacement and reification in cultural politics." B. Hobson (ed.). *Recognition Struggles and Social Movements: Contested Identities, Agency and Power*. Cambridge: Cambridge University Press.

Friedman, T. L. (1999). *The Lexus and the Olive Tree*. New York: Farrar, Straus, Giroux.

Fuentes, C. (1994). "Chiapas: Latin America's first post-communist rebellion." *New Perspectives Quarterly* 11(2): 54–8.

Fukuyama, F. (1989). "The end of history." *National Interest* 16(summer): 3–18.

Fukuyama, F. (1992). *The End of History and the Last Man*. London: Penguin.

Fukuyama, F. (2004). "Voile et controle sexuel." *Le Monde*, February 4. Paris.

Gaffney, P. D. (1994). *The Prophet's Pulpit: Islamic Preaching in Contemporary Egypt*. Berkeley: University of California Press.

Gamson, J. (1995). "Must identity movements self-destruct? A queer dilemma." *Social Problems* 42: 390–407.

Gamson, W. A. (1975). *The Strategy of Social Protest*. Homewood, Ill.: Dorsey.

García Márquez, G., and Pombo, R. (2001). "Habla Marcos." *Cambio*. Digital version available at <http://www.ezln.org/entrevistas/20010325.es.htm. English translation "The punchcard and the hourglass," *New Left Review*, 9, May–June 2001, pp. 69–79.

Garner, A. (2004). "Living history: trees and metaphors of identity in an English forest." *Journal of Material Culture* 9(1): 87–100.

Gates, B., with Myhrvold, N., and Rinearson, P. (1996). *The Road Ahead*. New York: Penguin.

Geertz, C. (1973.) *The Interpretation of Cultures*. New York: Basic.

Geertz, C. (1998). "The world in pieces: culture and politics at the end of the century." *Focaal* 32: 91–117.

Gell, A. (1975). *Metamorphosis of the Cassowaries: Umeda Society and Ritual*. London: Athlone.

Giddens, A. (1990). *The Consequences of Modernity*. Stanford, Calif.: Stanford University Press.

Giddens, A. (1999). *Runaway World: How Globalisation Is Reshaping Our Lives*. London: Profile.

Girardot, Norman J. (1983). *Myth and Meaning in Early Taoism: The Theme of Chaos (Hun-tun)*. Berkeley: University of California Press, 1983.

Gole, N. (1996). *The Forbidden Modern: Civilization and Veiling*. Ann Arbor: University of Michigan Press.

Gole, N. (2000). "Snapshots of Islamic modernities." *Daedalus* 129(1): 91–117.

Gole, N. (2002). "Islam in public: new visibilities and new imaginaries." *Public Culture* 14(1): 173–90.

Goodwin, J., and Jasper, J. M. (1999). "Caught in winding, snarling vine: the structural bias of political process theory." *Sociological Forum* 14(1): 27–54.

Goodwin, J., Jasper, J. M., and Polletta, F. (eds.) (2001). *Passionate Politics: Emotions and Social Movements*. Chicago: University of Chicago Press.

Goossaert, V. (2003). "Le destin de la religion chinoise au 20ème siècle." *Social Compass* 50(4): 429–40.

Gorz, A. (1982). *Farewell to the Working Class: An Essay on Post-Industrial Socialism*. Translated by Michael Sonenscher. London: Pluto.

Gossen, G. (1996). "Who is the comandante of Subcomandante Marcos?" *Indigenous Revolts in Chiapas and the Andean Highlands*. K. Gosner and A. Ouweneel (eds.). Amsterdam: Centre for Latin American Research and Documentation.

Grayck, T. (1996). *Rhythm and Noise: Aesthetics of Rock*. Durham, N.C.: Duke University Press.

Green, A. (2002). October 16 (blog) <http://www.urban75.net/vbulletin/showpost.php?p=443628&postcount=53>.

Griffiths, J. (1996). "Life in the fast lane on the M41." *Guardian*.

Habermas, J. (1979). *Communication and the Evolution of Society*. Translated and with an introduction by Thomas McCarthy. Boston: Beacon.

Habermas, J. (1984). *The Theory of Communicative Action*. London: Heinemann Educational.

Habermas, J. (1991). *The Structural Transformation of the Public Sphere: An Inquiry into a Category of Bourgeois Society*. Cambridge, Mass.: MIT Press.

Habermas, J. (1996). *Between Facts and Norms: Contributions to a Discourse Theory of Law and Democracy*. Translated by William Rehg. Cambridge: Polity.

Haenni, P. (2002). "Au-delà du repli identitaire. Les nouveaux precheurs égyptiens et la modernisation paradoxale de l'islam." <http://www.religioscope.com/articles/2002/029_haenni_precheurs.htm>.

Hage, J., and Powers, C. (1992). *Post-Industrial Lives: Roles and Relationships in the 21st Century*. Newbury Park, Calif.: Sage.

Hanjal, P. (2001). "Openness and civil society participation in the G8 and global governance." *New Directions in Global Political Governance: Creating International Order for the Twenty-first Century*. J. Kirton and J. Takase (eds.). Aldershot: Ashgate.

Hannerz, U. (1992). *Cultural Complexity: Studies in the Social Organization of Meaning*. New York: Columbia University Press.

Hansen, C. (2003). "Taoism." *The Stanford Encyclopedia of Philosophy*. Edward N. Zalta (ed.) <http://plato.stanford.edu/archives/spr2003/entries/taoism/>.

Hardt, M., and Negri, A. (2000). *Empire*. Cambridge: Mass.: Harvard University Press.

Harvey, D. (1990). *The Condition of Postmodernity: An Enquiry into the Origins of Cultural Change*. Oxford: Blackwell.

Hay, J. (1994). "The body invisible in Chinese art?" *Body, Subject and Power in China*. A. Zito and T. Barlow (eds.). Chicago: University of Chicago Press.

Hefner, R. (1998). "Multiple modernities: Christianity, Islam, and Hinduism in a Globalizing age." *Annual Review of Anthropology* 27: 83–104.

Hefner, R. (2001). "Public Islam and the problem of democratization." *Sociology of Religion* 62(4): 491–515.

Hetherington, K. (1998). *Expressions of Identity: Space, Performance, Politics*. London: Sage.

Hetherington, K. (2000). *New Age Travellers: Vanloads of Uproarious Humanity*. London: Cassell.

Higgins, N. (2001). "An interview with commandante David, a Tzotzil member of the Zapatista delegation to Mexico City, 2001." *Alternatives: Global, Local, Poltical* 26(13): 373–82.

Hirschkind, C. (1997). "What is Political Islam?" *Middle East Report* 205.

Hirschkind, C. (2001a). "Civic virtue and religious reason: an Islamic counterpublic." *Cultural Anthropology* 16(1): 3–34.

Hirschkind, C. (2001b). "The ethics of listening: cassette-sermon audition in contemporary Egypt." *American Ethnologist* 28(3): 623–49.

Hirschkind, C. (2004). "Hearing modernity: Egypt, Islam and the pious ear." *Hearing Cultures: Essays on Sound, Listening and Modernity*. V. Erlmann (ed.). Oxford: Berg.

Hoexter, M., Eisenstadt, S. M., and Levtzion, N. (eds.) (2002). *The Public Sphere in Muslim Societies*. Albany: State University of New York Press.

Hoggart, R. (1957). *The Uses of Literacy*. London: Chatto & Windus.

Hsu, E. (1999). *The Transmission of Chinese Medicine*. Cambridge: Cambridge University Press.

Hsu, E. (2000). "Spirit (Shen), styles of knowing, and authority in contemporary Chinese medicine." *Culture, Medicine and Psychiatry* 24: 197–229.

Huntington, S. P. (1996). *The Clash of Civilizations and the Remaking of World Order*. New York: Simon & Schuster.

Huntington, S. P. (2004). *Who Are We? The Challenges to America's National Identity*. New York: Simon & Schuster.

Ignatieff, M. (1998). *The Warrior's Honor: Ethnic War and the Modern Conscience*. London: Chatto & Windus.

Ion, J. (1997). *La fin des militants?* Paris: Editions Ouvrières.

Ion, J., and Peroni, M. (eds.) (1997). *Engagement public et exposition de la personne*. Paris: Editions de l'Aube.

Jacob, M. (1991). *Living the Enlightenment: Freemasonry and Politics in Eighteenth Century Europe*. Oxford: Oxford University Press.

Jacob, M. (1992). "Private beliefs and public temples: the new religiosity of the eighteenth century." *Social Research* 59: 59–84.

Jasper, J. M. (1997). *The Art of Moral Protest: Culture, Biography, and Creativity in Social Movements*. Chicago: University of Chicago Press.

Jauréguiberry, F. (1997). "L'usage du téléphone portatif comme expérience sociale." *Réseaux* (82–3): 149–64.

Joas, H. (1996). *The Creativity of Action*. Translated by Jeremy Gaines and Paul Keast. Cambridge: Polity.

Johnston, J., and Laxer, G. (2003). "Solidarity in the age of globalization: lessons from the anti-MAI and Zapatista struggles." *Theory and Society* 32: 39–91.

Joppke, C. (1993). *Mobilizing against Nuclear Energy: A Comparison of Germany and the United States*. Berkeley: University of California Press.

Jordan, A. G., and Maloney, W. A. (1997). *Protest Businesses? Mobilizing Campaigning Groups*. New York: Manchester University Press.

Jordan, T. (1999). *Cyberpower: The Culture and Politics of Cyberspace and the Internet*. London: Routledge.

Jordan, T., and Taylor, P. (2004). *Hacktivism and Cyberwars: Rebels with a Cause?* London: Routledge.

Jowers, P. (1999). "Timeshards: repetition, timbre and identity in dance music." *Time and Society* 8(2): 381–96.

Keane, J. (2003). *Global Civil Society?* Cambridge: Cambridge University Press.

Keddie, N. (1998). "The new religious politics: where, when, and why do 'fundamentalisms' appear?" *Comparative Studies in Society and History* 40(4): 696–723.

Keenan, T. (2002). "Publicity and indifference: media, surveillance, 'humanitarian intervention'" <http://www.bard.edu/hrp/keenan/publicity&indifference.htm>.

Keith, C. L. Z. (2003). "The Falun Gong problem: politics and the struggle for the rule of law in China." *China Quarterly*: 623–42.

Kepel, G. (1994). *The Revenge of God: The Resurgence of Islam, Christianity and Judaism in the Modern World*. Translated by Alan Braley. Cambridge: Polity.

Kepel, G. (2002). *Jihad: The Trail of Political Islam*. Translated by Anthony F. Roberts. Cambridge, Mass.: Harvard University Press.

Khagram, S., Riker, J., and Sikkink, K. (eds.) (2002). *Restructuring World Politics: Transnational Social Movements, Networks, and Norms*. Minneapolis: University of Minnesota Press.

Khilnani, S. (2003). *The Idea of India*. London: Penguin.

Khosrokhavar, F., and Touraine, A. (2000). *La recherche de soi. Dialogue sur le sujet*. Paris: Fayard.

Kirschner, S. R. (1996). *The Religious and Romantic Origins of Psychoanalysis: Individuation and Integration in Post-Freudian Theory*. New York: Cambridge University Press.

Kirshenblatt-Gimblett, B. (1999). "Playing to the senses: food as a performance medium." *Performance Research* 4(1): 1–30.

Klandermans, B. (1986). "New social movements and resource mobilization: the European and the American Approach." *International Journal of Mass Emergencies and Disaster* 4(2): 13–39.

Kleinman, A., and Kleinman, J. (1995). "Remembering the Cultural Revolution: alienating pains and the pain of alienation/transformation." *Chinese Societies and Mental Health*. T. Lin (ed.). Oxford: Oxford University Press.

Kleinman, A., and Kleinman, J. (1994). "How bodies remember: social memory and bodily experience of criticism, resistance and delegitimation following China's cultural revolution." *New Literary History* 25(3): 707–23.

Kleinman, A., Kleinman, J., and Lee, S. (1999). "Introduction to the transformation of social experience in Chinese Society." *Culture, Medicine and Psychiatry* (23): 1–6.

Kohlberg, L. (1981). *The Philosophy of Moral Development: Moral Stages and the Idea of Justice*. San Francisco: Harper & Row.

Koselleck, R. (1985). *Futures Past: On the Semantics of Historical Time.* Translated by Keith Tribe. Cambridge: Mass.: MIT Press.

Kouchner, B., and Burnier, M. (1970). *La France sauvage.* Paris: Publications premières.

Kouchner, B. (1991). *Le malheur des autres.* Paris: Odile Jacob.

Kuriyama, S. (1994). "The imagination of winds and the development of the Chinese conception of the body." *Body, Subject and Power in China.* A. Zito and T. E. Barlow (eds.). Chicago: University of Chicago Press.

Laidi, J. (2001). *Le sacre du present.* Paris: Flammarion.

Larson, K. (2003). "Art, politics mingle at Vermont Theater." *Miami Herald* <http://www.miami.com/mld/miamiherald/entertainment/6265918.htm>.

Law, J., and Urry, J. (2004). "Enacting the social." *Economy and Society* 33(3): 390–410.

Le Bot, Y. (1997). *Le rêve zapatiste. Sous-commandant Marcos.* Paris: Le Seuil.

Le Bot, Y. (2003). "Le zapatisme, première insurrection contre la mondialisation néolibérale." *Un autre monde.* M. Wieviorka (ed.). Paris: Balland.

Lee, M. (1995). *Earth First! Environmental Apocalypse.* Syracuse, N.Y.: Syracuse University Press.

Leites, E. (1986). *The Puritan Conscience and Modern Sexuality.* New Haven: Yale University Press.

Lerner, D. (1958). *The Passing of Traditional Society: Modernizing the Middle East.* With the collaboration of Lucille W. Pevsner, and an introduction by David Riesman. Glencoe, Ill.: Free.

Levi, M., and Murphy, G. (2002). "Coalitions of contention: the case of the WTO protests in Seattle." International Sociological Association, Brisbane; unpublished paper.

Leyton, E. (1998). *Touched by Fire: Doctors without Borders in a Third World Crisis.* Toronto: McClelland & Stewart.

Leyva Solano, X. (1998). "Catequistas, misioneros y tradiciones en las Cañadas." *Chiapas. Los rumbos de otra historia.* J. Viqueira and M. Humberto Ruz (eds.). Mexico City: CEM/UNAM.

Leyva Solano, X. (1999). "Chiapas es México: autonomías indígenas y luchas políticas con una gramática moral." *El Cotidiano* (93): 5–18.

Leyva Solano, X. (2001). "Regional, communal, and organizational transformations in Las Cañadas." *Latin American Perspectives* 28(117): 20–44.

Lewis, B. (1990). "The roots of Muslim rage." *Atlantic Monthly* (September): 47–60.

Lewis, B. (2002). "What went wrong?" *Atlantic Monthly* 289(1): 43–5.

Lewis, B. (2003). *The Crisis of Islam: Holy War and Unholy Terror.* New York: Modern Library.

Lichterman, P. (1996). *The Search for Political Community: American Activists Reinventing Commitment.* Cambridge: Cambridge University Press.

Li Hongzhi (1999) *Zhuan Falun* (Internet version). 3rd trans. New York: Universe.

Lindley, D. E. (1984). *The Court Masque.* Manchester: Manchester University Press.

Lubeck, P. M. (2000). "The Islamic revival: antinomies of Islamic movements under globalization." *Global Social Movements*. R. Cohen and S. M. Rai (eds.). New Brunswick, N.J.: Athlone.

Ma, G. X. (1999). *The Culture of Health: Asian Communities in the United States*. Foreword by Walter Tsou. Westport, Conn.: Bergin & Garvey.

Macleod, A. E. (1991). *Accommodating Protest: Working Women, the New Veiling, and Change in Cairo*. New York: Columbia University Press.

MacLeod, A. (1992). "Hegemonic relations and gender resistance: the new veiling as accommodating protest in Cairo." *Signs: Journal of Women and Culture in Society* 17(3): 533–57.

Macnaghten, P., and Urry, J. (2000). "Bodies in the woods." *Body and Society* 6(3–4): 166–82.

Maffesoli, M. (1996). *The Time of the Tribes: The Decline of Individualism in Mass Society*. Translated by Don Smith. Thousand Oaks, Calif.: Sage.

Mahmood, S. (2001a). "Feminist theory, embodiment, and the docile agent: some reflections on the Egyptian Islamic revival." *Cultural Anthropology* 16(2): 202–36.

Mahmood, S. (2001b). "Rehearsed spontaneity and the conventionality of ritual: disciplines of salat." *American Ethnologist* 28(4): 827–53.

Mahmood, S. (2003). "Ethical formation and politics of individual autonomy in contemporary Egypt." *Social Research* 70(3): 837–66.

Mahmood, S. (2004). *Politics of Piety: The Islamic Revival and the Feminist Subject*. Princeton: Princeton University Press.

Maldonado, E. (2001). "Los relatos Zapatistas y su vínculo con la oralidad tradicional." *Convergencia: Revista de Ciencias Sociales* (24): 141–53.

Maldonado, E. (2004). "Desde las voces cantarinas al testimonio indígena." *Tiempo y Escritura* (7): Archived at <http://www.azc.uam.mx/publicaciones/tye/vocescantarinas.htm>.

Mallet, S. (1975). *The New Working Class*. Nottingham: Spokesman.

Mandaville, P. G. (2001). *Transnational Muslim Politics: Reimagining the Umma*. London: Routledge.

Mann, M. (1993). *The Sources of Social Power*, vol. 2. Cambridge: Cambridge University Press.

Marcos, Subcommandante (1996). "Closing speech to the First Encuentro." Available at www.ezln.org.

Marcos, Subcommandante (2003). "Chiapas, the thirteenth stele: Part Two, A death." Z Net, July 25 <http://www.zmag.org/content/showarticle.cfm?SectionID=8andItemID=3957>.

Marshall, D. (2002). "Behavior, belonging and belief: a theory of ritual practice." *Sociological Theory* 20(3): 360–80.

Martin, G. (2002). "Conceptualizing cultural politics in subcultural and social movement studies." *Social Movement Studies* 1(1): 73–88.

McAdam, D. (1982). *Political Process and the Development of Black Insurgency, 1930–1970*. Chicago: University of Chicago Press.

McAdam, D., Tarrow, S., and Tilly, C. (2001). *Dynamics of Contention*. New York: Cambridge University Press.

McDonald, K. (1999). *Struggles for Subjectivity: Identity, Action and Youth Experience*. Cambridge: Cambridge University Press.

McDonald, K. (2002). "From Solidarity to Fluidarity: social movements beyond 'collective identity' – the case of globalization conflicts." *Social Movement Studies* 1(2): 109–28.

McIntosh, A. (1994). "Over the rainbow: an Irish pilgrimage." *Trumpeter* <http://trumpeter.athabascau.ca/content/v11.3/mcintosh.html>.

McKay, G. (2000). *Glastonbury: A Very English Fair*. London: Gollancz.

Meddeb, A. (2002). *La maladie de l'Islam*. Paris: Seuil.

Melucci, A. (1989). *Nomads of the Present, Social Movements and Individual Needs in Contemporary Society*. J. Keane and P. Mier (eds.). London: Hutchinson Radius.

Melucci, A. (1996a). *Challenging Codes: Collective Action in the Information Age*. Cambridge: Cambridge University Press.

Melucci, A. (1996b). "Individual experience and global issues in a planetary society." *Social Science Information* 35(5): 485–509.

Melucci, A. (2000). *Culture in gioco. Differenze per convivere*. Milan: Edizioni Il Saggiatore.

Mobini-Kesheh, N. (1999). *The Hadrami Awakening: Community and Identity in the Netherlands East Indies 1900–1942*, Ithaca: Cornell University.

Mol, A., and Law, J. (1994). "Regions, networks and fluids: Anaemia and social topology." *Social Studies of Science* 24: 641–71.

Monsiváis, C. (1997). *Mexican Postcards*. New York: Verso.

Morris, P. (2004). *Imagining Inclusive Society in Nineteenth-Century Novels: The Code of Sincerity in the Public Sphere*. Baltimore: Johns Hopkins University Press.

Mouzelis, N. (1998). "Beyond the normative and the utilitarian." *British Journal of Sociology* 49(3): 491–7.

Nash, J. (2001). *Mayan Visions: The Quest for Autonomy in an Age of Globalization*. New York: Routledge.

Nasser, M. (1999). "The new veiling phenomenon – is it an anorexic equivalent? A polemic." *Journal of Community and Applied Social Psychology* 9: 407–12.

Nast, H., and Pile, S. (eds.) (1998). *Places Through the Body*. London: Routledge.

Negri, A. (1991). *Marx beyond Marx*. Brooklyn: Autonomedia.

Oleson, T. (2004). "Globalizing the Zapatistas: from Third World solidarity to global solidarity." *Third World Quarterly* 25(1): 255–67.

Ohmae, K. (1990). *The Borderless World: Power and Strategy in the Interlinked Economy*. New York: HarperBusiness.

Ots, T. (1994). "The silenced body – the expressive Leib." *Embodiment and Experience: The Existential Ground of Culture and Self*. T. Csordas (ed.). Cambridge: Cambridge University Press.

Pahl, R. (2000). *On Friendship*. Cambridge: Polity.

Palmer, D. (2003). "Le qigong et la tradition sectaire chinoise." *Social Compass* 50(4): 471–80.

Park, L., and Hinton, D. (2002). "Dizziness and panic in China: associated sensations of zhang fu organ disequilibrium." *Culture, Medicine and Psychiatry* 26: 225–57.

Parker-Gumucio, C. (2002). "Les nouvelles formes de religion dans la société global-isée: un défi à l'interprétation sociologique." *Social Compass* 49(2): 167–86.

Passy, F. (2001). "Political altruism and the Solidarity movement." *Political Altruism? Solidarity Movements in International Perspective*. M. P. Giugni and Passy, F. (eds.). New York: Rowman & Littlefield.

Paugam, S. (2000). *La disqualification sociale: Essai sur la nouvelle pauvréte*. Paris: Presses Universitaires de France.

Paulson, J. (2001). "Peasant struggles and international solidarity: the case of Chiapas." *Socialist Register 2000: Working Classes: Global Realities*. Leo Panitch and Colin Leys (eds.). London: Merlin.

Penny, B. (2002). "The body of Master Li." Charles Strong Memorial Lecture, Australian Association of Religious Studies.

Pérez de Lama, J. (2000). "Urbanismo anarquista: La nava de los locos." *Boletín FIDAS* (23): digital version available at <http://www.hackitectura.net/osfavelados/osfavela2002/anarchogeographies/urbanarquista/urbanarquista.html>.

Perry, E. (2001). "Challenging the mandate of heaven: popular protest in modern China." *Critical Asian Studies* 33(2): 163–80.

Peterson, A. (2001). *Contemporary Political Protest: Essays on Political Militancy*. Aldershot: Ashgate.

Plows, A. (2002). "Twyford Down + 10." SchNEWS of the World, Yearbook 2002 <http://www.schnews.org.uk/sotw/twyford-down-plus10.htm>.

Plows, A. (2005). "Donga tribe." *The Encyclopedia of Religion and Nature*. B. Taylor (ed.). Bristol: Thoemmes Continuum.

Plows, A. (no date). "The Dongas tribe." Unpublished manuscript.

Polletta, F. (2001). "This is what democracy looks like." *Social Policy* (summer): 25–8.

Polletta, F. (2002). *Freedom Is an Endless Meeting: Democracy in American Social Movements*. Chicago: University of Chicago Press.

Poovey, M. (1995). *Making a Social Body: British Cultural Formation, 1830–1864*. Chicago: University of Chicago Press.

Poovey, M. (2002). "The liberal civil subject and the social in eighteenth-century British moral philosophy." *Public Culture* 14(1): 125–45.

Poulet, B. (1999). "À gauche de la gauche." *Le Débat* 103: 39–59.

Prigogine, I., and Stengers, I. (1997). *The End of Certainty: Time, Chaos, and the New Laws of Nature*. New York: Free.

Putnam, R. (2000). *Bowling Alone: The Collapse and Revival of American Community*. New York: Simon & Schuster.

Qutb, S. (1970). *Social Justice in Islam*. Trans. John B. Hardie. New York: Octagon.

Ravon, B., and Raymond, R. (1997). "Engagement bénévole et expérience de soi: l'ex-emple des Restos du coeur." *Engagement public et exposition de la personne*. J. Ion and M. Péroni (eds.). Paris: Editions de l'aube.

Riley, P. (1986). *The General Will before Rousseau: The Transformation of the Divine into the Civic*. Princeton: Princeton University Press.

Roadblock, London: Alarm UK, 1995 <http://www.antiroads.org.uk/roadblock/roadblock.pdf>.

Robertson, R., and Khonder, H. (1998). "Discourses of globalization." *International Sociology* 13(1): 25–40.

Roche, M. (2003). "Mega-events, time and modernity." *Time and Society* 12(1): 99–126.

Rodriguez, R. (1996). "Portrait de Rafael Guillén, alias le sous-commandant Marcos." *Esprit* 222 (June): 129–46.

Rootes, C. (1995). "Britain: greens in a cold climate." *The Green Challenge: The Development of Green Parties in Europe*. D. Richardson and C. Rootes (eds.). London: Routledge.

Rosanvallon, P. (2000). *The New Social Question: Rethinking the Welfare State*. Translated by Barbara Harshav, with a foreword by Nathan Glazer. Princeton: Princeton University Press.

Rosanvallon, P. (2002). "Histoire moderne et contemporaine du politique." Inaugural Lecture, 28 March 2002, Paris: Collège de France.

Roseneil, S. (1995). *Disarming Patriarchy: Feminism and Political Action at Greenham*. Bristol: Open University Press.

Roseneil, S. (2001). "A movement of moral remaking: the death of Diana, Princess of Wales." *Culture and Politics in the Information Age*. F. E. Webster (ed.). London: Routledge.

Routledge, P. (1997). "The imagineering of resistance: Pollok Free State and the practice of postmodern politics." *Transactions of the Institute of British Geographers* (22): 358–76.

Roy, O. (2004). *Globalized Islam: The Search for a New Ummah*. London: Hurst.

Rucht, D., and Neidhardt, F. (2002). "Towards a 'movement society'? On the possibilities of institutionalizing social movements." *Social Movement Studies* 1(1): 7–30.

Ruggiero, G., and Duncan, K. (1997). "On the growing free media movement." *Z Magazine*, 47–50.

Ryan, M. (1997). *Civic Wars: Democracy and Public Life in the American City during the Nineteenth Century*. Berkeley: University of California Press.

Ryan, M. (1999). "Civil society as democratic practice: North American cities during the nineteenth century," *Journal of Interdisciplinary History* 29(4) (spring): 559–84.

Ryder, A. (1995). "Peter Schumann: puppets, bread and art" <http://www.sagecraft.com/puppetry/papers/Schumann.html>.

Salmon, J.-M. (1998). *Le désir de société: Des restaurants du coeur au mouvement des chomeurs*. Paris: La Découverte.

Salomon, N. (2003). "Undoing the Mahdiyya: British Colonialism as religious reform in the Anglo-Egyptian Sudan, 1898–1914." Paper presented at Society for the Anthropology of Religion, Conference, 2003.

Salvatore, A. (1997). *Islam and the Political Discourse of Modernity*. Reading: Ithaca.

Salvatore, A. (2000). "Social differentiation, moral authority and public Islam in Egypt: the path of Mustafa Mahmud." *Anthropology Today* 16(2): 12–15.

Salvatore, A. (2004). "Making public space: opportunities and limits of collective action among Muslims in Europe." *Journal of Ethnic and Migration Studies* 30(5): 1013–31.

Saunders, R. (2002). "Uncanny presence: the foreigner at the gate of globalization." *Comparative Studies of South: Asia, Africa and the Middle East* 21(1–2): 88–98.

Schama, S. (1995). *Landscape and Memory.* London: HarperCollins.

Schipper, K. (1993). *The Taoist Body.* Berkeley: University of California Press.

Schoenfeldt, M. C. (1999). *Bodies and Selves in Early Modern England: Physiology and Inwardness in Spenser, Shakespeare, Herbert, and Milton.* Cambridge: Cambridge University Press.

Schumann, P. (1999). "What, at the end of this century, is the situation of puppets and performing objects?" *Drama Review* 43(3): 56–61.

Secor, A. (2002). "The veil and urban space in Istanbul: women's dress, mobility and Islamic knowledge." *Gender, Place and Culture* 9(1): 5–22.

Seligman, A. (1992). *The Idea of Civil Society.* New York: Free; Maxwell Macmillan Canada; Maxwell Macmillan International.

Seni, N. (1995). "Fashion and women's clothing." *Women in Modern Turkish Society: A Reader.* S. Tekeli (ed.). London: Zed.

Seremetakis, C. (1994). *The Senses Still: Perception and Memory as Material Culture in Modernity.* Boulder: Westview.

Sewell, W. H. (1980). *Work and Revolution in France: The Language of Labor from the Old Regime to 1848.* Cambridge: Cambridge University Press.

Sfez, L. (2001). *Le rêve biotechnologique.* Paris: PUF.

Sheller, M., and Urry, J. (2003). "Mobile transformations of 'public' and 'private' life." *Theory, Culture and Society* 20(3): 107–25.

Shildrick, M. (1999). "This body is not one: dealing with differences." *Body and Society* 5(2–3): 77–92.

Shildrick, M. (2002). *Embodying the Monster: Encounters with the Vulnerable Self.* London: Sage.

Singerman, D. (2004.) "The networked world of Islamist social movements." *Islamic Activism: A Social Movement Theory Approach.* Q. Wiktorowicz (ed.). Bloomington: Indiana University Press.

Siméant, J. (2001). "Entrer, rester en humanitaire: des fondateurs de Médecins Sans Frontières aux membres actuels des ONG médicales françaises." *Revue Française de Science Politique* 51(1–2): 47–72.

Smalley, D. (1994). "Defining timbre, refining timbre." *Contemporary Music Review* 10(2): 35–48.

Smelser, N. J. (1962). *Theory of collective behavior.* London: Routledge & Kegan Paul.

Snow, D. (2001). "Collective identity and expressive forms." eScholarship Repository, University of California <http://repositories.cdlib.org/csd/01-07>.

Snow, D., and McAdam, D. (2000). "Identity work processes in the context of social movements: Clarifying the movement/identity nexus." *Self, Identity, and Social Movements.* S. Stryker, T. J. Owens, and R. W. White (eds.). Minneapolis: Minneapolis University Press.

South Downs EarthFirst!, "Lessons from Twyford Down so far," unpublished manuscript.

Stahler-Sholk, R. (2001). "Globalization and social movement resistance: the Zapatista Rebellion in Chiapas, Mexico." *New Political Science* 23(4): 493–516.

Stallybrass, P., and White, A. (1986). *The Politics and Poetics of Transgression.* Ithaca: Cornell University Press.

Starrett, G. (1995). "The hexis of interpretation: Islam and the body in the Egyptian popular school." *American Ethnologist* 22(4): 953–69.

Strickmann, M. (2002). *Chinese Magical Medicine*. Bernard Faure (ed.). Stanford, Calif.: Stanford University Press.

Szerszynski, B. (2002). "Ecological rites: ritual action in environmental protest." *Theory, Culture and Society* 19(3): 51–69.

Summers, A. (1997). "The heart of the matter." *Sydney Morning Herald*, September 11, p. 15.

Tarleton, J. (2000) "Busted puppets: Philly police arrest puppetistas, toss their art into the trash" <http://www.johntarleton.net/philly_puppets.html,>.

Tarrow, S. (1994). *Power in Movement: Social Movements, Collective Action, and Politics*. Cambridge: Cambridge University Press.

Tarrow, S. (1998). "Fishnets, internets and catnets: globalization and transnational collective action." *Challenging Authority: The Historical Study of Contentious Politics*. M. Hanagan, L. Moch, and W. te Brake (eds.). Minneapolis: University of Minnesota Press.

Tarrow, S. (1999). "Paradigm warriors: regress and progress in the study of contentious politics." *Sociological Forum* 14(1): 71–7.

Tarrow, S. (2002). *The New Transnational Contention: Organizatons, Coalitions, Mechanisms*. Panel on "Social Movements and Transnational Social Movements," American Political Science Association, Chicago.

Tarrow, S. (2003). *Scale Shift in Transnational Contention*. Transnational Process and Social Movements, Bellagio, Italy.

Taylor, C. (1989). *Sources of the Self: The Making of the Modern Identity*. Cambridge: Mass.: Harvard University Press.

Taylor, C. (2004). *Modern Social Imaginaries*. Durham: Duke University Press.

Taylor, V. (2000). "Mobilising for change in a social movement society." *Contemporary Sociology* 29(1): 219–30.

Taylor, V., and Whittier, N. (1992). "Collective identity in social movement communities: lesbian feminist mobilization." *Frontiers in Social Movement Theory*. A. Morris and C. Mueller (eds.). New Haven: Yale University Press.

Taylor, V., and Whittier, N. (1995). "Analytical approaches to social movement culture: the culture of the women's movement." *Social Movements and Culture*. H. Johnston and B. Klandermans (eds.). Minneapolis: Minneapolis University Press.

Therborn, G. (2003). "Entangled modernities." *European Journal of Social Theory* 6(3): 293–305.

Thompson, E. P. (1963). *The Making of the English Working Class*. London: Gollancz.

Thornton, P. (2002) "Framing dissent in contemporary China: irony, ambiguity and metonymy," *China Quarterly*, 661–81.

Thrift, N. (1999). "The place of complexity." *Theory, Culture and Society* 16(3): 31–69.

Tilly, C. (1982). "Britain creates the social movement." *Social Conflict and the Political Order in Modern Britain*. J. Cronin and J. Schneer (eds.). London: Croom Helm.

Tilly, C. (1984a). *Big Structures, Large Processes, Huge Comparisons*. New York: Russell Sage Foundation.

Tilly, C. (1984b). "Social movements and national politics." C. Bright and S. Harding (eds.). *Statemaking and Social Movements: Essays in History and Theory.* Anne Arbor: University of Michigan Press.

Tilly, C. (1993–4). "Social movements as historically specific clusters of political performances." *Berkeley Journal of Sociology*(38): 1–30.

Tilly, C. (1997). "Social movements as political struggle." New York: Columbia University   <http://www.sociology.columbia.edu/people/faculty/tilly/papers/social_movements.html>.

Tilly, C. (2002). "Violence, terror and politics as usual." *Boston Review* 27(3–4): 21–4.

Tilly, C. (2003). "Political identities in changing polities." *Social Research* 70(2): 605–20.

Tilly, C. (2004). *Social Movements, 1768–2004.* Boulder: Paradigm.

Tong, J. (2002). "An organizational analysis of the Falun Gong: structure, communications, financing." *China Quarterly* (171): 636–60.

Touraine, A. (1955). *L'évolution du travail ouvrier aux usines Renault.* Paris: CNRS.

Touraine, A. (1966). *La conscience ouvrière.* Paris: Seuil.

Touraine, A. (1971). *The May Movement; Revolt and Reform: May 1968 – the Student Rebellion and Workers' Strikes – the Birth of a Social Movement.* Translated by Leonard F. X. Mayhew. New York: Random House.

Touraine, A. (1974). *The Post-Industrial Society: Tomorrow's Social History – Classes, Conflicts and Culture in the Programmed Society.* Translated by Leonard F. X. Mayhew. London: Wildwood House.

Touraine, A. (1977). *The Self-Production of Society.* Translated by Derek Coltman. Chicago: University of Chicago Press.

Touraine, A. (1981). *The Voice and the Eye: An Analysis of Social Movements.* Translated by Alan Duff, with a foreword by Richard Sennett. Cambridge: Cambridge University Press.

Touraine, A. (1983). *Anti-Nuclear Protest: The Opposition to Nuclear Energy in France.* Translated by Peter Fawcett. Cambridge: Cambridge University Press.

Touraine, A. (1988). *Return of the Actor: Social Theory in Postindustrial Society.* Foreword by Stanley Aronowitz, and translation by Myrna Godzich. Minneapolis: University of Minnesota Press.

Touraine, A. (2000). *Can We Live Together? Equality and Difference.* Cambridge: Polity.

Touraine, A. (2002). "From understanding society to discovering the subject." *Anthropological Theory* (2): 387–98.

Touraine, A. (2005). *Un nouveau paradigme: pour comprendre le monde d'aujourd'hui.* Paris: Fayard.

Touraine, A., Wieviorka, M., Dubet, F. (1987). *The Workers' Movement.* Translated by Ian Patterson. Cambridge: Cambridge University Press.

Trejo, G. (2002). "Redefining the territorial bases of power: peasants, Indians and guerrilla warfare in Chiapas, Mexico." *International Journal on Multicultural Societies* 4(1): 99–129.

Turetzky, P. (2002). "Rhythm: assemblage and event." *Strategies* 15(1): 121–38.

Turner, B. (2001). "Cosmopolitan virtue: on religion in a global age." *European Journal of Social Theory* 4(2): 131–52.

Turner, V. (1995). *The Ritual Process: Structure and Anti-Structure*. With a foreword by Roger D. Abrahams. New York: de Gruyter.

Urry, J. (2000). *Sociology beyond Societies: Mobilities for the Twenty-First Century*. London: Routledge.

Urry, J. (2002). "Mobility and proximity." *Sociology* 36(2): 255–74.

Urry, J. (2003). *Global Complexity*. Malden, Mass.: Polity.

Vermander, B. (2001). "Looking at China through the mirror of Falun Gong." *China Perspectives* 35(May–June): 4–13.

Vidal, J. (2001). "White knights say 'enough' to G8." *Guardian*, July 19 <http://www.guardian.co.uk/international/story/0,3604,523842,00.html>.

Villalón, L. (1999). "Generational changes, political stagnation, and the evolving dynamics of religion and politics in Senegal." *Africa Today*: 129–47.

Wacquant, L. (2004). "Pointers on Pierre Bourdieu and symbolic politics." *Constellations* 11(1): 3–15.

Wall, D. (1999). *Earth First! and the Anti-Roads Movement: Radical Environmentalism and Comparative Social Movements*. London: Routledge.

Wall Street Journal Europe, "Adieu Seattle?" Editorial, September 24, 2001, p. 10.

Wallerstein, I. (1996). *Open the Social Sciences. Report of the Gulbenkian Commission on the Restructuring of the Social Sciences*. Stanford, Calif.: Stanford University Press.

Weber, E. (1976). *Peasants into Frenchmen: The Modernization of Rural France, 1870–1914*. Stanford, Calif.: Stanford University Press.

Wei-ming, T. (1997). "Destructive will and ideological holocaust: Maoism as a source of social suffering in China." *Social Suffering*. A. Kleinman, V. Das, and M. Lock (eds.). Berkeley: University of California Press.

Welsh, I. (2001). "Anti nuclear movements: failed projects or heralds of a direct action milieu?" *Sociological Research Online* 6(3) <http://www.socresonline.org.uk/6/3/welsh.html>.

Werner, K. (1998). "Deconstructing the issue of Islamic fundamentalism: approaching the issue." *Islam – Motor or Challenge of Modernity*. G. Stauth (ed.). Hamburg: Lit.

Wieviorka, M. (2003). *The Making of Terrorism*. Translated by David Gordon White, with a new preface. Chicago: University of Chicago Press.

Wieviorka, M. (2005a). "After new social movements." *Social Movement Studies* 4(1): 1–19.

Wieviorka, M. (2005b). *La tentation antisémite. Haine des Juifs dans la France d'aujour-d'hui*. Paris: Laffont.

Wiktorowicz, Q., and Taji-Farouki, S. (2000). "Islamic NGOs and Muslim Politics: a case from Jordan." *Third World Quarterly* 21(4): 685–99.

Wiktorowicz, Q. (2000). "The Salafi movement in Jordan." *Journal of Middle East Studies* 32: 219–40.

Wilson, E. O. (1997). *Consilience: The Unity of Knowledge*. New York: Knopf.

Winslow, L. (2002). "Puppets and protest: street theater, art and vigil in the 21st century." *Whole Earth* (fall).

Womack, J. (1999). *Rebellion in Chiapas: An Historical Reader*. New York: New.

Wright, S. (2000). "'A love born of hate': autonomous rap in Italy." *Theory, Culture and Society* 17: 117–35.

Wuthnow, R. E. (1998). *The Encyclopedia of Politics and Religion*. Washington, D.C.: Congressional Quarterly.

Xiao, H. (2001). "Falun Gong and the ideological crisis of the Chinese Communist Party: Marxist atheism versus vulgar theism." *East Asia: An International Quarterly* 19(1–2): 123–43.

Xiaoyang, Z., and Penny, B. (1994). "The qigong boom," *Chinese Sociology and Anthropology* 27(1): 1–94.

Xu, J. (1999). "Body, discourse and the cultural politics of contemporary Chinese Qigong." *Journal of Asian Studies* 58(4): 961–91.

Yang, G. (2003). "The Internet and the rise of a transnational Chinese cultural sphere." *Media, Culture and Society* 25: 469–90.

Yashar, D. (1998). "Contesting citizenship: indigenous movements and democracy in Latin America." *Comparative Politics* 31(1): 23–42.

Zakin, S. (1993). *Coyotes and Town Dogs: Earth First! and the Environmental Movement*. New York: Viking.

Zarcone, T. (2003). "View from Islam, view from the West." *Diogenes* 50(4): 49–59.

Index